What People Are Sa ... Book

No holds barred, this book ... were many secrets that weren't ... those who were not attuned. So many ... mean there were things taught that you're not supp... to share with others until they pay to take the class. I understand how this book must have shocked many Reiki Masters because it shows the secret Reiki Symbols and how to use them. And you know what? I think it's time to share the powers of this healing technique to anyone and everyone who wants/needs it. It should be taught at an affordable price. This book does all that. ***WHQ***

This book goes with me wherever I go. It is a great quick reference guide for the symbols, how to give an attunement, and answers any questions you may have. After reading this book, I was able to give myself Reiki with a renewed belief and spirit. After purchasing this book, I purchased Steve's DVDs. They are indeed awe-inspiring. ***JS***

Compared to the other books I have purchased, this one is the best, and most valuable. Other books merely "talk" about Reiki and attunements instead of explaining them. I remember having many questions about Reiki and not being able to find the answers. Ever since I got this book I've been very pleased, and so have others who have borrowed it from me. ***HM***

Steve is a true pioneer! Another good thing about Steve's book is that he leaves out people's opinions, history and research about Reiki and gets right down to how to use it without wasting time or space. Just about every book you pick up has the history of Reiki, which is okay to a degree, but after reading it once or twice, that's enough. Steve's is a true "How To Do It" book. ***SP***

Kudos! Steve's Reiki book is clear and concise, and it's an easy, excellent read with awesome attributes. I read it cover to cover as soon as it arrived and read it again the next day. As a result, I ordered all Steve's Reiki DVDs for important instructional use in my work. They are beneficial for the beginner or the Reiki Master. The Reiki community is richer for his informative and creative contribution. ***CR***

I have read many books about Reiki and this one is by far the most complete, easy to read and a joy. A great adjunct to Steve's videotapes as well, I have them all and THEY WORK. If you are looking for one Reiki book to buy, this one should be on top of your list. Steve Murray's Reiki teachings have brought my experience to a higher level. What more can you ask for? ***JG***

I have been a Reiki Master for years now and have read many books. I find the *Reiki The Ultimate Guide* one of the best I've read. It is simple like Reiki was meant to be. It is very simple to read and understand. Remember this, there is no right or wrong way to use Reiki. True Reiki also teaches us not to criticize or judge others' beliefs or works. My recommendation is simply, read it! I believe it can help enhance your use of Reiki by helping you understand the concept of Reiki as a whole! Keep up the good work, Steve. ***DR***

Reiki The Ultimate Guide is brilliantly written and an easy read! The book includes clear illustrations of attunements and symbols. It answered questions I wouldn't have thought to ask. Steve has covered all the aspects in simple language. This book has greatly improved my healing abilities among all the topics covered and has raised my vibration. I say it is "A MUST " to reach the highest levels! Steve's wisdom is of the highest order! ***ML***

Reiki Master Attunement Become a Reiki Master DVD, along with the book, "*Reiki The Ultimate Guide,* Learn Sacred Symbols & Attunements Plus Reiki Secrets You Should Know" was a powerful and rich experience. The guides help make the attunement process clear and easy to follow. I especially appreciated reading Steve Murray's personal journey through the pitfalls and roadblocks associated with becoming a Reiki Master. Reiki is something that needs to be shared. ***FK***

Overall, this is a great book. I find myself reading it on many occasions for reinforcement, and being a practitioner myself, I find it very valuable. Great work Steve! ***BM***

Reiki

The Ultimate Guide Vol. 2
Learn Reiki Healing with Chakras plus New Reiki Healing Attunements for All Levels

Steve Murray

Third Printing

Body & Mind Productions, Inc.

Reiki
The Ultimate Guide Vol. 2
Learn Reiki Healing with Chakras *plus*
New Reiki Healing Attunements for All Levels

Published by
Body & Mind Productions, Inc.
820 Bow Creek Lane, Las Vegas, NV 89134
Website: www.healingreiki.com
Email: bodymindheal@aol.com

Third Printing January 2009

Library of Congress Cataloging-in-Publication Data
Murray, Steve
Reiki The Ultimate Guide 2: Learn Reiki Healing with Chakras *plus*
New Reiki Healing Attunements for All Levels / Murray, Steve - 1st ed.
Library of Congress Control Number 2004097114
ISBN # 0-9752648-3-4
Includes bibliographical references and index.
1. Reiki 2. New Age 3. Alternative Health
4. Self-Healing 5. Spiritual 6. Healing

Cover design: Alan Berrelleza, armb-design@cox.net
Type design, production: armb-design, Alan Berrelleza
Photography: Gracie Garcia
Editors: 1ST edit, Sonya Baity. Final edit Carol von Raesfeld
Drawings: © 2005, Robert Finkbeiner

Printed in U.S.A.

DVDs-CDs-BOOKS

BOOKS BY STEVE MURRAY

Cancer Guided Imagery Program
For Radiation, Chemotherapy, Surgery, And Recovery

Reiki The Ultimate Guide
Learn Sacred Symbols and Attunements
Plus Reiki Secrets You Should Know

Reiki The Ultimate Guide Vol. 3
Learn New Reiki Aura
Attunements Heal Mental & Emotional Issues

Reiki The Ultimate Guide Vol. 4
Past Lives and Soul Retrieval
Remove Psychic Debris and Heal your life

Animal Psychic Communication
Plus Reiki Pet Healing

Reiki The Ultimate Guide Vol. 2
Learn Reiki Healing with Chakras
plus New Reiki Attunements for All Levels

Reiki False Beliefs Exposed
For All Misinformation
Kept Secret By a Few Revealed

Reiki The Ultimate Guide Vol. 5
Learn New Psychic Attunements to Expand Psychic Abilities & Healing

DVDS BY STEVE MURRAY

Reiki Master Attunement
Become A Reiki Master

Reiki 2nd Level Attunement
Learn and Use the Reiki Sacred Symbols

A Reiki 1st
Aura and Chakra
Attunement Performed

Successfully Preparing for Cancer Radiation
Guided Imagery and Subliminal Program

Preparing Mentally & Emotionally
For Cancer Surgery
A Guided Imagery Program

Preparing Mentally & Emotionally
For Cancer Radiation
A Guided Imagery Program

Reiki 1st Level Attunement
Give Healing Energy To Yourself and Others

Reiki PsychicAttunement
Open and Expand Your Psychic Abilities

Reiki Healing Attunement
Heal Emotional-Mental-Physical-Spiritual Issues

Reiki Psychic Attunement Vol. 2
New Attunements to Expand Psychic Abilities

Preparing Mentally & Emotionally
For Cancer Chemotherapy
A Guided Imagery Program

Preparing Mentally & Emotionally
For Cancer Recovery
A Guided Imagery Program

Pain Relief Subliminal Program
Let Your Unconscious Mind Do It

Destroying Cancer Cells
Guided Imagery and Subliminal Program

30-Day Subliminal Weight Loss Program Let Your Unconscious Mind Do The Work!

Cancer Fear and Stress Relief Program

Successfully Preparing for Cancer Chemotherapy
Guided Imagery and Subliminal Program

MUSIC CDs BY STEVE MURRAY

Reiki Healing Music
Attunement Volume I

Reiki Healing Music
Attunement Volume II

Reiki Psychic Music
Attunement Volume I

Reiki Psychic Music
Attunement Volume II

Reiki Aura Music Attunement

Reiki Chakra Music Attunement

DVDs BY BODY & MIND PRODUCTIONS

Learning To Read The Tarot
Intuitively

Learning To Read The Symbolism
Of The Tarot

Mind Fitness Workout:
"Program the Mind for Weight Loss as you Exercise" Dance Workout

How to Contact Spirits, Angels &
Departed Loved Ones:
A step-by-step Guide

Mind Fitness Workout:
"Program the Mind for Weight Loss as you Exercise" Walking Workout

How to Contact Spirits Vol. 2
Learn to use a Spirit/Ouija Board and Hold a Séance

Mind Fitness Workout:
"Program the Mind for Weight Loss as you Exercise" Fitness Workout

Remove Psychic Debris & Heal Vol.1
Access a Past life

Remove Psychic Debris & Heal Vol.2
Soul Retrieval

Remove Psychic Debris & Heal Vol.3
Detach Negative Psychic Cords

This Guide is Dedicated to

All my students around the world who have helped with my Reiki Mission Statement.

Steve Murray's Reiki Books now available

Reiki The Ultimate Guide Learn Sacred Symbols & Attunements plus Reiki Secrets You Should Know

Reiki The Ultimate Guide, Vol. 2: Learn Reiki Healing with Chakras, plus New Reiki Healing Attunements for All

Reiki The Ultimate Guide, Vol. 3: Learn New Reiki Aura Attunements Heal Mental & Emotional Issues

Reiki The Ultimate Guide, Vol. 4: Past Lives and Soul Retreival, Remove Psychic Debris and Heal plus View Future Events

Reiki The Ultimate Guide, Vol. 5: Learn New Psychic Attunements to Expand Psychic Abilities & Healing

Reiki False Beliefs Exposed For All Misinformation Kept Secret By a Few Revealed

Animal Psychic Communication Plus Reiki Pet Healing

CONTENTS

Special Note to the Reader

Throughout this book I emphasize that Reiki Healing Attunements are only for physical ailments and diseases, which they are. I use different Reiki Attunement techniques and formulas for spiritual, mental and emotional conditions and disorders. I originally planned on including this information in this book, but halfway through my manuscript I realized I would need at least another 300 pages to do it. So, there will be another Reiki The Ultimate Guide Vol. 3 in the near future to complete a trilogy. The third book will include the techniques and formulas I use for performing Reiki Attunements for specific spiritual, mental and emotional conditions and disorders.

Any questions or comments, feel free to contact me at my website www.healingreiki.com

Namaste,

Steve Murray

"O, happy the soul that saw its own faults..."

-Rumi

The Journey Continues

Being a two-finger typist, I was relieved when my first Reiki book was finally published. I assumed I would never write another Reiki book again, and my days of being an active author were over. Now, I really should have known better than to assume anything…

First Reiki Book

I authored my first Reiki book for the many, many thousands of students around the world who received Reiki Attunements through my DVD and video programs. They needed additional Reiki information and guidance to continue on their Reiki journey. Given the nature of the content and time constraints, I could not include all the information and guidance in a new DVD or video program, so I had to write a book.

Soon after *Reiki The Ultimate Guide* was published, I was caught off guard by how the book was accepted and embraced around the world. Sales took off without any mass-marketing, just word of mouth. I knew that a market existed for this type of Reiki book, but I was genuinely surprised by how large it was.

Looking back, I understand that the need for this type of book existed partly because a few Reiki Masters did not convey enough Reiki information and guidance to their students, and what they did convey led to unanswered questions about Reiki. I feel the main reason is simply Reiki Healers needed a concise guide they could refer to for help with Reiki.

More Fallout?

Once my first Reiki book was published, I fully expected some fallout from a few within the Reiki community, just like I experienced when I first released my Reiki Attunement videos years ago. To my surprise, this really did not happen.

Instead, I was taken aback by the first generous wave of e-mails and letters from Reiki Healers around the world thanking me for writing the book. I was also encouraged by the feedback from my fellow Reiki Masters saying they wished a guide like this had been available when they were learning Reiki, and they now recommend and use the book with their students.

A New Book Is Born

In many of the e-mails and letters from Reiki Healers throughout the world, there were always questions about additional ways to use Reiki for specific physical ailments and diseases, and how to use Chakras in healing. Reading all this correspondence, I soon realized it was my Karma to write another Reiki book, so before long I was back at my keyboard, pecking away.

About the Book

As in my first book, I keep the Reiki information and guidance simple and concise. The book includes a review of Reiki, Reiki Symbols and Attunements, plus knowledge about Chakras, back Chakras, Meridians and Nadis. A large part of the book is devoted to learning techniques and a formula for using Reiki with Chakras in helping with all specific physical ailments and diseases for yourself and others. I call these techniques "Reiki Healing Attunements."

My definition of an Attunement is "A sacred process, initiation and/or meditation with a specific purpose or intent." So I call these healing techniques Reiki Healing Attunements for two main reasons. One, you will be performing a sacred process of placing a Reiki Symbol or Symbols into one or multiple major Chakras during a Healing Attunement. Two, there is a specific purpose and intent during each Healing Attunement – to channel Reiki to help a specific physical ailment or disease. Of course, which symbol(s) and Chakra(s) you will use, in what order, and for what physical ailment or disease, you will learn in the later chapters.

Reiki Healing Attunements are additional healing tools you can use for yourself and others. You can perform the Attunements by themselves or include them in your healing sessions when you feel they are needed. The Attunements will make your healing sessions faster, and I believe you will experience stronger results with your Reiki Healing.

All Levels and Healing Attunements

If you are a Reiki 1st Level Healer, you will be shown how to perform Reiki Healing Attunements without the symbols. If you fall into this category, as soon as you are ready, I would suggest that you receive your 2nd Level Reiki Attunement. This will enable you to use Reiki Symbols, thereby, giving you many more options when using Reiki.

I explain three ways to perform Reiki Healing Attunements: one for the 1st Level Healer (as mentioned before), one for the 2nd Level Healer, and one for the Reiki Master. I give examples of performing Healing Attunements with step-by-step photos, plus I have included illustrations, a formula and guidelines to make your learning process easy.

Even if you have been attuned to another Reiki system or healing method, you will be able to perform Reiki Healing Attunements with the information I provide.

Goal of the Book

Various levels of expertise and ability exist in all modes of healing and Reiki Healers are no exception. For example, one medical doctor will say a medical procedure is impossible because of his skills, ability, and teachings. Another doctor will say it can be done because of his ability, skills, and teachings and will perform the procedure successfully.

Every Reiki Healer has his or her own level of expertise and skills in healing. The primary goal of this book is to give you options with Reiki so you can take your ability and expertise in Reiki Healing to a higher level.

Up to You

In this book I express and share my beliefs, teachings, and opinions. If, for whatever reason(s), you do not agree or feel comfortable with some or all of these statements, that's all right. Just use what resonates with you and leave the rest. All I ask is that you keep an open mind and heart while reading the book, and please keep in your thoughts my favorite quote throughout your life's journey. I believe it will make the journey easier.

"Believe nothing, no matter where you read it, or who said it, no matter if I have said it, unless it agrees with your own reason and your own common sense."

-Buddha

“The middle path is the way to wisdom.”
-Rumi

"Everything in the universe is a pitcher brimming with wisdom and beauty."

-Rumi

Controversial Beliefs

This chapter is about my sometimes-controversial Reiki beliefs.

My Reiki Mission Statement

To make Reiki knowledge, guidance, and Attunements available to everyone who seeks them. To make Reiki

1st, 2nd and Master Level Attunements affordable for everyone so healing is spread throughout the world.

Commercializing Reiki

I have received e-mails with comments that I have been commercializing Reiki by making the knowledge accessible to everyone. As for being accessible to everyone, that's exactly what I am trying to do as my Reiki Mission states. To address the comments that I am commercializing Reiki, I wholeheartedly disagree – that's not my intent.

My intent is to spread Reiki information and guidance in the best and most effective way I know how in today's world. My goal is to reach people around the globe who have never heard of or experienced Reiki, or perhaps could never afford it without my programs. Without today's technology, I would never be able to communicate and interact with these people.

A few ministers, preachers, and doctors use television, radio, DVDs, video, the Internet, and books to help communicate and multiply their messages and information. As a Reiki Master, I am using these same options to communicate my Reiki message and information around the world. I understand the majority of Healers just want to interact only within their local spheres of influence, which include family, friends and clients.

The bottom line is that this is the Information Age and we need to adapt and accept this, of course, only as we feel inclined. The new generation of Reiki Healers and the majority of experienced Reiki Healers understand this and are at one with the evolving times. They have a desire to be informed and share Reiki information and healing with others. This ultimately will make Reiki more accessible to people throughout the world. My Reiki Mission Statement is now becoming a reality.

Reiki Healer

I believe any individual can become a Reiki Healer and use Reiki if he or she receives an Attunement. You do not have to have a certain belief system, be spiritual, or have a religion and engage in elaborate studies of Reiki for it to work, but you will find yourself seeking more information on Reiki and sharing experiences and techniques with other Healers after becoming a Healer yourself. The book you are reading now is an example of seeking out further information on Reiki and healing.

Once you start a Reiki journey, you will find your life altered for the best, and usually will develop a higher level of consciousness and spiritual awareness in addition to healing abilities.

Other Healers and Reiki

I believe Reiki is the life force that keeps us alive. Once the life force is no longer flowing, our physical bodies cease to exist. All cultures have their own name for the life force or energy that is essential to our physical being. For example, it can be the *Chi* of the Chinese culture or the *Prana* of the Indian culture. I believe all Healers use Reiki, although it can be called by other names, but ultimately all healing energy is one and the same.

Everyone can naturally channel this life force to a certain extent. There are even a few gifted natural Healers who have never received a Reiki Attunement. Some successful Healers have been attuned to this life force in a different method because of their culture. But, Reiki Attunements are needed and used by most people to open, focus and increase their natural abilities with this life force.

Reiki Secrets Revisited

I am always getting questions from concerned students about whether they should keep Reiki Symbols, Attunements and other Reiki information a secret. They state they were instructed to do so from books they read or from Reiki teachers and other Reiki Healers. All three sources give various reasons for this cult-like secrecy. I feel it is important to go over my beliefs again because of these often-asked questions. The following paragraphs are excerpts from my first Reiki book, which explain my position on this sensitive subject that evokes strong feelings and opinions in some Reiki Healers.

There is a belief with some Reiki schools and Masters that Reiki Symbols and Attunements, and the whole process should be kept secret – that is, until there is an energy exchange, which is usually money, and the secrets are told and taught. The person is then instructed to keep these secrets for various reasons, including the Reiki tradition.

I do not believe in this. Traditions evolve and need to change with the times. I believe if people seek information about anything, including Reiki, they should be informed. Now this does not mean I believe in free Reiki classes, sessions and/or Attunements. It means I do not believe in secrets for any reasons, including control. I also believe this secret mentality has hurt the spread of Reiki and kept it from many people in need of it.

It has been said, if a person sees the symbols and knows how the Attunement is performed, negative energy can be created, so when the person does decide to try Reiki, it will not work or be as strong. I believe this is all nonsense because the life force does not work that way.

A Reiki Healer or a person contemplating becoming a Reiki Healer or having a Reiki session, should be fully informed if they want to be. I understand some people do not care about the process or how it works, just that it does. I was never one of those people.

Over the years, I have been told other reasons for keeping Reiki secrets, but none have ever made sense to me, especially in this day and age. What does stand out in my mind is that with some Reiki Masters the secrecy is a control issue, and some Reiki groups act like a cult by keeping the information secret. Only a select few have it. The reality now is the majority of the information is out there piecemeal via the Internet, newsletters, word-of-mouth, books, and even a few songs, although most of the time it is incorrect.

Look at it this way, say you would like and/or need a medical procedure. You want to obtain more information about the process before you experience it, but the doctor does not want to tell you anything about it until it is done, then they instruct you to keep it a secret. Depending on the level of the procedure, it could be kept a secret until you become a doctor. I have been told this is not a valid comparison, but in my mind it is. The only difference is that the medical doctor does invasive procedures to your physical body. A Reiki Healer works at times with all your bodies, which gives you even more reason to be informed.

Different Reiki Energy

I understand a few schools and teachings call their Reiki a “special” energy, different from any other life force energy, more powerful, etc. I have even heard individuals say their Reiki brand (some have added names to Reiki and even trademarked or copyrighted them) is more powerful and effective than other Reiki.

I do not subscribe to the above beliefs. I believe Reiki is your "universal life force energy" and there are not different brands of Reiki or stronger versions of this life force.

Now some Reiki Healers do channel Reiki stronger than others, but it is not because of the type of Reiki (or the brand or trademark.) The reasons they channel Reiki stronger can be many: natural abilities, stronger intent, balance in all their bodies (mental, physical, spiritual, emotional), more experience or more practiced techniques. All of these are within your power to work on to improve your strength of Reiki, except the natural ability.

In every line of work, sport, creative endeavor, etc., there are a few people who have a higher level of natural ability and Reiki is no exception. A Reiki Healer can make up for any lack of natural ability by having stronger intent when channeling Reiki, keeping balanced and clear on all their bodies, and practicing and learning new healing techniques. However, having said all that, any Healer can have days when his or her Reiki is not quite as strong and the reasons why are not always known. When this happens, I recommend taking a week off from Reiki and when you resume Reiki Healing, you will be back to normal.

Length of a Session

My belief is that the 45 to 90 minute sessions are too long. These long sessions sometimes discourage and distract people. After a while, they lose interest or maybe do not have the time and stop using Reiki. I believe a session can be just as effective in 15 to 30 minutes and the Healing Attunements you will learn in this book accomplish this.

I feel a person in a weakened state may become irritable and uncomfortable if flooded with too much Reiki during a lengthy session. Of course, if you feel long sessions have merit, and they sometimes do in certain circumstances, by all means continue with the practice. You can always extend the time of a Reiki Healing Attunement if you desire.

Reiki Lineage

I will close this chapter with my beliefs on Reiki lineage. A few Reiki Masters and schools put a lot of emphasis on Reiki lineage. I do not feel this is essential, especially now with all the branches of Reiki that have surfaced. I do feel that there is confusion at times with the symbols used in the different lineages. There are Reiki symbols that are being called "Usui" which are not Usui. This is not a problem if you have been attuned to these symbols. What is a problem and causes confusion is people stating their Reiki Symbols are stronger, more powerful than other Reiki Symbols. This type of statement is very subjective and usually ego or other motives are behind it. I believe the symbols to which you are attuned are the right symbols for you, so please do not be concerned if your symbols are different.

In Chapter Four I will review the classic Usui Reiki Symbols and you can compare these symbols with the symbols to which you have been attuned. If your symbols are different and you would like to be attuned to the symbols in this book, you can find a Reiki Master who uses these symbols, or you may use one of my programs to become attuned to them.

“Patience is the key to joy.”

-Rumi

“People of the world don’t look at themselves, and so they blame one another.”

-Rumi

Reiki and Usui Attunements

Reiki originates from two Japanese words, **Rei** and **Kei**, and is pronounced *ray-key*. The most common definition of **Rei** is *universal*. The most common definition of **Kei** is *life energy* or *life force*. So, Reiki translated is *Universal Life Energy* or *Universal Life Force.*

There have been other interpretations of "Rei" which include Spiritual, God-Conscious, and Higher Self, and they all can be used. Reiki is the life force that animates us all and is found all around us and throughout our physical bodies.

Reiki is a healing technique using this "universal life energy" channeled through the Healer to the recipient through the Palm Chakra of the hands. This type of healing is referred to as "Hands-on-Healing."

Hands-on-Healing has been used in just about all cultures for many, many centuries. Although with Reiki, you do not have to place hands on the body for it to be effective.

There are many theories and books written on the origin of Reiki: Lemuria, Atlantis, Egypt, India, Tibet, etc., and then the method vanished. Reiki was "awakened " in Japan by Dr. Mikao Usui during the early part of the 20th century.

Reiki Can Never Cause Harm

It is important to know that Reiki can never cause harm because it is our life force. Reiki can only help heal. If it is the person's Karma (destiny) not to receive or accept Reiki on any level, it still will not harm them.

Channeling Reiki

Channeling Reiki is the same as giving Reiki. When channeling Reiki you become connected to its source and you become a conduit for this life force. It then flows through you and out your Palm Chakras. Receiving a 1st, 2nd, or Master Level Reiki Attunement will enable you to connect to the unlimited source of Reiki and have it channel (flow) through you when you desire to use it. The majority of the Reiki you channel flows from the source into the Crown Chakra and out your Palm Chakras, but some of it also flows in from your other Chakras and even from breathing in air. Reiki Healers channel Reiki to themselves or others with their palms on the body or a few inches off. The channeling of Reiki can also be done with beaming and sending Reiki long distance, to the past present and future. These techniques are fully explained in my first Reiki book.

Reiki Metaphor

Here's a metaphor I always give for how Reiki works. Though simplistic, it will illustrate the concept. When you are channeling Reiki, you are like a powerful battery charger connected to an unlimited source of energy. You give this powerful charge to a person whose battery is low or drained for whatever reason (illness, stress, etc.), and they use the energy where it is needed to heal.

How Reiki Heals

When a person's Reiki flows smoothly and uninterrupted through the Chakras, Meridians and Nadis within the physical body, Reiki is able to reach the part of the body where it is needed (Chakras, Meridians, and Nadis are explained in later chapters.) A benefit of Reiki flowing smoothly and unrestricted is that it will help balance, cleanse, and clear the Chakras, Meridians, and Nadis, which, in turn, will maintain the Reiki flow throughout the body. This means good physical health will result and can be maintained.

However, when the Reiki flow becomes blocked, limited, or weakened, it causes a chain reaction throughout the body. The results are imbalances from a surplus of Reiki backing up and/or a shortage of Reiki. This causes certain parts of our bodies to fail to function naturally, so pain, physical ailments, and disease can occur. Basically, Reiki is needed in every living cell in the body and when it is low or cannot reach these cells, imbalances occur and disease and physical ailments can manifest within the body.

Take your immune system for example. Bacteria and viruses are always present in our bodies, but our immune system keeps them in check. The immune system needs a constant and uninterrupted flow of Reiki to be strong and fight these disease-causing micro-organisms. When the body is without the steady flow of Reiki, it is weakened and this allows bacteria and viruses to get a foothold.

Receiving Reiki Healing Attunements will help remove blockages and increase your life force flow throughout your body. This enables your body to be nourished by Reiki so it can return to a natural healthy state and healing can occur.

Different Attunements

There are now variations of ways to perform Reiki Attunements around the world. Most have developed and evolved from the Usui System of Attunements. This means when people talk about Attunements, they can be referring to different processes. The following is a summary of the Classic Usui Attunements which I teach and use.

Usui Reiki

In the classic Usui System of Reiki there are three Reiki levels. There are three Reiki Attunements that correspond and are given with these levels. The levels are 1st, 2nd and Master. In this system of Classic Usui Reiki there are only four symbols used in Reiki Healing and in passing Reiki Level Attunements.

The symbols available for use by the Reiki Healer depend on the Reiki level to which they have been attuned. The four Reiki Symbols are Power, Long Distance, Mental/Emotional, and the Master. Only the Reiki Master and Reiki 2nd Level Healers can use these symbols with intent for a specific purpose with Reiki.

In the 1st Level Reiki Attunement the symbols are used in passing the Attunement, but none are made available to the student to use. In the 2nd Level, the first three Reiki Symbols: Power, Long Distance, and Mental/Emotional, are attuned to the student and the student can use them. The Master Symbol is attuned and passed on to the student for use in the Reiki Master Attunement. All the Reiki Symbols are used in the process of giving all three Reiki Attunements. If you are a 2nd Level or Reiki Master, you will be using these symbols with the Chakras during the Reiki Healing Attunements.

Usui Attunements

In the Usui Reiki Attunement system, the 1st Level Attunement has four separate Attunements. The 2nd Level Reiki has only one Attunement, as does the Reiki Master Attunement. During the 1st Level Reiki Attunement, only the Power Symbol is placed into the hands. During the 2nd Level Reiki Attunement the Power, Long Distance, and the Mental/Emotional Symbols are placed into the hands. During the Master Attunement, all four symbols are placed into the hands.

One major difference in the Usui Attunement, when compared with other Reiki Attunement methods, is that the symbols are placed in the third eye during the Attunement, which I feel is very important and powerful.

The three Usui Reiki Level Attunements are also different from other Reiki Attunements in respect to which symbols are placed into the hands during the Attunements.

This happens when the hands are held over the head in a prayer position and the palms held opened in front of the Heart Chakra. I explain and show all the differences in detail in my first Reiki book.

The 4th Attunement

There is a 4th Level Reiki Attunement that has been created and now used by some Usui Reiki Masters. The 4th is an advanced Attunement given after the 2nd Level Attunement. This Attunement only attunes a person to the Master Reiki energy and Master Symbol. The difference is they can use the Master Symbol and its energy, but there are steps left out of the Attunement. One of the steps left out in this advanced Attunement is Reiki Symbols are not placed in the Palm Charkas during the Attunement. I disagree with this because the symbols need to be placed into the Palm Chakras to enable the person to perform Reiki Level Attunements on students, clients, relatives, and friends. If you look in my first book, I show the symbols being placed into the Palm Chakras during the Reiki Master Attunement.

There are two main reasons why a few Reiki Masters and schools use the 4th Level Attunement. One is to keep students coming back and prevent them from being able to perform Reiki Level Attunements themselves, which they feel would limit their future students; and two, the additional fee they charge for the extra Attunement.

In the next chapter, I will review the four Usui Reiki Symbols.

"Conventional opinion is the ruin of our souls."

-Rumi

The Symbols

This chapter is an overview of the Reiki Symbols that will be used in the Reiki Healing Attunements. In my first Reiki book I explain the symbols in more depth and detail.

As I mentioned earlier, if you are only a 1st level Reiki Healer, you will be shown a way to perform the Healing Attunements without the symbols. Even if your Reiki

Symbols look different, you still will be able perform them. I will explain how you can use the symbols you have been attuned to in a later chapter.

Usui Reiki Symbols

The Reiki Symbols that I use during the Reiki Healing Attunements are the classic Usui Symbols and the truest from the Usui lineage. There are only minor variations with these Reiki Symbols when they are traced from this lineage.

There are other symbols that a few Reiki Masters and schools are using and teaching, but they are not part of the Usui System. These symbols have been developed and created by different Reiki schools and Reiki Masters.

Variations of the Symbols

If you discover that the Reiki Symbols you have been taught and to which you have been attuned vary from the ones in this book, do not worry about it because you still received a Reiki Attunement. This can include Reiki Symbols with different lines, extra lines, and lines that go in reverse directions. The symbols you received from your Reiki Master are the right symbols for you to use because you have been attuned to them. What is important is activating and using the Reiki Symbols to which you have been attuned.

There are a few reasons for the variations of the Reiki Symbols. In the past, Reiki Symbols were taught orally.

Students were not allowed to write them down for hundreds of years. So when it was time for students to teach the Reiki Symbols, they taught them orally, from memory. That was not the best system for accuracy and variations in the symbols developed. Now, most of the time, Reiki Symbols are written on paper, which keeps variations to a minimum.

Another recent reason for variations of the symbols is that some Reiki Masters have intentionally changed the Reiki Symbols. They have done this to make their Reiki unique, personal, and to blend with their current beliefs, or they have been told by their Reiki guides to make the changes.

Translation of the Symbols

I have seen many different translations and interpretations of the Reiki Symbols. I use the most traditional and accepted ones here in this book. Translations and interpretations are tough, especially when you go from several languages. The Bible is a prime example of that. It has been translated into many languages from the original. This has resulted in some discrepancies in some parts of the Bible and its translations.

Feel free to use an interpretation that you were taught and feel comfortable with, but be aware and open to the different interpretations. There is no right or wrong concerning this, it's a matter of where you received your information. The important issue is the intent on the symbol's meaning when you use it.

The Four Usui Reiki Symbols

Cho Ku Rei

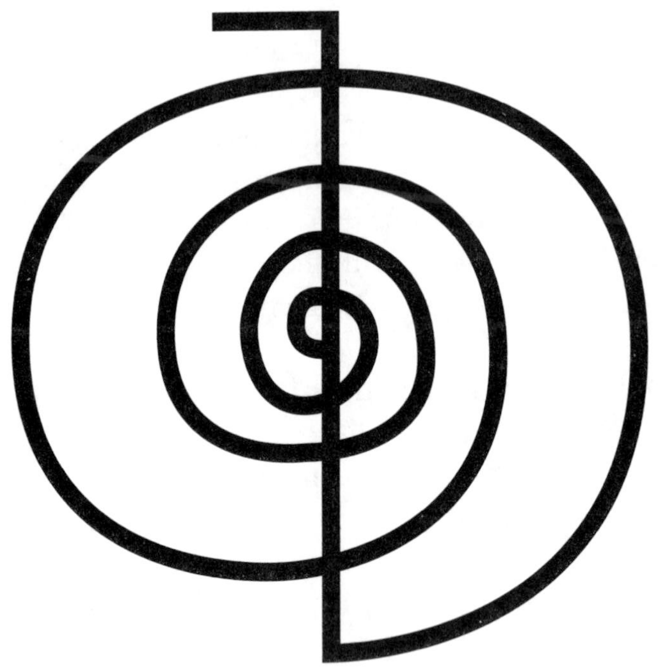

This is the Usui Power Symbol. It is also called the "Power Increase" Symbol. Its name is Cho Ku Rei, which means "Put all the power in the universe here." The Power Symbol has many uses when activated, but it is primarily used to increase the power of Reiki or to focus Reiki on a specific location and for protection.

Sei He Ki

This is the Usui Mental/Emotional Symbol. It is also called the "Emotional/Mental" Symbol, the "Mental" Symbol or the "Mental/Emotional/Addiction" Symbol. Its name is Sei He Ki and it means "God and humanity become One." This symbol has many uses when activated, but is commonly used in emotional, mental, and addictive healing situations.

Hon Sha Ze Sho Nen

This is the Usui Long Distance symbol. It is also referred to as the "Long Distance" and the "Absentee" Symbol. Its name is Hon Sha Ze Sho Nen. The name of this symbol has a few different interpretations. I was taught that it means "May the Buddha in me connect to the Buddha in you to promote harmony and peace." The symbol is very powerful and flexible and most healers do not utilize its full ability. When activated with specific intent, Reiki can be sent anywhere, anytime in the past, present, or future. Distance, time, and space are not a barrier when you use this symbol.

Dai Koo Myo

This is the Reiki Usui Master Symbol. Its name is "Dai Koo Myo." With this symbol, there are also several translations, but the one I use is "Great Being of the universe shine on me, be my friend." The Master Symbol is the ultimate Reiki Symbol in all aspects. It intensifies Reiki, takes it to a higher level and creates a stronger connection with your source. When you activate other Reiki Symbols with the Master Symbol, the symbols are then taken to their highest level of effectiveness.

Drawing and Activating the Symbols

I receive a lot of mail from students around the world concerned about drawing the Reiki Symbols correctly and/or perfectly for them to be activated. I am going to tell you now – the power of the Reiki Symbols does not come from drawing them perfectly. It comes from your intent to activate the symbol(s) once you have been attuned to them. So do not worry when you draw the symbols and they are not perfect. Just draw and activate them the best that you can, the way you were shown when you received your Attunement.

I feel there is not a correct or incorrect way to use or activate these symbols as long as the intent is there. It is what you intuitively feel is right for you. As time goes on with your use of the symbols you will develop the techniques that work best for you.

“Indeed envy is a defect; worse than any other.”

-Rumi

"It is God's kindness to terrify you in order to lead you to safety."

-Rumi

Healing and Reiki

The key to a healthy life while we are on our earthly journey is a holistic balance in all aspects of our lives. Unfortunately, it is the human condition that all of us will experience ill health at one time or another. The key is to keep that to a minimum and when it does occur, to use a balanced approach to healing.

I believe in the benefits of the Eastern Philosophy of Preventive Medicine to keep illness at a minimum, and

I practice it. I have been extremely successful with this philosophy in my life. I also believe in the power and technology of Western medicine in healing and would not hesitate to use it if needed, although I would take responsibility for myself and research Western medications and/or treatments before I proceeded with them. I would combine Reiki with any treatment(s) I decided upon.

Miracles and Healing

Miracles can and do happen using only Reiki or prayers or Western medicine, etc., but usually in a successful healing there are no shortcuts, rather it is a balanced process with a treatment plan that's best for the circumstances. I believe that plan includes Reiki, other healing modalities, perseverance, and patience.

Reiki is Not a Substitute

It is important to understand that Reiki Healing Attunements are not a substitute for conventional medical care or any condition requiring immediate medical attention. With major health issues, Reiki should be used in conjunction with professional medical treatment, instead of by itself. Depending on the health issue, treatments can include conventional medical doctors and/or one or more other medical practitioners such as a naturopath, osteopath, chiropractor, hypnotherapist, acupuncturist, or dietician, etc., whichever you determine is appropriate for your circumstances.

Reiki as an adjunctive therapy can be a very effective and important element of a healing program. For example, if you break your arm, you should go to the doctor to have it set and put into a cast, then channel Reiki to the arm so it can heal faster. You would not expect Reiki to set the bone.

I understand that the above might be obvious for most people, but I do receive e-mails from people who state that although they became ill over the course of many years without addressing the problem, they expect to receive a few Reiki Healing Attunements and become healed. It does not work that way. Usually becoming sick is a process and becoming well is also a process. Using Reiki or any healing modality, including Western medicine, pills and drugs is not going to heal you instantly. I do believe if you include Reiki Healing Attunements with other healing modalities that are suited for the physical problem, the majority of the time the healing process will become easier and faster.

Patience and Healing

Since everyone's circumstances are different and unique concerning physical ailments and disease, it can be a few days to a few weeks or a month before any physical changes are experienced or felt after receiving Reiki Healing Attunements. The key for a successful outcome is to be consistent with the Healing Attunements and all other treatments prescribed for the ailments and disease, and most of all, to be patient.

When Reiki Does Not Heal

Every person's life journey and circumstances are different. Throw in life's big picture and it's impossible for any Healer to figure out or understand why Reiki does not help at all times.

I have heard many reasons why Reiki sometimes does not heal and I assume some are correct at times. They include, it was too late for the physical body to heal, or it was the person's Karma not to heal. Metaphysics laws state if a person does not desire healing, either unconsciously or consciously, it can be rejected, so that can come into play with healing.

I believe Healers should never make judgments on whether Reiki is not healing or give a reason why it is not healing any person, even if they believe it is one of the reasons I mentioned. The reality is that nobody really knows why Reiki does not work at times. Most importantly, I believe a healer should never give up, unless told to do so.

"Let's ask God to help us to self-control for one who lacks it, lacks his grace."

-Rumi

"Looking up gives light, although at first it makes you dizzy."

-Rumi

Chakra Teachings

The following chapters contain my teachings on Chakras and the physical body. The whole Chakra system is very complex with many teachings and books written that are very in depth on the subject. It would take another book just to review some of the information, opinions, teachings, and beliefs that are available. The information I convey is only about the physical body and Chakras. This is what you need to know to perform the

Reiki Healing Attunements for physical ailments and disease. If you would like to continue research on Chakras, I have listed a few books you can start with in the bibliography in the back of the book. The following is a sample of the additional information Chakra books contain:

- How Chakras affect you mentally, emotionally, and spiritually.
- Chakra areas of consciousness and how they affect you.
- Psychological and spiritual characteristics of each Chakra and its symbolism.
- How Chakras affect all your bodies: physical, mental, spiritual, emotional, and additional non-physical bodies.
- How Chakras affect basic needs, fears, and human behavior.

Different Teachings

There are teachings and books that differ or have conflicting information on Chakras and the physical body. There is no right or wrong with these differences. They all are correct within the healing modalities in which they are taught. It's what information resonates and works best for you. The following are just a few examples to give you an idea of the different teachings that relate to Chakras and the physical body.

- The Chakras spin. Some teachings state they spin clockwise, others say counterclockwise. A few say they alternate with the 1st, 3rd, 5th, and 7th Chakras spinning in one direction, and the 2nd, 4th, and 6th Chakras spinning in another direction.
- 1st Chakra points up and down and not front to back.
- Back Chakras are not mentioned, or if they are, their importance is not emphasized.
- Differences of secondary and minor Chakras.
- How many Chakras there are (major, secondary, minor), and their locations and functions.
- Which Chakras are associated with the Pituitary and Pineal glands – the 6th or 7th.
- Chakras names. Some names are associated with their location and others with their function.
- Colors of Chakras are different.

As you can see, there are conflicting and subjective teachings with Chakras. If you discover your teachings differ on one or several points from mine regarding Chakras and the physical body, do not worry about it. The difference(s) will not change how you perform or the effectiveness of the Reiki Healing Attunements. If you feel it is necessary, you can make any adjustments when doing the Reiki Healing Attunements that are in line with your teachings.

"Loosen the bonds of avarice from your hands and neck."

-Rumi

Chakra

Chakra is a Sanskrit word meaning "spinning wheel" or "vortex" and usually it is used in reference to each of the seven major energy centers in our physical body.

There are also many secondary or minor Chakras in the body that I will talk about later in the chapter, but the Seven Major Chakras, front and back, are what you will be working with during the Healing Attunements.

Each major Chakra has important individual functions in the body and works in conjunction with all the other major Chakras and secondary and minor Chakras. The major Chakras manage our most critical functions, while the secondary and minor Chakras regulate less fundamental needs. Each Chakra is an individual, but is also an important part of the whole Chakra System.

The wheel-like spinning vortexes are not physical, but are in your physical body, although a portion of the vortexes extends out of the body front and back. The whirling circular motion forms a cavity or vacuum in the center of the Chakra drawing in Reiki. It then steps down the Reiki to a lower frequency of vibration so it can enter the body smoothly and be utilized within the body. Next, the Chakra processes the Reiki and acts as a pump or valve, regulating its flow throughout the body. Essentially, Chakras are portals through which Reiki can flow in, be processed and circulated throughout your body.

7 Major Chakras

The Seven Major Chakras are aligned and connected to an energy channel that is behind and parallel with the spine. The following are the Seven Major Chakras locations (Fig.1).

Seven Major Chakras and Locations

◆ The 1st Chakra is also known as the "Root" Chakra, "Base" Chakra, or *Muladhara* (Sanskrit). Muladhara translated means "root." Located at the base of the spine, it's the root or foundation of the major Chakras.

◆ The 2nd Chakra is also known as "Sacral" Chakra, "Sexual" Chakra, or *Svadhisthana* (Sanskrit). Svadhisthana translated means "sacred home of the self." It is located below the navel in the lower abdomen.

◆ The 3rd Chakra is also known as the "Solar Plexus" Chakra or *Manipura* (Sanskrit). Manipura translated means "inner sun" or "seat of the soul." It is located at the base of the sternum.

◆ The 4th Chakra is also known as the "Heart" Chakra or *Anahata* (Sanskrit). Anahata translated means "unstruck or unbeaten." It is located at the center of the thoracic cavity behind the heart, the center of the chest.

◆ The 5th Chakra is also known as the "Throat" Chakra or *Vishuddha* (Sanskrit). Vishuddha translated means "purification." It is located in the throat area, at the base of the larynx.

◆ The 6th Chakra is also known as the "Brow" Chakra, "Third Eye," "Forehead" Chakra or *Ajna* (Sanskirt). Ajna translated mean "perception." It is located in the center of the head, slightly above and between the eyebrows.

◆ The 7th Chakra is also known as the "Crown" Chakra or *Sahasrara* (Sanskrit). Sahasrara translated means "crown." It is located on top of the head, at the soft spot on a newborn baby's head. This spot is commonly

7 Major Chakras

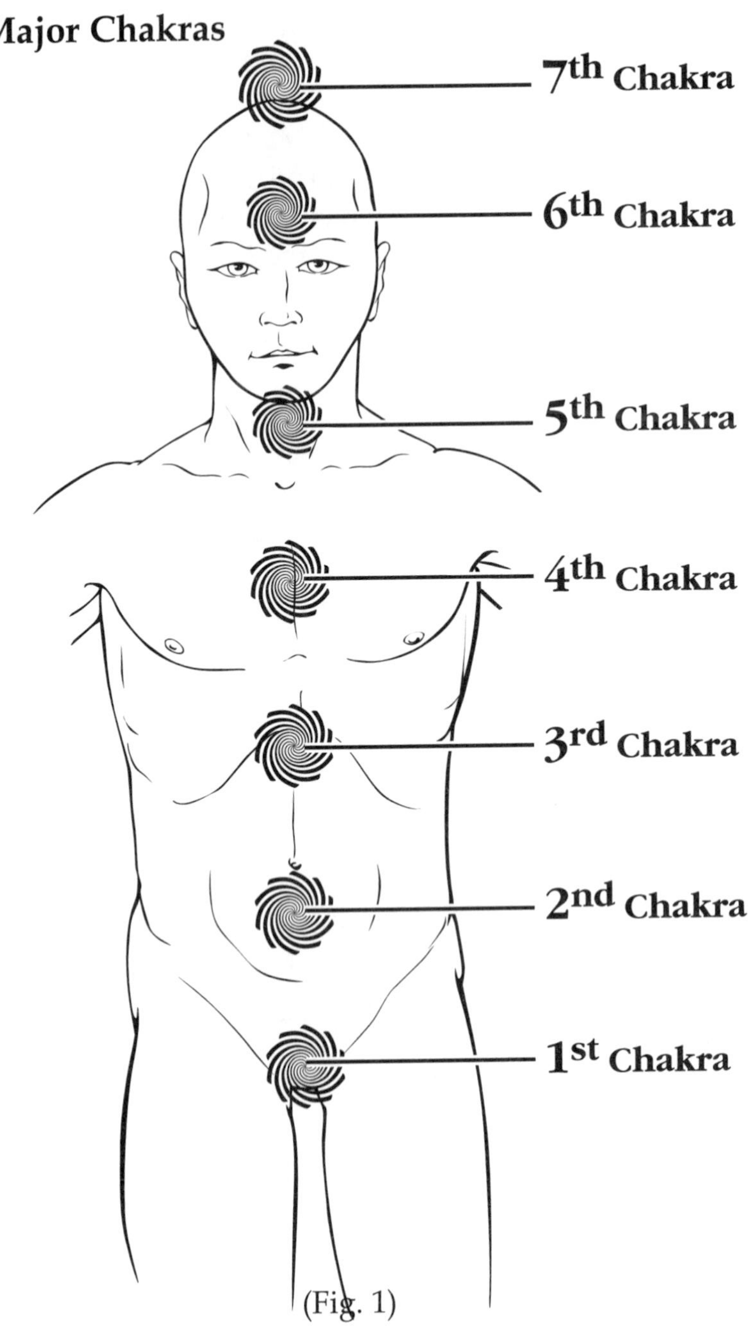

(Fig. 1)

thought to be where the soul enters the physical body at birth and departs at the time of death.

Chakra Descriptions

People who can see Chakras describe them as being about the size of your hand and when looked at directly, they resemble a spinning wheel. A Chakra is cone-shaped with its point plugging into your energy channel along your spine. Its opening (vortex) extends (Fig 2.) about four to six inches away from your body, front and back. Some teachings claim Chakras can even extend farther outside the body. The Chakra funnel is tight and compact near the surface of the skin, gradually widening as it extends outside the physical body. When viewed from the side, a Chakra looks more like an energy vortex similar to the shape of a tornado. Notice on the drawing that some front Chakras are deeper than others in the body because of their connection to the spine, while the back Chakras are not deep at all.

A Chakra spins on its own axis and can spin fast or slow, vibrating at different frequencies. I believe when they are healthy, the front Chakras spin in a clockwise direction if you are standing in front and looking straight at them. The back Chakras spin the opposite direction, counter-clockwise. The Chakras' spin is debatable in different teachings, but their spin and frequency are determined by their location and the person's health. The lowest rate of spin is in the 1st Chakra with the rate increasing in each

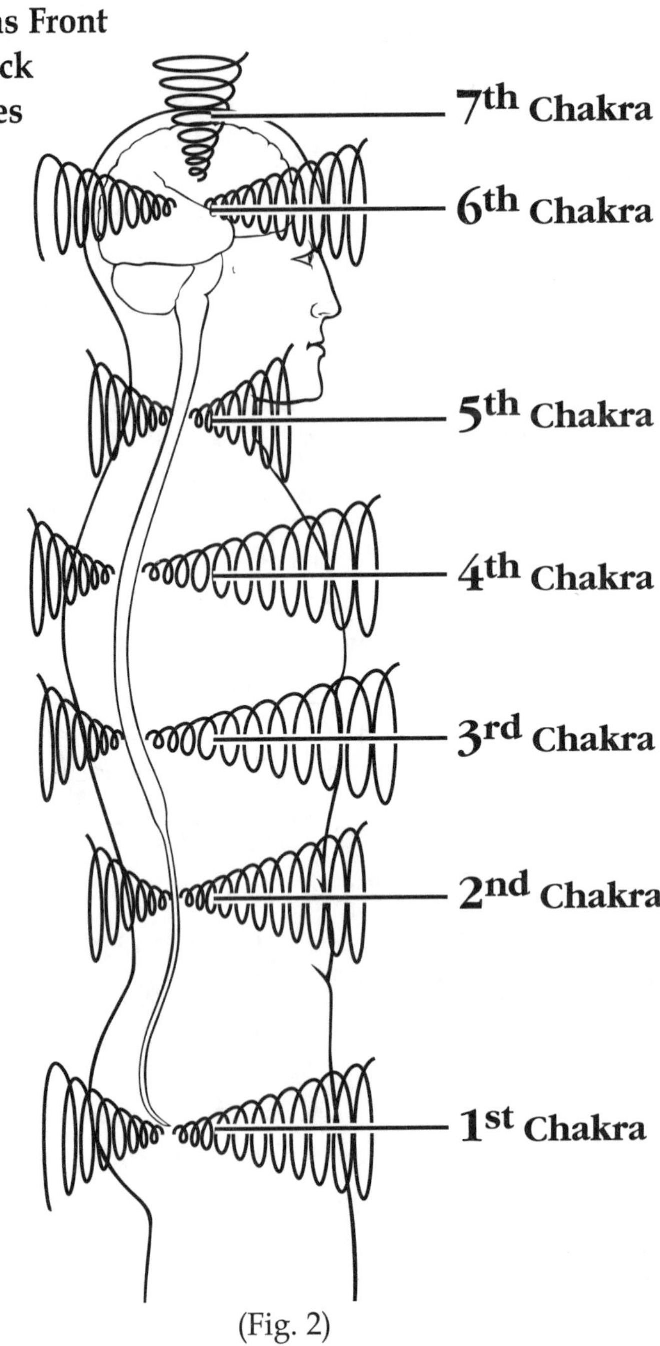
Chakras Front
and Back
Vortexes
7th Chakra
6th Chakra
5th Chakra
4th Chakra
3rd Chakra
2nd Chakra
1st Chakra

(Fig. 2)

subsequent Chakra, the fastest being the 7th Chakra. No matter what your belief or theory on the Chakra spin, the successes of Reiki Healing Attunements are not based on its direction.

Chakra Colors

Since Chakras spin at different speeds (again, the slowest is the 1st Chakra, then on up to the 7th which is the fastest), each emits a different light frequency resonating as a color that can be detected by some people. The following are the most common colors associated with the Chakras.

- 1st Chakra - Red.
- 2nd Chakra - Orange.
- 3rd Chakra - Yellow.
- 4th Chakra - Two colors are most frequently associated with this Chakra: Green and Pink.
- 5th Chakra - Blue.
- 6th Chakra - Indigo.
- 7th Chakra - Three colors are most frequently associated with this Chakra: White, Violet, and Gold.

Chakra Influence In the Body

Basically, the physical body's systems are responsible for different functions. They are: sensory, breathing, circulation, digestion, reproduction, and secretion, with one major Chakra influencing each one of these bodily functions. Sometimes the influence will overlap to a surrounding Chakra, although the influence will not be as strong. Usually a physical ailment or disease will manifest symptoms in one or more of these bodily functions.

The knowledge of what each Chakra influences, which body systems, body parts, internal organs and glands, is an important element in the Reiki Healing Attunements. I will give you complete, detailed instructions in later chapters on how to determine this.

Secondary or Minor Chakras

Most cultures and teachings refer to Seven Major Chakras, which I have described, but some speak of only six, and others even describe as many as eight or more. The biggest differences in cultures and teachings are the secondary Chakras and minor Chakras and how many there are. Some state there are 122 to more than 300 secondary and minor Chakras throughout your body. I believe secondary and minor Chakras are the same, so I just use the term "secondary" Chakras. As for the number of these Chakras throughout the body, I believe it is closer to 300. No matter what your teachings, the secondary Chakras are very important in maintaining your health. Just remember, the major Chakras are portals to the secondary Chakras, making the whole Chakra system connected.

Secondary Chakras

The secondary Chakras have most of the same characteristics as the Seven Major Chakras, although they are much smaller and vary in size. They are located wherever there is a joint in the body, the palms of the hands, soles of the feet, and the ends of the fingers and toes.

Secondary Chakras are attached to joints, glands, and nerve clusters throughout the body. It is important to note that one of the reasons Reiki Healing is so powerful is because of all the secondary Chakras used in channeling Reiki with the hands. This includes the ones in the palms, all the joints in the fingers, and in the tips of the fingers.

People who can see secondary Chakras say they appear as spikes of energy emanating from the body rather than the spinning vortices of the major Chakras. This information corresponds with physical signs of Reiki energy coming from the palms of the hands when channeling it.

Healthy Chakras

There is a clear connection between the condition of a Chakra and the condition of the corresponding organs, glands, and nerves in the area surrounding it. If the Chakra is in good condition and balanced, there is not a health challenge. If a Chakra is blocked, physical problems can manifest.

So, the goal for good health is having strong, clear Chakras that are "spinning" unblocked, bright and clean. When this is achieved, our Chakra system is balanced. "Balanced" means Reiki is flowing smoothly and unblocked and can access where it is needed for healing, building, and nourishing the physical body.

Chakra Blocks

A "block" is the term commonly used when a Chakra is not functioning well and this can be for a variety of reasons. Some of the reasons are that it may be spinning too slowly, spinning in the wrong direction, or not spinning at all. It could also be that it is over-active or under-active. Since every person's situation is different, it may not be exactly clear why a Chakra is blocked. The good news is, that for whatever reason one is blocked, it can be returned to a healthy state and Reiki Healing Attunements will help with this.

Some teachings disagree with this, but I believe Chakras cannot be opened or closed, however they can be blocked. When a Chakra becomes blocked, an imbalance occurs and this can affect corresponding body systems, body parts, organs, glands, and nerves in the area the Chakra is located.

If the block is not cleared, a physical illness could manifest. If the block continues, there can be a domino effect on the other Chakras, which can compound any physical illness that has manifested and create more physical problems.

Back Chakras

All the major Chakras have a corresponding back vortex (Fig. 3) except the 7th Chakra. A few teachings state there is a back Chakra for the 7th located where all dimensions/time zones become one, but you will work only with the six during Reiki Healing Attunements. Working with these six back Chakras is a very important key element in success of the Attunements.

I strongly believe in clearing and balancing both sides of the Chakras, which is essential for good health and healing. Also, it's a key element to the success of Reiki Healing Attunements.

Usually the back Chakras are neglected, under-used, and become blocked because so few people are aware of them. If they are aware of them, they fail to work with them because they do not realize their importance.

The main reason you have to work with both sides of the Chakras is simple. If one side is still blocked, then the whole Chakra is blocked and complete healing will be difficult, if not impossible.

If you only learn one thing from this book, let it be that you have back Chakras, which must be balanced and cleared like the front Chakras in order to maintain the health of your body.

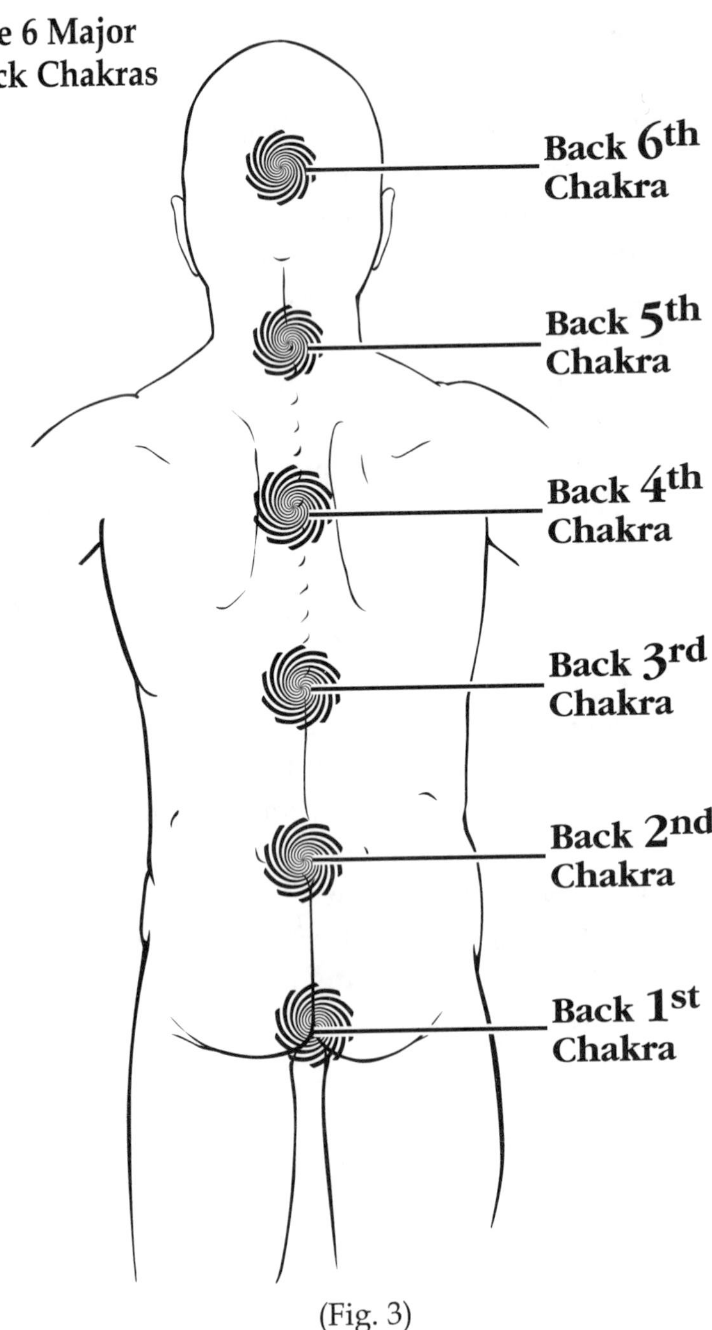
The 6 Major
Back Chakras
Back 6th
Chakra
Back 5th
Chakra
Back 4th
Chakra
Back 3rd
Chakra
Back 2nd
Chakra
Back 1st
Chakra

(Fig. 3)

Back Chakra Teachings

A majority of Chakra teachings focus on the front side of the Chakras and the information that's available on the back Chakras is sometimes confusing and conflicting. All you really need to know about the back Chakras for Reiki Healing Attunements is this:

- Each back Chakra correlates with the same body systems and body organs as its front Chakra.
- The front side of the major Chakras corresponds to our conscious, physical being and the laws of the physical universe.
- The back Chakras of the major Chakras correspond to our unconscious, non-physical being and to the laws of the non-physical universe.

Upper and Lower Chakras

I have heard at times that the upper Chakras, 4th, 5th, 6th and 7th are good and the lower 1st, 2nd and 3rd are bad. Some of the reasons for this are that the three lower bad Chakras are linked to basic primary needs, those of survival and procreation, which can bring about the worst in humans in certain circumstances. The four higher good Chakras are linked with our psychological makeup, love, communication, knowledge, and connection with the spiritual realms, which can bring about the best in humans in certain circumstances.

The fact is, all Chakras are important and they all need to be balanced and cleared for health and harmony. I believe there is no distinction between good or bad Chakras because each one has its purpose and is part of the whole, so they are all good.

Chakras and Reiki Healing Attunements

As I stated before, there is a whirling circular motion that forms a cavity or vacuum in the center of the Chakra. During the Reiki Healing Attunements, you are going to channel Reiki and embed Reiki Symbols with intent to help heal a specific physical ailment or disease directly into the Chakra's cavity (vortex). Once this is done, Reiki is then processed, transformed, and sent to help the ailment or disease you are focusing on, and then flows through the rest of the Chakra system.

Reiki Healing Attunements are effective because they work directly with the Chakra(s) where the physical ailments or diseases are manifested, so Reiki is processed there first. The Chakra you will use will be determined by its influence over the body systems and organs where the physical illness has manifested.

“No prayer is complete without presence.”

-Rumi

“On the way there is no harder pass than this: fortunate is he who does not carry envy as his companion.”

-Rumi

Meridians

During the Healing Attunements, Reiki flows into the Chakras and on through connecting pathways or channels named "Meridians" or "Nadis" that exist throughout the body. These connecting pathways transport Reiki to other major Chakras which, in turn, process the Reiki and transport it through secondary Meridians throughout the whole body.

People who are sensitive to the Reiki flowing from one Chakra to another through these connecting pathways say it is a rushing water sensation, a spreading warmth, and/or a tingling feeling.

Meridians or Nadis?

There is a conflict in some teachings on what these energy channels are called, Meridians or Nadis. Some teachings mention both as one and the same. There are also differences in how the energy system is mapped throughout the body. My teachings on the energy pathways have a mixed influence from India and China. It really doesn't matter what your beliefs are, Meridians or Nadis, they both serve the same function in transporting Reiki throughout the body.

Nadis are referred to mainly in India's energy healing systems. In the Chinese energy healing system these pathways are called Meridians, as I prefer to call them.

China has a very sophisticated tradition of energy medicine which focuses on Meridians throughout the body. The Meridians have a major role in Chinese healing systems. In the Chinese system, each of the 12 major Meridians is named for the main organ it is related to or a function it corresponds with, for example, Lung Meridian, Heart Meridian, etc.

The Japanese adapted some aspects of the Chinese healing systems for their healing methods. It is now believed Reiki originated in Tibet, China and resurfaced in Japan.

Because of this Chinese influence on Reiki, I call the energy channels throughout the body Meridians, not Nadis.

Twelve Major Meridians

There are two systems of Meridians forming the network of energy channels throughout the body, major Meridians and secondary Meridians. There are 12 Major Meridians and, just like secondary Chakras, there are hundreds of secondary Meridians.

The Twelve Major Meridians (Figs. 4 & 5) run up and down the body and are interconnected with the Chakras. Major Meridians pass through major internal organs, but secondary Meridians do not.

When in a healthy state, the Meridian System transports Reiki in a continuous circulation throughout the body, but blockages can also occur in Meridians. Reiki Healing Attunements can dissolve these blockages and restore the body's healthy flow of Reiki through the Meridian System.

Meridian Metaphor

The Meridians are the equivalent of our blood vessels throughout the body, but instead of transporting blood, they transport Reiki.

Here's an excellent metaphor that many teachers use to described how Meridians function and what happens

Major Front Meridians

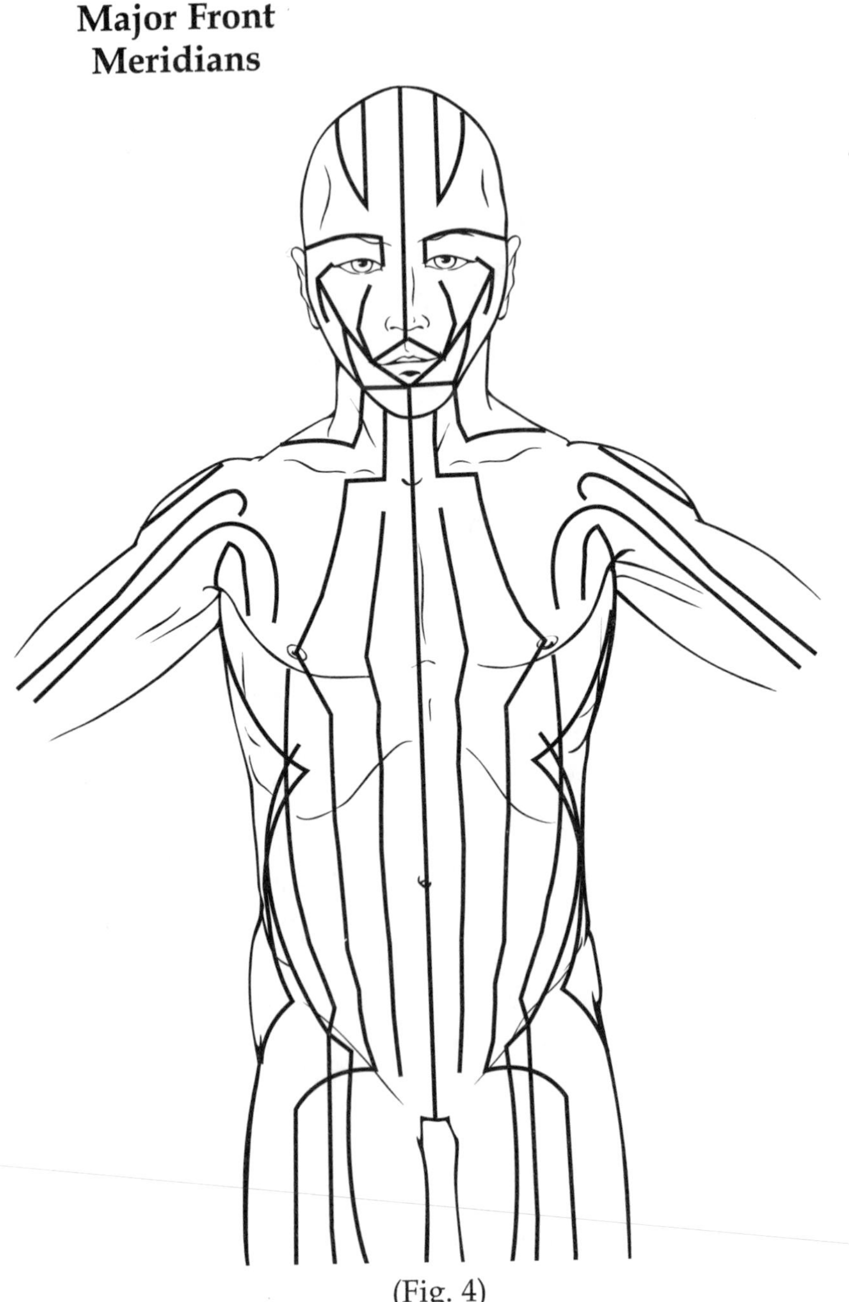

(Fig. 4)

Major Back Meridians

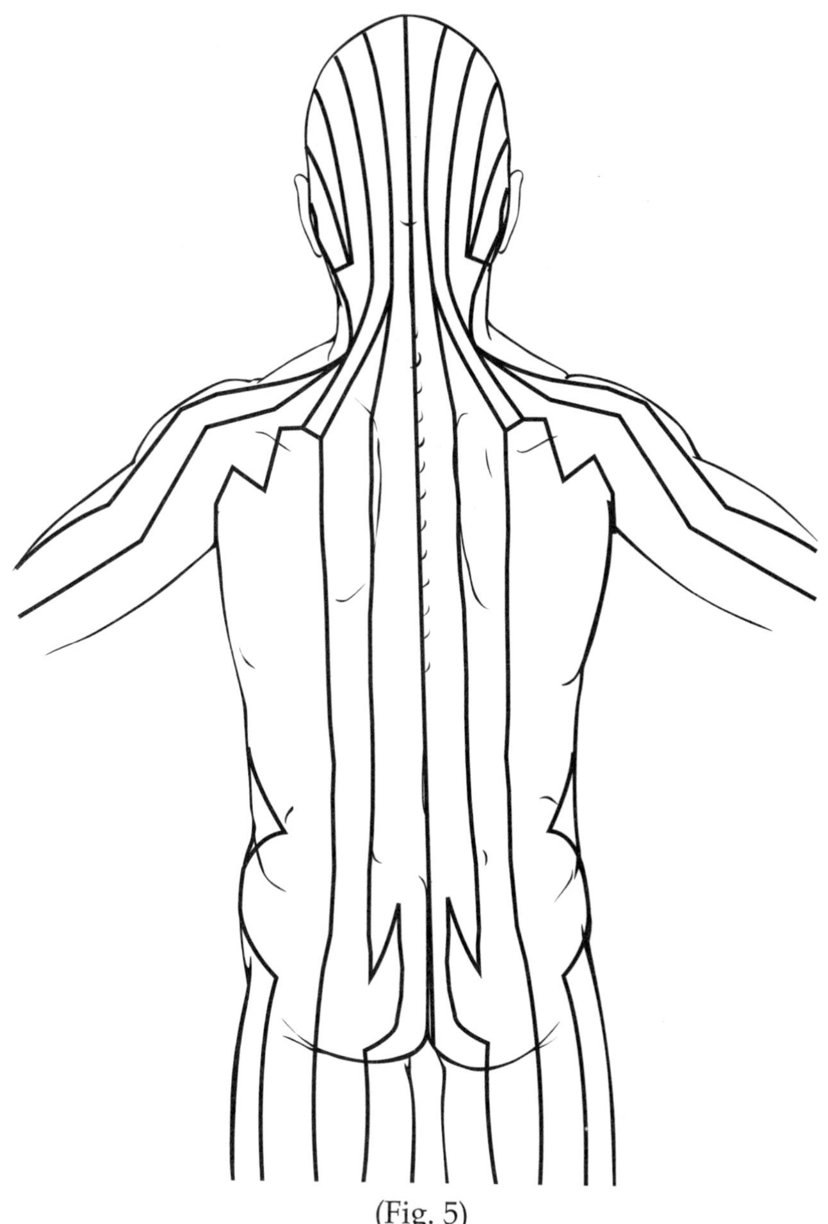

(Fig. 5)

when they become blocked. Imagine the Meridians as a riverbed over which water flows and irrigates the land, feeding, nourishing, and sustaining the substance through which it flows. If a dam were placed at any point along the river, the nourishing effect that the water had on the whole river would stop at the point the dam was placed. Of course, the water represents Reiki.

**"Paradise is surrounded by what we dislike;
the fires of hell are surrounded by what we desire."**

-Rumi

"Since in order to speak, one must first listen, learn to speak by listening."

-Rumi

Reiki Signs

Students always like to know what they should experience during and after a Reiki Healing Attunement. Before we proceed into the chapters on how to prepare for and how to perform Reiki Healing Attunements, let's review that. Please keep in mind, Reiki experiences can be different each time you give or receive a Healing Attunement.

Reiki: Subtle and Powerful

Reiki is very powerful as your life force should be, but it

is very subtle when it flows into and throughout the physical body so it can be absorbed and used. If Reiki entered the body like a charge of electricity or any stronger than it does, there would be major problems with your body accepting and utilizing it. The more you perform Reiki Healing Attunements or receive Reiki Healing Attunements, it will become easier for you to sense Reiki and know when it is flowing.

Reiki Physical Signs

People like to have physical signs to affirm that Reiki is flowing during a Reiki Healing Attunement. This includes the Healer performing the Healing Attunement and the person receiving the Healing Attunement. It is human nature to want to have physical signs to wrap the conscious mind around, to confirm something is actually happening.

The majority of the time there are indeed physical signs when channeling Reiki, but sometimes there are no physical signs. Please do not worry or be concerned about this when and if this happens. This does not mean the Reiki is not flowing, or the Reiki Healing Attunement is not working, because it is. When there are minimal or no physical signs during a Healing Attunement, ultimately there are the same positive results after this Attunement as a Healing Attunement with the physical signs.

Some of the possible physical signs you may manifest when you are channeling (giving) Reiki to a person during a Reiki Healing Attunement include warm to very hot hands; tingling sensations in hands or throughout the body; hands cold to ice cold; possibly even numbness in the hands and/or arms.

You may experience a combination of the above signs or have your own unique signs. On occasion, the person receiving the Healing Attunement can feel the same physical signs as the Healer. At times you may not feel anything if you are performing the Healing Attunement, but the person receiving it will, or vice versa. Usually, both the Healer and the receiver of the Attunement will experience their own Reiki signs.

Mental and Spiritual Signs

Mental and spiritual signs of Reiki can manifest when a person is receiving a Reiki Healing Attunement, and even when the Healer is performing the Attunement. Some of the possible mental and spiritual signs are spiritual visions, flashes of insight, knowing of certain information, out-of-body experiences, colors experienced, music heard, different smells, or departed loved ones and guides might appear. There could be just one of these, or a combination.

Emotional Signs

A person might have an emotional release during the Healing Attunement and start crying, or their nose starts running, or various fluids are released from the physical body. This can happen at times from the release of Psychic Debris[1] (explained in my first book) that has been blocked and/or trapped in the Chakras and Meridians.

[1]An emotional charge created by anger, fear, grief, etc. that is never processed or released. The emotional charge is experienced over and over again and accumulates over time creating Psychic Debris.

Of course, all of the mentioned experiences do not happen during every Reiki Healing Attunement. The manifestations of these experiences are a harmless part of the healing process and should not be feared. If it happens to you or a client, just embrace the experience, or at least understand and accept it as part of a cleansing, releasing process that you must go through for healing. It is always temporary.

Chakra Signs

Physical Chakra signs experienced during a Reiki Healing Attunement vary from person to person and can be different each time a Healing Attunement is received. You should be aware of some of the possibilities and be able to describe them to the person receiving the Healing Attunement so there will be no fear or surprises.

The physical signs range from Chakras feeling warm or hot, to a rushing and flowing sensation in and around the Chakras, then spreading throughout the body. The signs might be as simple as a relaxed feeling or tingly, vibrating sensations throughout the body spreading from the Chakra with which you're working. The signs experienced can be a combination of any of the above, or a person will have their own unique signs.

Maybe nothing at all will be experienced consciously with the Chakras during a Reiki Healing Attunement. As I mentioned before, if this happens, it does not mean the Healing Attunement has not been received or will not work. The Attunement will still be successful when there are minimal or no signs. Ultimately, the Healing

Attunement will produce the same outcome as if physical Chakra signs were experienced.

After an Attunement

After a Reiki Healing Attunement your Chakras will be shifting and processing Reiki very rapidly, especially the one you were working with during the Attunement. This will clear and balance your body thereby allowing healing to take place and Reiki to flow uninterrupted where it is needed.

Because of individual circumstances, everyone progresses differently in terms of time regarding healing. You might not consciously sense or physically feel anything at first, but healing can be taking place. Eventually you will start to sense and feel the change and healing on a physical level. You will have more awareness consciously of the healing as time goes on and you receive additional Reiki Healing Attunements.

"That which is false troubles the heart, but truth brings joyous tranquility."

-Rumi

Preparing for the Attunements

In the following chapters you are going to learn step-by-step everything you need to know to perform Reiki Healing Attunements on yourself and others. This will include directions, photos, illustrations, and guidelines.

Preparation Before and After the Attunement

Doctors have certain steps they follow before and after a surgery. This includes knowing what surgery they are about to perform and how they are going to perform it; cleaning the area and themselves before surgery; and taking certain precautions during and after the surgery to clean the room and themselves.

The same applies to Healing Attunements. There are certain steps to follow before and after a Reiki Healing Attunement. If you have your own method, or wish to develop your own method for doing these steps and it will accomplish the same goal, feel free to do so.

Steps Before a Healing Attunement

- Decide on the Healing Attunement
- Preparation
- Wash Hands
- Grounding and Clearing
- Protection

Decide on the Attunement

Before performing a Reiki Healing Attunement, you need to know two important things: one, what physical ailment or disease it is for; and two, which Chakra you will be working with during the Attunement.

If you are performing the Attunement on yourself, you certainly will know for what purpose the Healing Attunement is to be used, but, if the Healing Attunement is for another person, you need to find out in advance why it is needed.

Once you know what the Healing Attunement is for, you then can determine which Chakra to work with during the Attunement. Chapter 11 explains the formula for this.

Preparation

Below are preparation suggestions I recommend before receiving a Reiki Healing Attunement. Follow as many on the list as you can. The Reiki Healing Attunement still will be received if you cannot do every suggestion, but follow as many as you can to ensure an effective Attunement.

- Limit or stop eating all animal protein 24 hours before the Attunement.
- Consume only water or juice four to six hours before the Attunement.
- Limit or stop use of caffeine drinks four to six hours before the Attunement.
- Stop drinking alcohol 24 hours before the Attunement.
- Limit sugar 24 hours before the Attunement.
- Limit or stop smoking four to six hours before the Attunement.
- One day before the Attunement, meditate a few minutes upon the reason you need the Reiki Healing Attunement.

Wash Hands

This is a simple step, but an important one. Wash your hands before an Attunement, even if you are going to perform it on yourself. The easiest way is to buy disposable cleaning packets and use them when needed.

Grounding and Clearing

The Healer should always clear and ground him or herself before performing a Reiki Healing Attunement. This ensures Reiki will flow through strongly and uninterrupted. Healers usually have their own method and process for doing this before any Reiki session, and that will work.

One simple and effective way to do this for all levels is by taking a moment to bring Reiki Energy through the top of the head (7th Chakra) all the way down through your body and out both legs into the earth, then wait a few seconds and bring it back from the earth, all the way back up both legs and out the top of the head. This whole process should only take a few minutes and usually you will sense a feeling of balance after the process is complete. Again, you can follow your own method, as long as it clears and grounds you before performing the Healing Attunement.

Protection

Here is a brief overview why protecting yourself and others is important. I believe that what I call "Psychic Debris" can be released during a Healing Attunement. Healers call Psychic Debris different names, but most are aware of it and have experienced it during a healing session with others. The source of Psychic Debris is debatable among Healers, but most agree it can be released during a healing session. The amount released during a session, if any, can vary depending on the individual and his or her condition and circumstances.

I believe the source of Psychic Debris to be emotions that have accumulated over a period of time because they were not processed or released by the individual. (This can be years.) These accumulated emotions can be fear, grief, anger, hate, etc.

Normally, if processed and released in a timely manner, these emotions are not negative and are a part of the human experience, but when they are held onto by the conscious or unconscious mind and are not processed and released in a timely manner, they can accumulate in and around a person's body, and that's when the emotions become negative. I am sure you have sensed or felt a stranger's anger, fear, hate, etc. just by standing next to or walking by them. Perhaps you have walked into an empty room and felt strange or maybe sensed a wave of stress, fear, or anger? This is Psychic Debris. Actually, when Psychic Debris is released during a Healing Attunement, it is a good thing and helps with the healing process. You just need to protect yourself from it.

When released during an Attunement, Psychic Debris can attach itself to you and/or linger in the room waiting to attach itself to somebody else or change future circumstances in a negative way. When Psychic Debris attaches to you or another person, negative emotional charges can be experienced as long as it stays attached and is not destroyed. This is why new Healers who do not protect themselves during a healing session sometimes feel drained or sick and experience strange emotions to which they are unaccustomed. As soon as they clear and balance themselves, they are back to normal.

Below are several suggestions regarding protection. You can also use your own methods.

- Visualize or imagine white or golden light filling the area and surrounding you and/or your client.
- You can smudge or sage the room, yourself and/or your clients.
- Place Reiki Crystals or Reiki Healing Stones in the corners of the room.
- State a prayer asking your higher power, guides, angels, etc., to protect you and/or your client during this time.
- Clear the room with the symbols to which you have been attuned by drawing and activating them in all corners of the room. 1st Level Healers will not be able to use this suggestion.

Please make sure you do some or all of the above or your own method for protection. Either way, it can be done rapidly, and in less than a minute once you are experienced at it.

Extra Help

If you are a 2nd Level Reiki Healer or Reiki Master you can send Reiki to the room or area where the Reiki Healing Attunement will take place ahead of time. This can be done when you anticipate working with a difficult physical ailment or disease. Reiki can be sent a few days or any length of time before the Attunement. Just send Reiki with the intent to start cleansing, clearing, and preparing the area where the Attunement will be performed and it will be there when you arrive.

Steps After a Healing Attunement

- Break the Connection
- Clearing Room and Self
- Wash Hands and Shower
- Sleep and Rest

Break the Connection

After performing the Attunement on another person, rub and/or shake your hands to break the energy connection you formed with them during the Attunement.

Clearing Room

Even though you had protection during the Healing Attunement, you still want to clear the area and yourself when you are through. This should only take about 30 seconds to do.

Many Healers have their own method for this which can be used. Here's what I do after the Healing Attunement. I bring additional golden light into the room, filling it up and at the same time surrounding me. I then ask my source to remove and dissolve any and all residual Psychic Debris (or whatever you call it), from the room and myself now.

Wash Hands and Shower

Wash your hands after performing the Attunement and take a shower as soon as possible.

Sleep and Rest

After receiving a Reiki Healing Attunement, the best thing to do is sleep when there is a chance. This allows the body to integrate the Attunement without other distractions. In the days after a Reiki Healing Attunement, your body will be detoxifying, so drink plenty of water during that time to help your body flush out the toxins that are released.

“The lion who breaks the enemy’s ranks is a minor hero compared to the lion who overcomes himself.”

-Rumi

"There is no worse sickness for the soul, O you who are proud, than this pretense of perfection."

-Rumi

Chakra Formula

As I mentioned earlier, in many Chakra teachings there are diverse opinions about which Chakra influences or corresponds with a certain body system, body part, organ, or gland, and just as many diverse opinions about which Chakra to use with healing a specific ailment or disease.

This chapter has a Chakra formula that will give you continuity in determining which Chakra to use during a Reiki Healing Attunement for any physical ailment or disease. The formula includes guidelines and illustrations to make it user friendly. The Chakra Formula can also be used with other healing modalities.

Two-Step Chakra Formula

By following the steps below you will determine which Chakra to use during the Reiki Healing Attunement for any physical ailment or disease.

1. You must identify the specific physical ailment or disease for which the Reiki Healing Attunement is going to be performed and where it has manifested in the body. This information is usually available from a medical diagnosis. You need this information before you can proceed to Step Two.

2.You will then need to ascertain which Chakra's area of influence corresponds to that area of the body the ailment or disease has manifested in, and that will be the Chakra you will use in the Healing Attunement. The guidelines and illustrations in Step Two show you how to find this Chakra.

Review the illustrations (Figs 6-12) at the end of this chapter and find the one that shows the organ, body part, body system, etc., where the ailment or disease has manifested: then look at the Chakra's area of influence in which it is located in and that's the Chakra you will use during the Healing Attunement.

If, for example, the Healing Attunement is for a kidney stone in the right kidney, look at the illustration that shows the kidneys and find the right kidney; then see which Chakra's area of influence in which the right kidney is located and that's the Chakra you will use during the Attunement. In this example, it is the 3rd Chakra.

If the area where the ailment or disease is located overlaps two Chakras, you must use the Chakra that has the largest area of influence. For example, if there is a tumor in the brain and it is located in the 6th Chakra and 7th Chakra, but a larger portion is in the 7th Chakra, the 7th Chakra would be used for the Healing Attunement.

Additional Guidelines

On occasion, the illustrations might not show the organ, gland, etc., that was diagnosed as the problem. If that happens, all you need to know is the location or the body system it is in. To get this information you need to ask the doctor or do some research; then look for that area on an illustration and see in which Chakra's area of influence it is located and that's the Chakra you will use in the Attunement.

For ailments or diseases of the skin, muscles, joints, soft body tissue and bones, use the Chakra's area of influence where it has manifested to determine the Chakra to use. A few examples: arthritis, tumors, growths, muscle spasms, joint problems, broken bones and tendons. If the same ailment or disease has manifested in two or more locations (e.g., arthritis of the fingers and knees, or a skin problem on the face and stomach), you do a separate Healing Attunement for each location.

The majority of the time you will just use the illustrations to find the Chakra for the Healing Attunement. Sometimes, however, a physical ailment or disease is not localized, but is manifested throughout a body system. Use the guidelines below when this is the situation.

- For ailments or diseases within the lower body, legs, feet, etc. use the 1st Chakra.
- For ailments or diseases within the shoulders, arms and hands use the 4th Chakra.
- For colds, flus, or viruses use the 4th Chakra.
- For ailments or diseases that are in the central nervous system use the 7th Chakra.
- For ailments or diseases that are in the autonomic nervous system use the 6th Chakra.
- For ailments or diseases that are in the Lymphatic/Immune system use the 4th Chakra.
- For ailments or diseases that are blood specific use the 3rd Chakra.
- For ailments or diseases that are in the circulatory system use the 4th Chakra.
- For ailments or diseases that are in the Skeletal System or Muscular System use the 7th Chakra.

Illustration Descriptions

There are seven illustrations to use with Step Two. Each illustration diagrams the Seven Major Chakras with the surrounding organs, glands, nerves, etc. located in their area of influence. The illustrations include the following body systems:

◆ **Muscular System (Fig.6)**

Muscles make up half of the body's systems. These include voluntary muscles to lift objects, move, etc., and involuntary muscles, which include heart muscle and smooth muscle to provide power for the Digestive, Cardiovascular and Respiratory Systems.

◆ **Skeletal System (Fig.6)**

The skeletal system is the structure (bones) on which the body is built. It is the body's foundation.

◆ **Nervous System (Fig.7)**

The brain is the site of conscious and unconscious thought. Through the nerves of the spinal cord and the nerves that spread throughout the body, the brain controls all body movement.

◆ **Endocrine System (Fig.8)**

The endocrine system plays a major role in the body's daily health. The glands release hormones directly into the bloodstream and control all aspects of growth, development, and daily bodily functions.

◆ **Reproductive System (Fig.9)**

The gonads, the primary reproductive organs, are the testes in the male and the ovaries in the female. These organs are responsible for producing the sperm and ova, but they secrete hormones and are also considered to be endocrine glands.

◆ **Urinary System (Fig.9)**

This system's primary function is the kidneys' production of urine to eliminate waste and excess fluids.

◆ **Digestive System (Fig.10)**
The digestive system starts at the mouth and ends at the anus. The system has many functions, but the main ones are storing food, digesting it, and eliminating waste.

◆ **Respiratory System (Fig.11)**
The respiratory system carries air in and out of the lungs where oxygen and carbon dioxide are exchanged.

◆ **Cardiovascular System (Fig.11)**
This system's main purpose is to pump oxygenated blood throughout the body. Blood circulation also removes waste products from the body.

◆ **Lymphatic / Immune System (Fig.12)**
The lymphatic system functions include the transport of lymphatic fluid, which can carry bacteria and cancer cells. Lymphatic glands are found throughout the body and swell up when infected to prevent the spread of disease and infections. The lymphatic system is a major element in our physical body's defense system.

Additional Information

Here are a few definitions to help you with the illustrations and a brief overview of the glands in the Endocrine System. Endocrine glands are identified with Chakras in most teachings. When you understand what they do within the body, you will see why it is vital to your well-being that they are healthy.

Organ and Nerve Plexus

An organ is a structure that contains at least two different types of tissue functioning together for a common purpose. Every major Chakra is associated with the functioning of corresponding organ(s) in our body as the illustrations show.

A nerve plexus is a network of intersecting nerves that come together to supply a particular area with nerves.

Endocrine Glands

◆ **Gonads**

Gonads secrete hormones that affect all aspects of sexuality in men and women throughout their lives. This includes reproduction, puberty, fertility, menstruation, pregnancy, menopause, sex drive, etc.

◆ **Pancreas**

The pancreas secretes two major hormones, insulin and glucagon. The human body needs blood glucose (blood sugar) balanced, and insulin and glucagon are the hormones that do this. Glucose is the only food substance utilized by the brain.

◆ **Adrenal Glands**

The Adrenal Glands have two separate parts, the medulla and the cortex. The medulla secretes adrenaline which acts directly on the heart, blood vessels, lungs, and muscles in the fight or flight response. The cortex secretes steroids which balance the physical and emotional energy levels. This helps with shock and stress. It also produces Aldosterone which balances water, sodium, and potassium. This helps maintain normal blood pressure.

◆ **Thymus**

Although all the functions of the Thymus are not fully understood, we do know it is important to the body's immune response, especially the production of T-cells. Auto-immune diseases, including AIDS, are affected by the thymus, as are some forms of cancer.

◆ **Thyroid and Parathyroid**

The Thyroid gland affects metabolism in several ways–growth, temperature control, energy production, and carbohydrate and fat metabolism. The Parathyroid consists of four glands that are vital to calcium metabolism which is needed for healthy teeth, bones, and muscles, including the heart.

◆ **Pituitary and Hypothalamus**

The Pituitary gland regulates the entire endocrine system. The Hypothalamus secretes hormones which, in turn, regulate the flow of hormones from the Pituitary. The Hypothalamus gland also directs the body's thirst, hunger, sexual desire, and the biological clock that determines our aging process. Some teachings place the Pituitary and Hypothalamus glands under the influence of the 7th Chakra. I place the Pineal gland with the 7th Chakra.

◆ **Pineal**

The pineal secretes melatonin which stimulates sleep and controls our body clock and our daily biological rhythms. The area where this gland is located is considered the connecting link between the physical and spiritual worlds.

The following pages have the seven illustrations (Figs. 6-12) you will use with Step Two of the Chakra Formula.

Skeletal / Muscular System

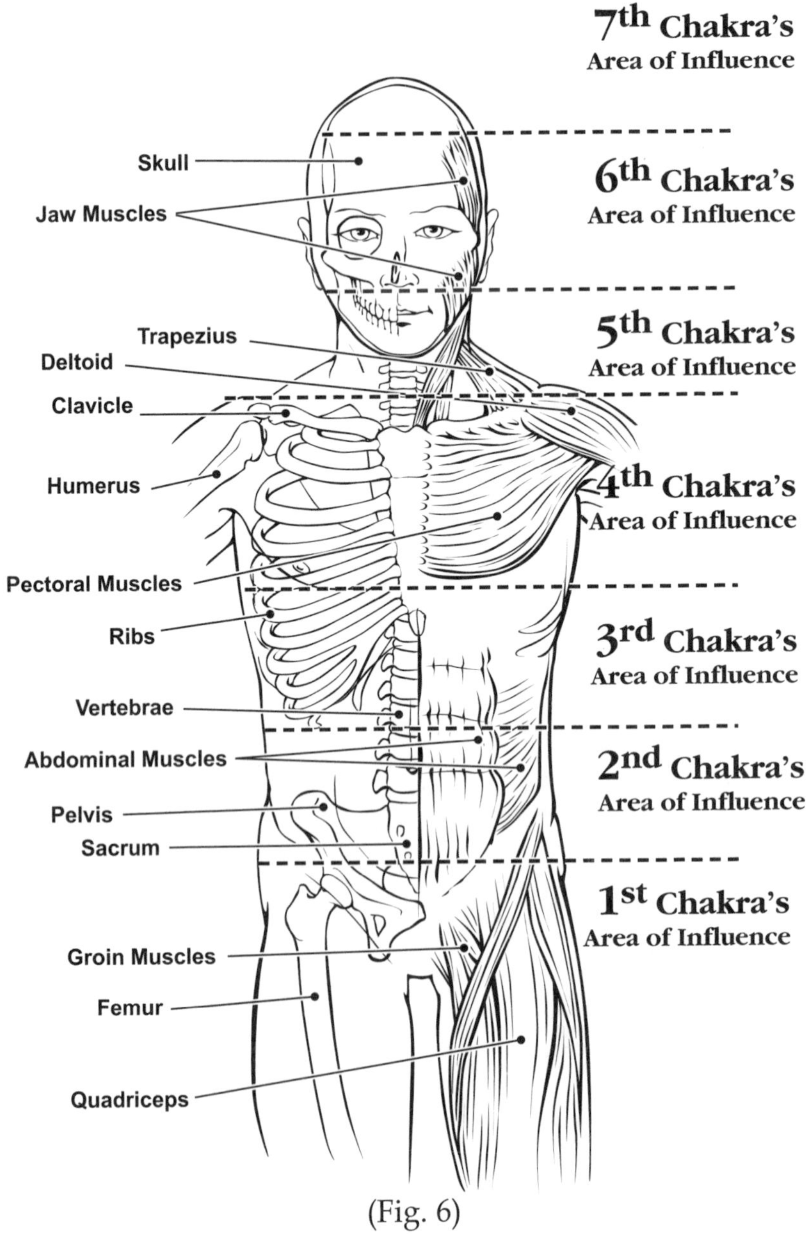

(Fig. 6)

Nervous System

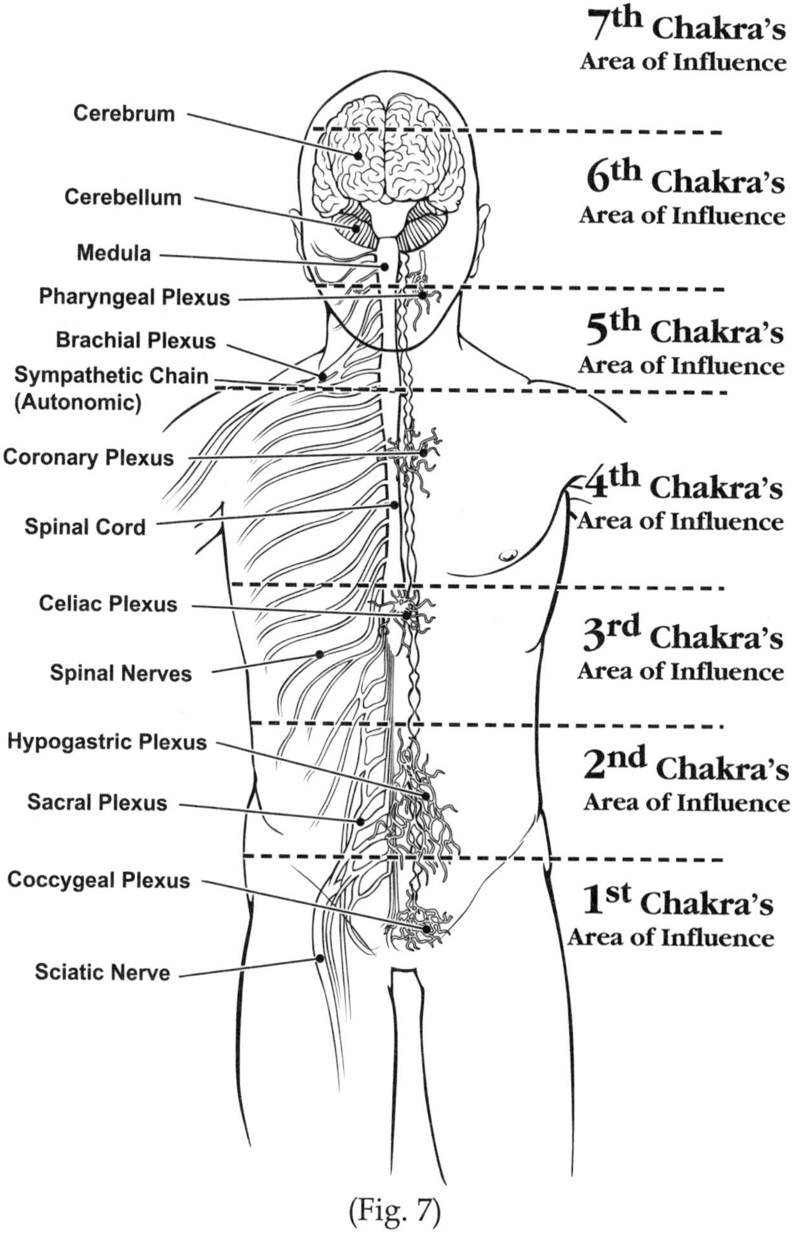

(Fig. 7)

Endocrine System

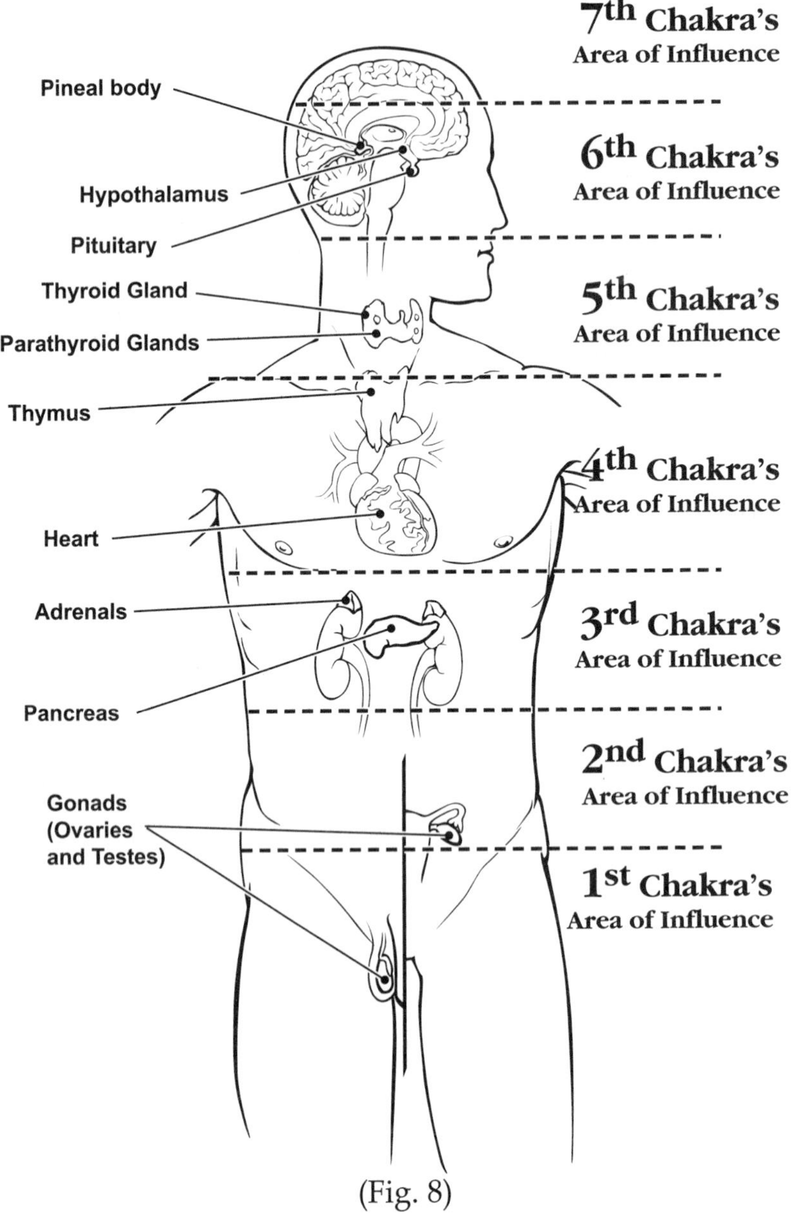

(Fig. 8)

Reproductive / Urinary System

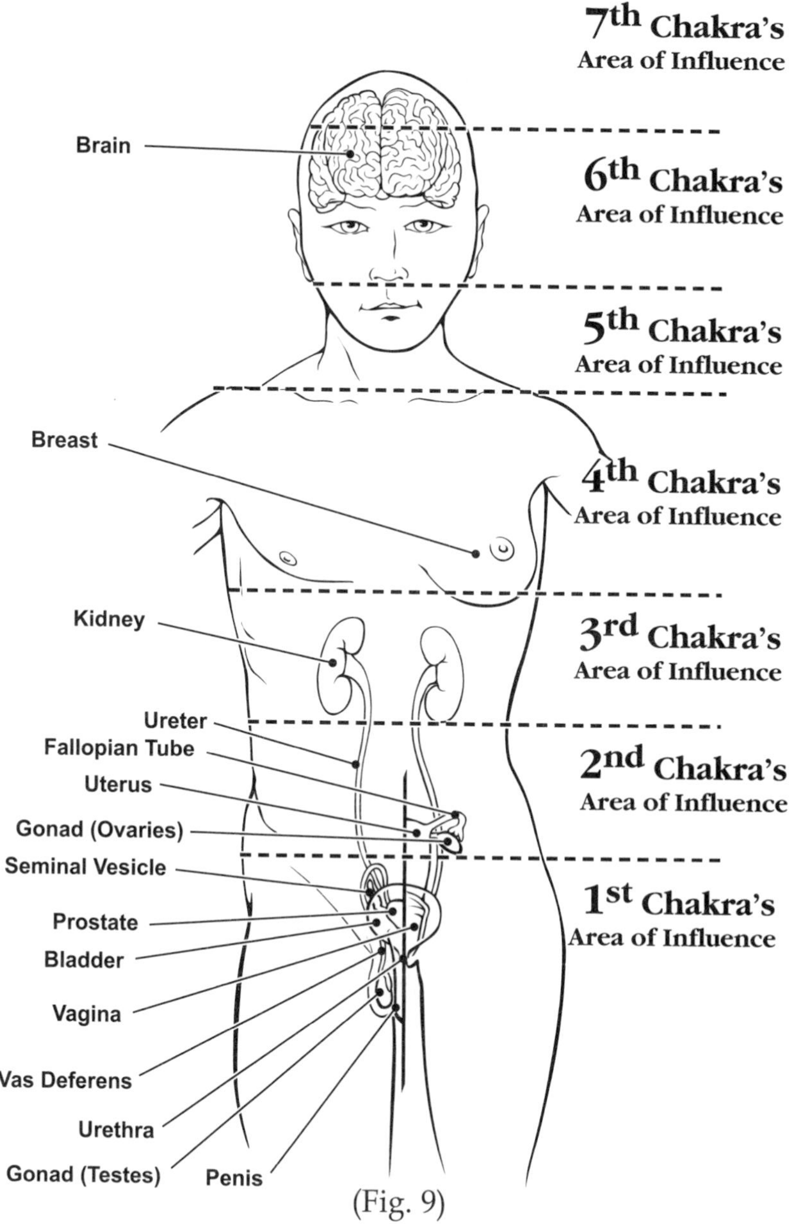

(Fig. 9)

Digestive System

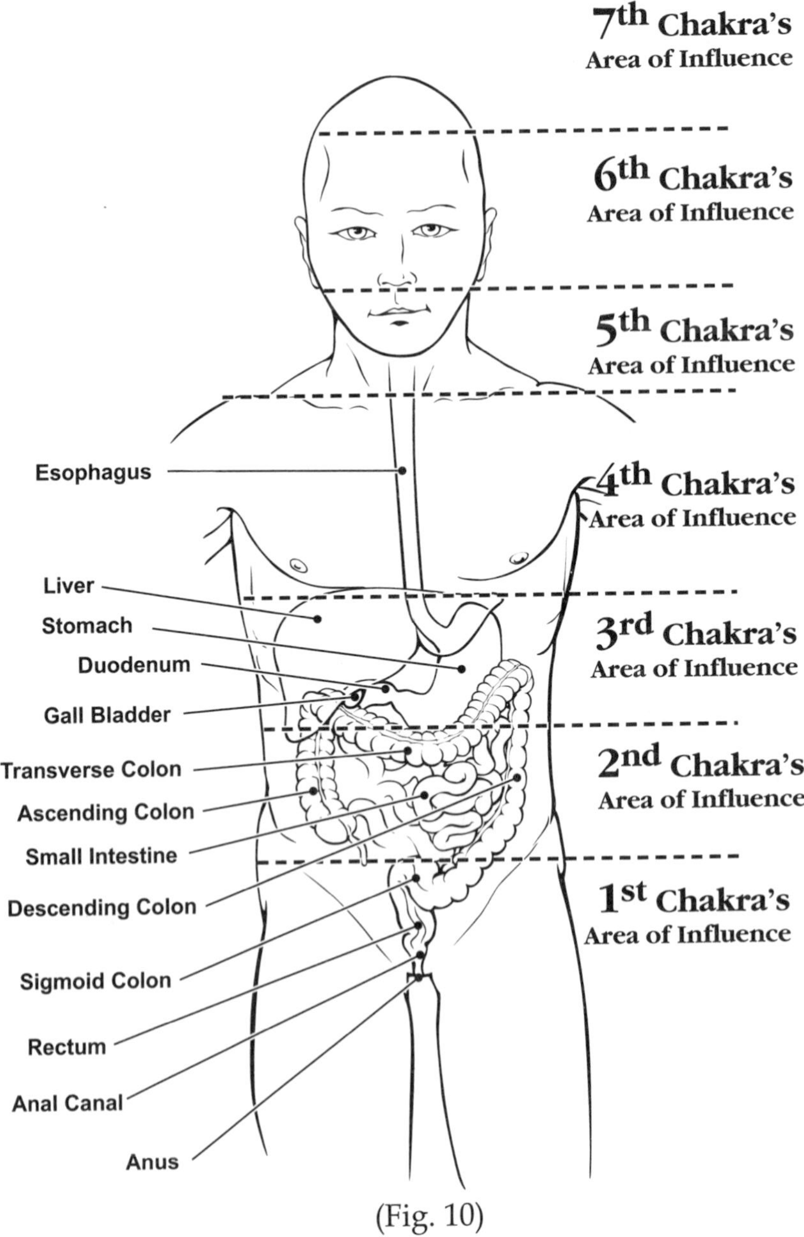

(Fig. 10)

Cardiovascular / Respiratory System

7th Chakra's
Area of Influence

6th Chakra's
Area of Influence

5th Chakra's
Area of Influence

4th Chakra's
Area of Influence

3rd Chakra's
Area of Influence

2nd Chakra's
Area of Influence

1st Chakra's
Area of Influence

Larynx
Cartoid Artery
Trachea
Aorta
Lung
Heart
Diaphragm
Liver
Vena Cava
Descending Aorta
Femoral Artery

(Fig. 11)

Lymphatic / Immune System

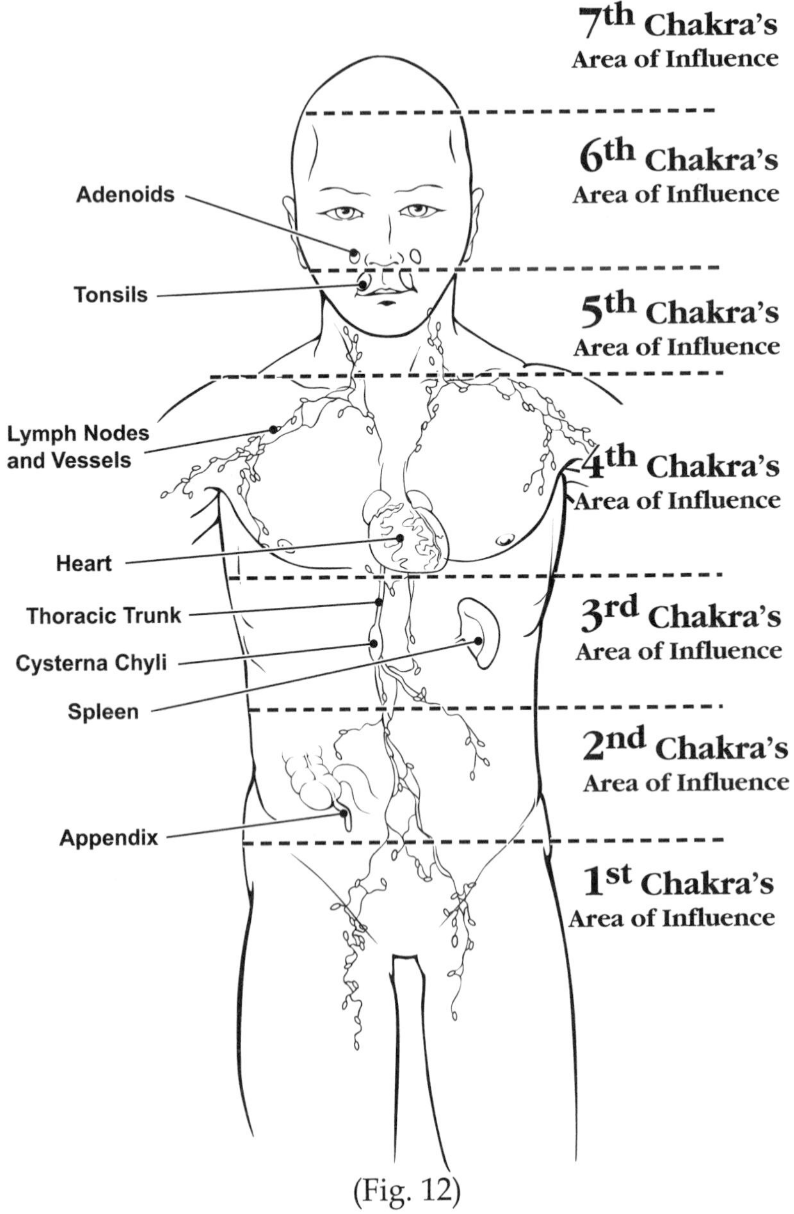

(Fig. 12)

“The only lasting beauty is the beauty of the heart.”

-Rumi

“Let the beauty of what you love, be what you do.”

-Rumi

Reiki Healing Attunements

You have now learned how to prepare before a Reiki Healing Attunement, what to do afterward, and the formula for finding which Chakra to use during the Attunement. This chapter gives you the steps for performing a Reiki Healing Attunement. With each step, there is an explanation. At first glance it might seem like a lot to learn, but after performing a few Attunements, the process will become second nature.

Before I give the steps, I would like to explain a few words and terms that I use in explaining the steps so you will have an understanding of them.

Visualize

In the Attunement directions, I ask you to visualize the Reiki Symbols. Visualization is seeing a picture in your mind's eye. In this case, it is Reiki Symbols. Some Healers have a challenge visualizing and I am one of them. If you have a difficult time visualizing, just imagine or know the symbols are there when asked to do so, or you can draw them in the air like I do.

Activate Symbols

When you activate a Reiki Symbol, it generally means you turn it on, make it work, or put it into action, etc. There are many ways to activate a Reiki Symbol and it depends on the way you were taught or your preference. A few ways to activate a symbol are thinking of its name, saying it out loud if no one is around or silently if non-attuned people are present, or you can just use your intent to activate the symbol. Activate Reiki Symbols the way that works the best for you.

Visualize and Activate = All in One

At the point in the Reiki Healing Attunement Steps when I say *Visualize* the symbol, then activate it. This is done almost simultaneously. In fact, when some Healers visualize a symbol, it's activated automatically.

Embed the Symbol

Once you have the Reiki Symbol visualized and activated over the Chakra, I ask you to embed the symbol into it. This means to place the symbol into the center of the Chakra in the body. You can do this several ways such as by visualizing it there, imagining it there, or knowing it is there with your intent. What I do is visualize the symbol, then lower and guide it into the center of the Chakra with my finger, not touching the client. Use the method that is the easiest for you.

Intent and Focus

Intent is your state of mind in knowing Reiki's purpose and where it should flow during the Healing Attunement. For example, I am performing a Healing Attunement for a kidney stone. When I am channeling Reiki during the Attunement, my *intent* for the Reiki is to flow to the kidney stone.

Focus is staying in the moment and concentrating on the task at hand. For example, you are *focusing* your intent on channeling Reiki into the Chakra for the kidney stone.

It is taught by some Masters and schools that you can channel Reiki without intent and focus. Some even say both are really not needed during a Reiki session, that you do not have to do anything special. You can let your mind wander and even talk when channeling Reiki. In performing Reiki Healing Attunements, it's completely the opposite.

During the Healing Attunements only talk when necessary and you must have strong intent and focus. This is especially important during the five minutes in Step 9 when you are channeling Reiki into the Chakra. Let me make this clear, *intention* and *focus* are crucial elements for a successful Reiki Healing Attunement.

Healing Attunement Length

Once you become experienced performing a Reiki Healing Attunement, it should never last longer than fifteen to thirty minutes. Of course, there are always exceptions to this and you will know intuitively when an Attunement needs to be longer.

Healing Attunement Steps

1. You have prepared for the Healing Attunement.

- You have completed the steps outlined in Chapter 10.

2. You are in the correct position to either perform an Attunement on yourself or another person.

- If you are giving the Reiki Healing Attunement to yourself or another person, I fully recommend lying down, though a sitting position can be used. If you are performing the Healing Attunement on another person, make sure you have room to move around and are in a quiet area where you will not be disturbed.

3. State the intent for the Healing Attunement silently to yourself before you begin. At this time, you can also ask for guidance during the Attunement. *Step should only take a few seconds.*

- You must make your intent clear on which Attunement you are going to perform. For example, if you are going to give a Reiki Healing Attunement for an ulcer, state "This Healing Attunement I am about to perform is for an ulcer." You do this silently and it should only take a few seconds. You can use your own wording as long as the intent is clear.
- You can also ask your higher power, source, Guardian Angel(s), Reiki Guide(s), etc., for guidance during the Attunement.

4. Visualize the Mental/Emotional Symbol in front of the 7th Chakra, activate it, and then embed it into middle of the Chakra. *Step should only take 15 seconds.*

- You visualize (or imagine, know, or draw) the Mental/Emotional Symbol in front of the 7th Chakra, activate it and then embed it into the Chakra. Use the embedding method that works best for you.

How I Do Step Four

Since the same process for step four is used for other steps, but with different Symbols and Chakras, I will stop right here and explain how I personally do it. I draw the symbol, which is the best method of visualization for me, in front of the Chakra. I then activate it by thinking of its name (Photo A), then guide the symbol into the Chakra (Photo B) with my two fingers, without touching the client. This whole process only takes about 15 seconds. As I stated before, there are several ways you can accomplish this step and you can decide the best way for you.

Step Four: Additional Information

The Reiki Healing Attunements are only for physical ailments or diseases, so this is the only time the Mental/Emotional symbol is used during a Healing Attunement. This step is performed at the beginning of every Healing Attunement to help clear any mental and/or emotional blockages that a person has about their physical ailment or disease that might hinder the Healing Attunement.

5. Channel Reiki into the 7th Chakra. *Step should take only take about 2 minutes.*

- After the Mental/Emotional Symbol is embedded into the 7th Chakra, channel Reiki for a few minutes into the center of it. Channel the Reiki with intent for it to clear any mental or emotional blocks associated with the physical ailment or disease for which the Attunement is being performed.

(Photo A)

(Photo B)

6. Proceed to the Chakra you will be working with during the Healing Attunement. Visualize the Power Symbol over it, activate it, and embed it into the Chakra. *Step should only take 15 seconds.*

- You visualize (or imagine, know, or draw) the Power Symbol over the front of the Chakra, activate it, and then embed it into the Chakra using the method that works best for you.

- By embedding the Power Symbol into the Chakra, you will increase the Reiki and make the intent stronger when you perform Step 9.

7. Stay with the same Chakra. Visualize the Long Distance Symbol over it, activate it, and embed it into the Chakra. *This step should only take 15 seconds.*

- You visualize (or imagine, know, or draw) the Long Distance Symbol over the front of the Chakra, activate it, and then embed it into the Chakra using the method that works best for you.

- By embedding the Long Distance Symbol into the Chakra, it will be there for present and future healing for the intent you channel in Step 9.

8. Stay with the same Chakra. Visualize the Master Symbol over it, activate it, and embed it into the Chakra. *Step should only take 15 seconds.*

- You visualize (or imagine, know, or draw) the Master Symbol over front of the Chakra, activate it, and then embed it into the Chakra using the method that works best for you.

- By embedding the Master Symbol into the Chakra, it will take the intent you channel in Step 9 to the highest level.

9. The Reiki symbols are now embedded into the Chakra. Next, channel Reiki into the center of the Chakra with the intent for what the Reiki Healing Attunement is being performed. *Step should only take 5 minutes.*

- Example: the Reiki Healing Attunement is for an ulcer. Your intent for the Reiki you are channeling into the Chakra is to flow to the ulcer for healing.

10. Next, go to the back Chakra of the Chakra you have been working with. Channel Reiki into the center of the back Chakra with the intent for what the Reiki Healing Attunement is being performed. *Step should only take 5 minutes.*

- Example: the Reiki Healing Attunement is for an ulcer. Your intent for the Reiki you are channeling into the back Chakra is to flow to the ulcer for healing.

11. The Attunement is complete.

- Perform the finishing steps outlined in Chapter 10.

1st Level Healers and Healing Attunements

If you are a 1st Level Healer, you can perform the Reiki Healing Attunements. The difference is, you omit the steps with the symbols. I do recommend receiving your 2nd Level Attunement as soon as you are ready.

2nd Level Healers and Healing Attunements

If you are a 2nd Level Healer, you can perform all the steps except Step 8. As for becoming a Reiki Master and doing Step 8, it is really not necessary for successful Healing Attunements. Becoming a Reiki Master is a process that not every person desires, or they wait until they feel they are ready to become one and this can take time. There are powerful Reiki Healers who have never become a Reiki Master.

When Symbols are Different

If your Reiki Symbols have variations in the way they are drawn from what is shown in this book, it is not a problem in using them during the Healing Attunement. You have been attuned to them, so they will be effective.

If you have completely different Reiki Symbols, you can still use them in Reiki Healing Attunements; however, you have to make sure the symbols you use equate to a Power Symbol, a Long Distance Symbol, a Mental/Emotional Symbol, and a Master Symbol.

To make the steps easy to follow, here they are without the explanations. You can make a copy to use during your first Attunements.

Healing Attunement Steps for 1st Level

1. You have prepared for the Healing Attunement.

2. You are in the correct position to either perform the Attunement on yourself or another person.

3. State the intent for the Healing Attunement silently to yourself before you begin. At this time, you can also ask for guidance during the Attunement. *Step should only take a few seconds.*

4. Channel Reiki into the 7th Chakra with the intent to clear any mental or emotional blocks associated with the physical ailment or disease for which the Attunement is being performed. *Step should only take about 2 minutes.*

5. Proceed to the Chakra you will be working with during the Healing Attunement. Focus and channel Reiki into the center of the Chakra with the intent for what the Reiki Healing Attunement is being performed. *Step should only take 5 minutes.*

6. Next, go to the back Chakra of the Chakra you have been working with. Channel Reiki into the center of the back Chakra with the intent for what the Reiki Healing Attunement is being performed. *Step should only take 5 minutes.*

7. The Attunement is complete. Perform the finishing steps outlined in Chapter 10.

Healing Attunement Steps for 2nd Level

1. You have prepared for the Healing Attunement.

2. You are in the correct position to either perform the Attunement on yourself or another person.

3. State the intent for the Healing Attunement silently to yourself before you begin. At this time, you can also ask for guidance during the Attunement. *Step should only take a few seconds.*

4. Visualize the Mental/Emotional symbol in front of the 7th Chakra, activate it, and then embed it into middle of the Chakra. *Step should only take 15 seconds.*

5. Channel Reiki into the 7th Chakra with the intent to clear any mental or emotional blocks associated with the physical ailment or disease for which the Attunement is being performed. *Step should only take about 2 minutes.*

6. Proceed to the Chakra you will be working with during the Healing Attunement. Visualize the Power Symbol over it, activate it, and embed it into the Chakra. *Step should only take 15 seconds*

7. Stay with the same Chakra. Visualize the Long Distance Symbol over it, activate it, and embed it into the Chakra. *Step should only take 15 seconds.*

8. The Reiki symbols are now embedded into the Chakra. Next, channel Reiki into the center of the Chakra with the intent for what the Reiki Healing Attunement is being performed. *Step should only take 5 minutes.*

9. Next, go to the back Chakra of the Chakra you have been working with. Channel Reiki into the center of the back Chakra with the intent for what the Reiki Healing Attunement is being performed. *Step should only take 5 minutes.*

10. The Attunement is complete. Perform the finishing steps outlined in Chapter 10.

Healing Attunement Steps for the Master

1. You have prepared for the Healing Attunement.

2. You are in the correct position to either perform the Attunement on yourself or another person.

3. State the intent for the Healing Attunement silently to yourself before you begin. At this time, you can also ask for guidance during the Attunement. *Step should only take a few seconds.*

4. Visualize the Mental/Emotional Symbol in front of the 7th Chakra, activate it, and then embed it into middle of the Chakra. *Step should only take 15 seconds.*

5. Channel Reiki into the 7th Chakra with the intent to

clear any mental or emotional blocks associated with the physical ailment or disease for which the Attunement is being performed. *Step should only take about 2 minutes.*

6. Proceed to the Chakra you will be working with during the Healing Attunement. Visualize the Power Symbol over it, activate it, and embed it into the Chakra. *Step should only take 15 seconds*

7. Stay with the same Chakra. Visualize the Long Distance Symbol over it, activate it, and embed it into the Chakra. *Step should only take 15 seconds.*

8. Stay with the same Chakra. Visualize the Master Symbol over it, activate it, and embed it into the Chakra. *Step should only take 15 seconds.*

9. The Reiki symbols are now embedded into the Chakra. Next, channel Reiki into the center of the Chakra with the intent for what the Reiki Healing Attunement is being performed. *Step should only take 5 minutes.*

10. Next, go to the back Chakra of the Chakra you have been working with. Channel Reiki into the center of the back Chakra with the intent for what the Reiki Healing Attunement is being performed. *Step should only take 5 minutes.*

11. The Attunement is complete. Perform the finishing steps outlined in Chapter 10.

“Everyone has been made for some particular work, and the desire for that work has been put in every heart.”

-Rumi

Points To Remember

Here are important points to remember in performing Reiki Healing Attunements. You should review them thoroughly before performing your first Healing Attunements.

Points

- The Reiki Healing Attunements are only for physical ailments and/or diseases. They are not for any spiritual, mental or emotional conditions or illness. I define an *ailment* as "a body disorder" and a *disease* as "an abnormal body condition which impairs functioning." Both are recognized by signs and symptoms in the body.

- Perform only one Healing Attunement for one ailment or disease at a time. Wait a minimum of three days before performing another. You can receive as many Healing Attunements as needed for an ailment or disease every three days. Since every person has different circumstances, the amount of Healing Attunements needed will vary from person to person.

- If a person has multiple ailments and/or diseases that require Healing Attunements, start with just one, then you can alternate Healing Attunements every three days to address others.

- Perform a Reiki Healing Attunement only if you know the physical ailment and/or disease and where it has manifested. You need this information anyway to prepare and perform a Healing Attunement. If you do not have this information, you can do your typical Reiki Healing until you are able to acquire this information.

- If you are a Reiki 2nd Level or Master, you can perform the Healing Attunements without embedding the symbols if you desire. Just follow the Reiki 1st Level steps.

- The symbols I have drawn as examples in the photographs have been made larger for demonstration purposes. You may visualize or draw the Reiki Symbols any size you desire.

- You do not use a back 7th Chakra during a Healing Attunement.

- When channeling Reiki during the Healing Attunement, you can use one or two hands. They can be either on or off the body.

- What makes each Healing Attunement different is the intent for the Healing Attunement, even though the same Chakras are used.

- If there are differences in your Chakra teachings compared to mine, do not worry. Teachings can be very subjective and usually the differences are minor. If you feel it is necessary to make adjustments in the Healing Attunements because of this, feel free to do so.

- There might come a time when you have an ailment or disease that falls into a gray area regarding which Chakra to use during an

Attunement, even after using the Chakra guidelines and illustrations. If this happens, just take a few minutes and use your intuitiveness to decide which Chakra to use.

Channeling the Back Chakras

When you are performing a Healing Attunement on another person, working with a back Chakra is easy. The person is on their stomach and you are over them with complete access to the Chakra. When working on your own back Chakra, it can be a challenge for most people, unless you are really flexible or double-jointed.

If you cannot reach a back Chakra, all you have to do is direct your palm towards the Chakra area (Photo 1) and intend for the Reiki to channel there the best you can, and it will.

Next Chapters

The next seven chapters are examples on to perform Reiki Healing Attunements to help you get a better understanding of the process. The chapters include step-by-step photos with each chapter using a different Chakra. I show both ways to perform the Healing Attunement (on yourself and others) in the first chapter for all Reiki Levels. After that, I alternate chapter by chapter, first showing how to perform an Attunement on yourself, then how to perform an Attunement on another person. Each chapter explains how to perform the Attunements for all Reiki levels.

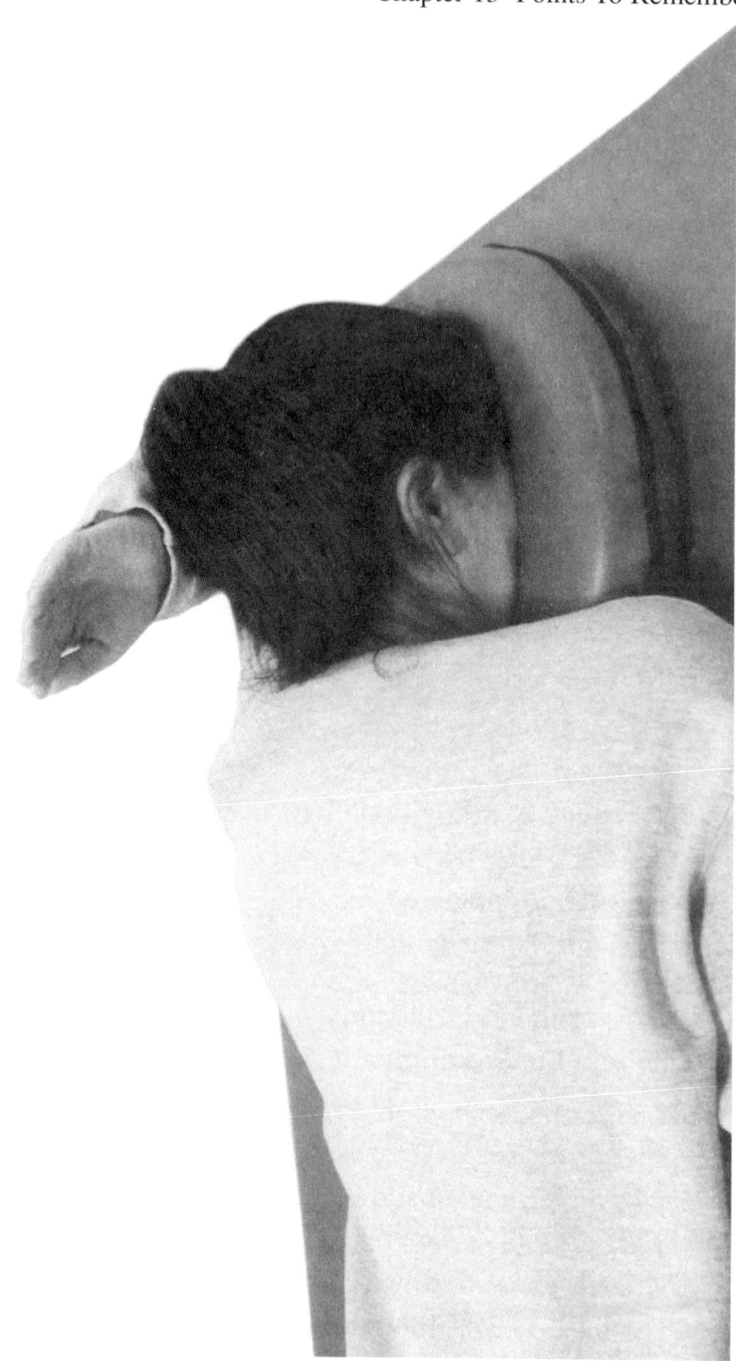

(Photo 1) Showing how to channel Reiki to the back 4th Chakra.

“Don’t grieve. Anything you lose comes round in another form.”

-Rumi

Example One: Reiki Healing Attunement

Example of a Reiki Healing Attunement for Sciatica, performed on yourself and performed on another person using the 1st Chakra.

Healing Attunement for 1st Level Reiki: Performed on Yourself

1. You have prepared for the Healing Attunement.

2. You are in the correct position to perform the Attunement on yourself.

3. State the intent for the Healing Attunement (Sciatica) silently to yourself before you begin. At this time, you can also ask for guidance during the Attunement. *Step should only take a few seconds.*

4. Channel Reiki into the 7th Chakra with the intent to clear any mental or emotional blocks associated with the Sciatica. (Photo 2) *Step should only take about 2 minutes.*

5. Proceed to the 1st Chakra. Focus and channel Reiki into the center of the Chakra with the intent for it to flow to the Sciatica. (Photo 3) *Step should only take 5 minutes.*

6. Next, turn on your stomach and proceed to the back 1st Chakra. Channel Reiki into the center of the back 1st Chakra with the intent for it to flow to the Sciatica. (Photo 4) *Step should only take 5 minutes.*

7. The Attunement is complete. Perform the finishing steps outlined in Chapter 10.

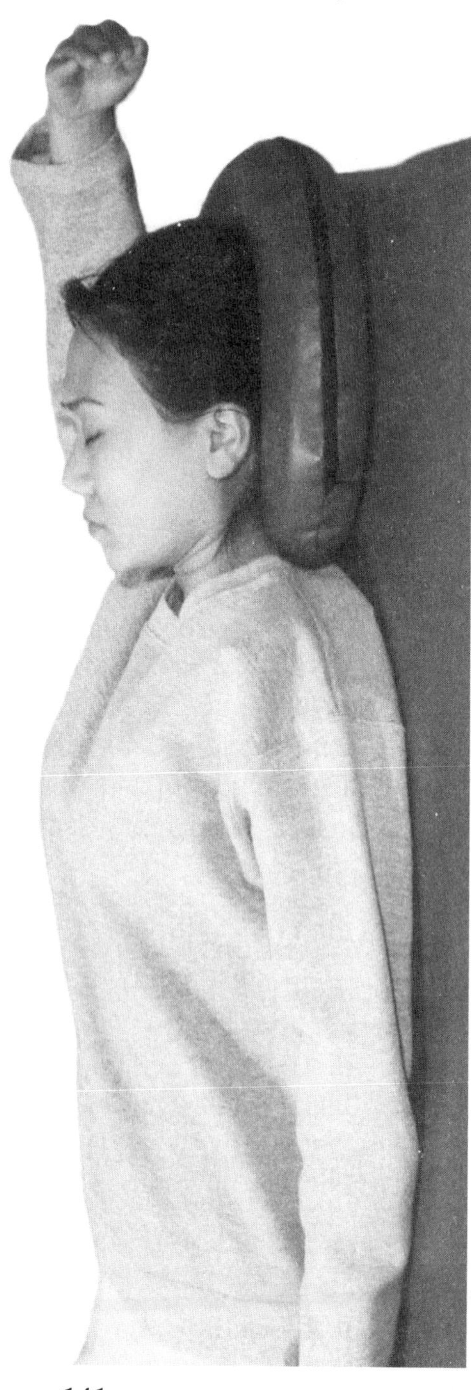

(Photo 2) Channel Reiki into the 7th Chakra with the intent to clear any mental or emotional blocks associated with the Sciatica. *Step should only take about 2 minutes.*

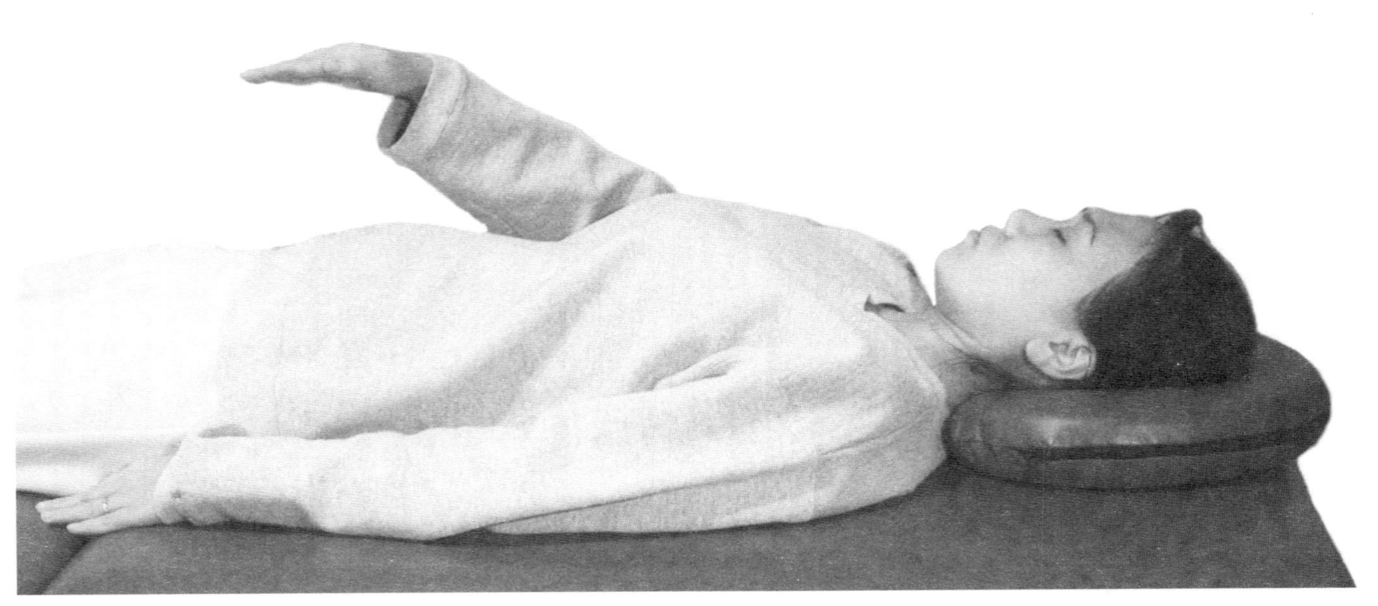

(Photo 3) Proceed to the 1st Chakra. Focus and channel Reiki into the center of the Chakra with the intent for it to flow to the Sciatica. *Step should only take 5 minutes.*

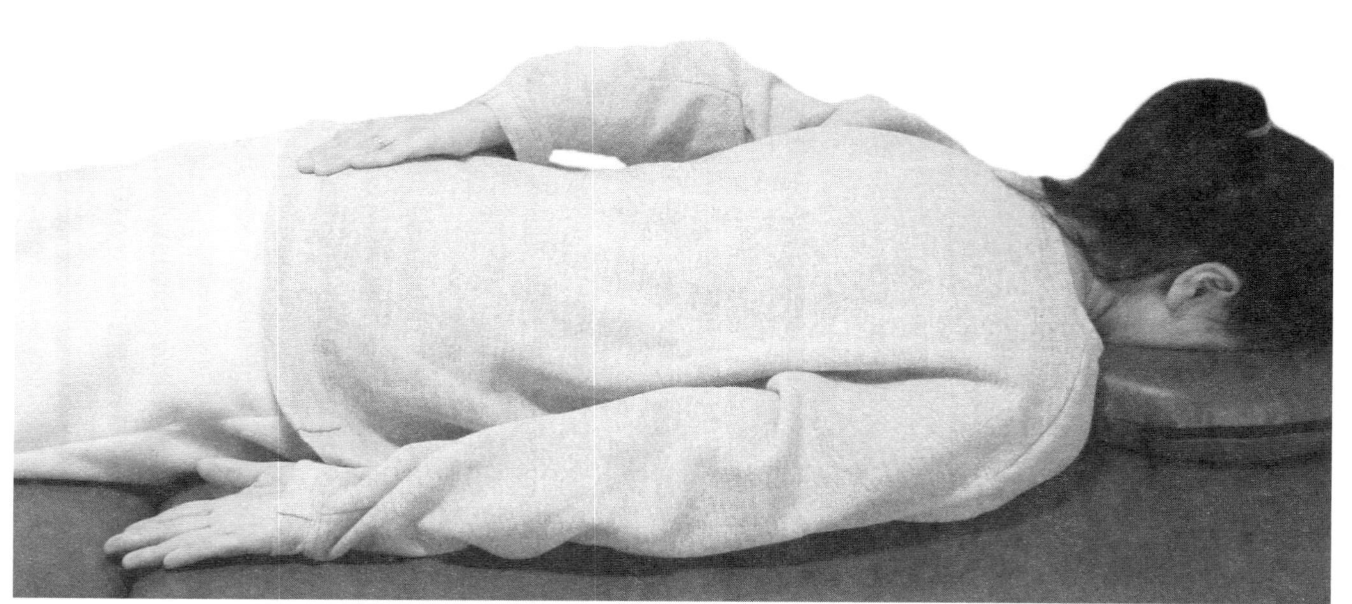

(Photo 4) Next, turn on your stomach and proceed to the back 1st Chakra. Channel Reiki into the center of the back 1st Chakra with the intent for it to flow to the Sciatica. *Step should only take 5 minutes*

Healing Attunement for 1st Level Reiki: Performed on Another Person

1. You have prepared for the Healing Attunement.

2. You are in the correct position to perform the Attunement on another person.

3. State the intent for the Healing Attunement (Sciatica) silently to yourself before you begin. At this time, you can also ask for guidance during the Attunement. *Step should only take a few seconds.*

4. Channel Reiki into the 7th Chakra with the intent to clear any mental or emotional blocks associated with the Sciatica. (Photo 5) *Step should only take about 2 minutes.*

5. Proceed to the 1st Chakra. Focus and channel Reiki into the center of the Chakra with the intent for it to flow to the Sciatica. (Photo 6) *Step should only take 5 minutes.*

6. Next, have the person turn on their stomach and proceed to the back 1st Chakra. Channel Reiki into the center of the back Chakra with the intent for it to flow to the Sciatica. (Photo 7) *Step should only take 5 minutes.*

7. The Attunement is complete. Perform the finishing steps outlined in Chapter 10.

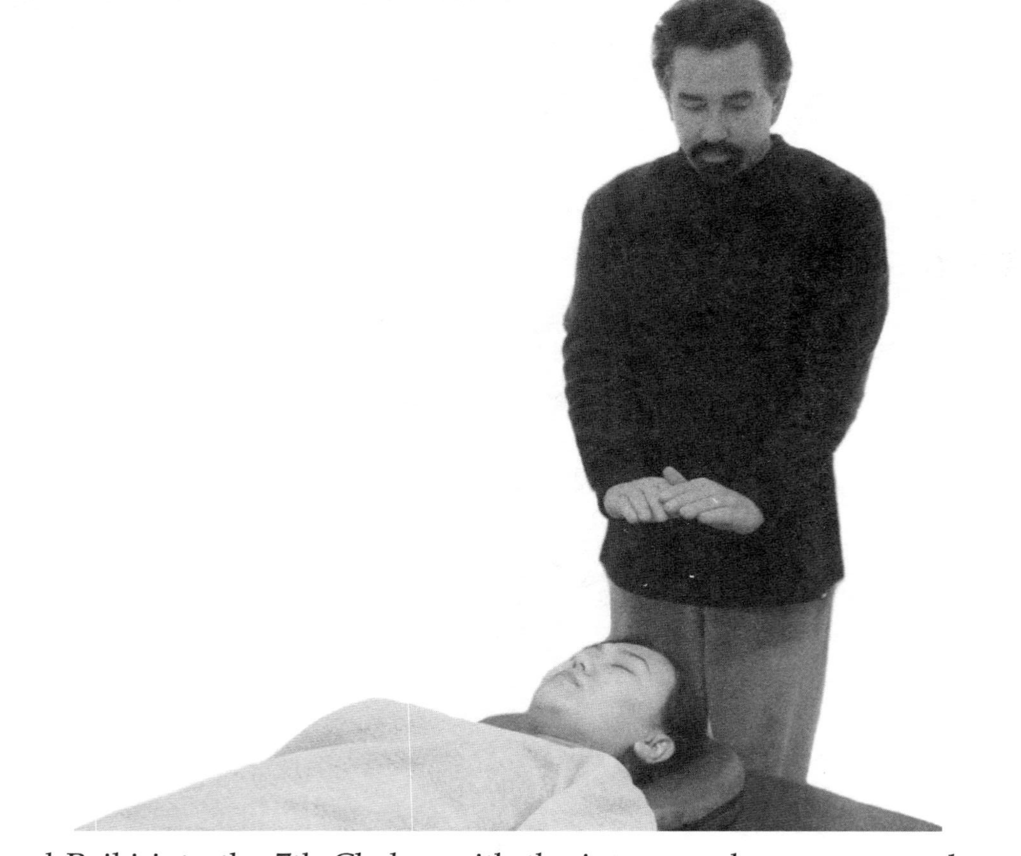

(Photo 5) Channel Reiki into the 7th Chakra with the intent to clear any mental or emotional blocks associated with the Sciatica. *Step should only take about 2 minutes.*

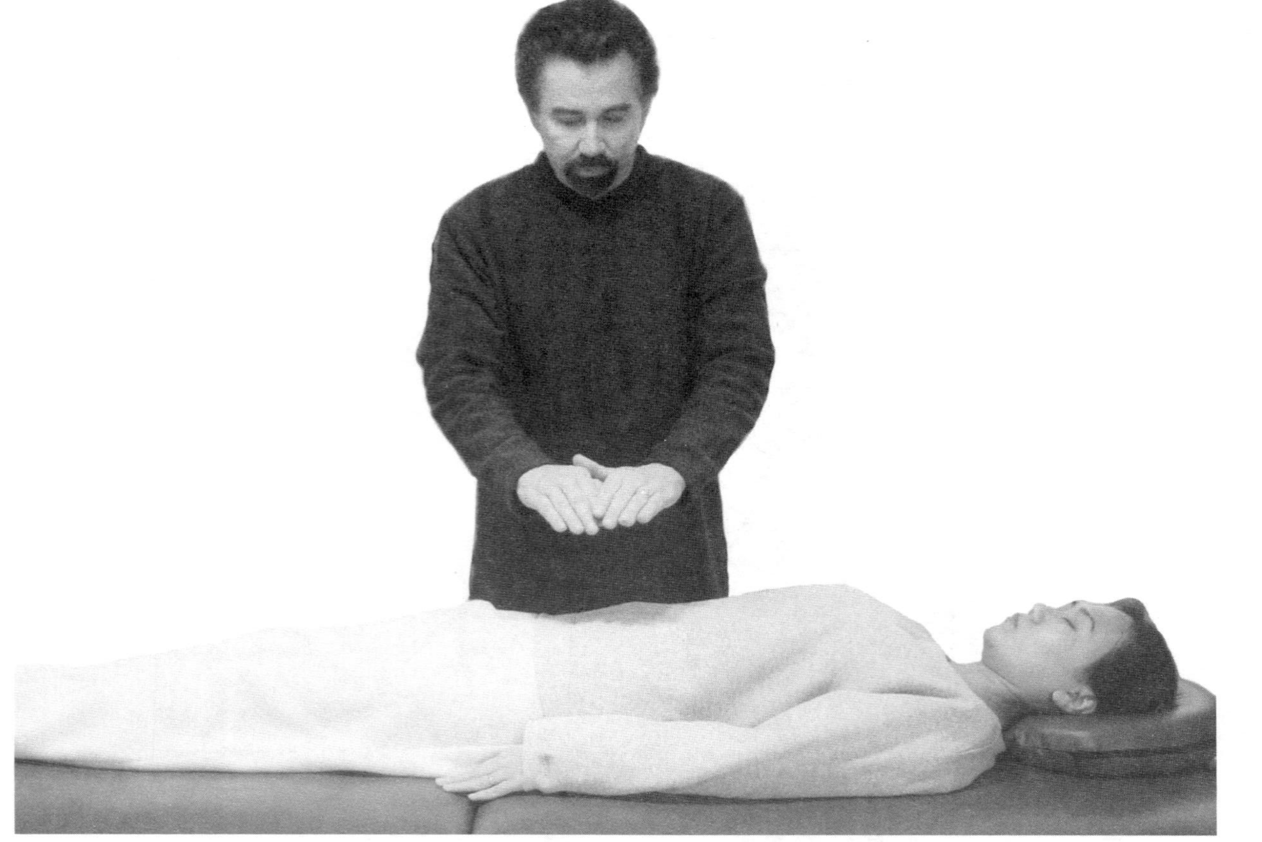

(Photo 6) Proceed to the 1st Chakra. Focus and channel Reiki into the center of the Chakra with the intent for it to flow to the Sciatica. *Step should only take 5 minutes.*

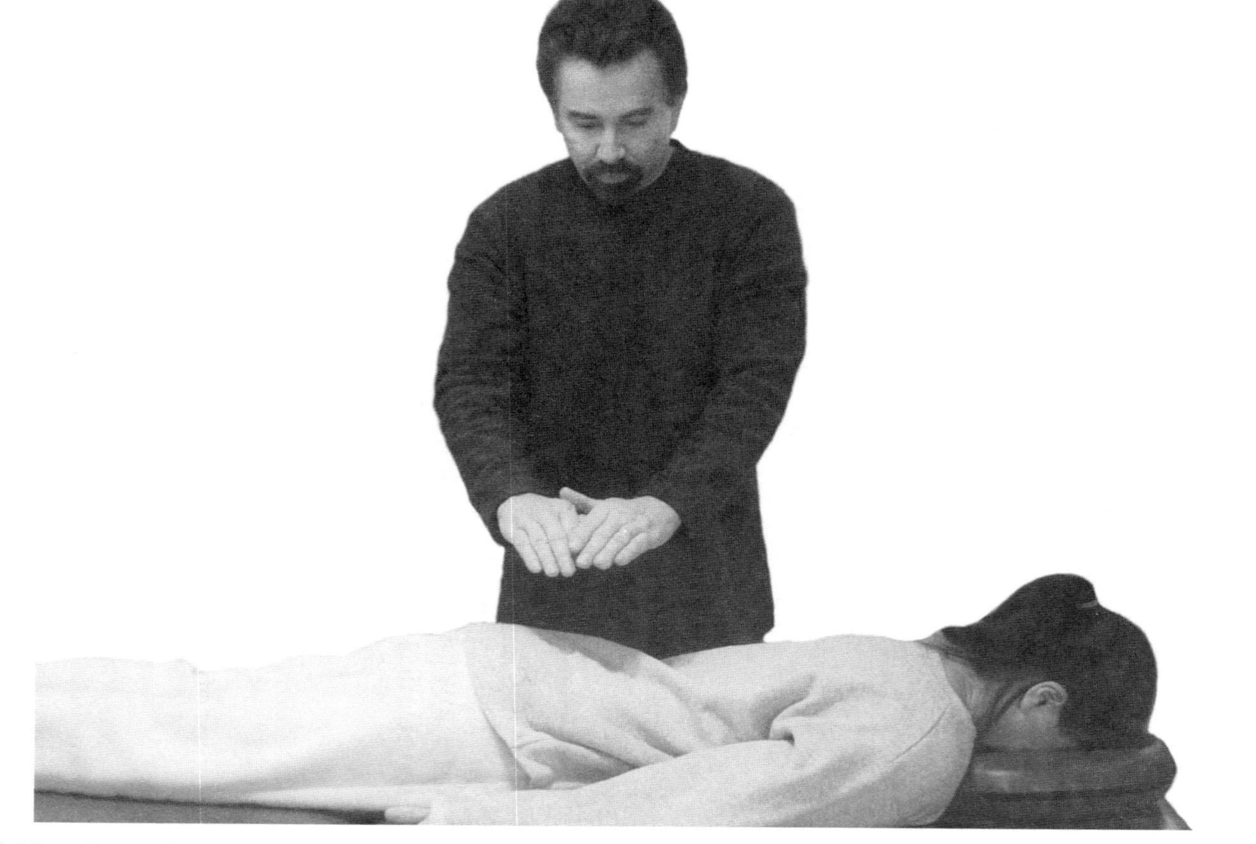

(Photo 7) Next, have the person turn on his or her stomach and proceed to the back 1st Chakra. Channel Reiki into the center of the back Chakra with the intent for it to flow to the Sciatica. *Step should only take 5 minutes.*

Healing Attunement for Reiki 2nd Level and Master: Performed on Yourself

1. You have prepared for the Healing Attunement.

2. You are in the correct position to perform the Attunement on yourself.

3. State the intent for the Healing Attunement (Sciatica) silently to yourself before you begin. At this time, you can also ask for guidance during the Attunement. *Step should only take a few seconds.*

4. Visualize the Mental/Emotional Symbol in front of the 7th Chakra, activate it (Photo 8), then embed it into the center of the Chakra. (Photo 9) *Step should only take 15 seconds.*

5. Channel Reiki into the 7th Chakra with the intent to clear any mental or emotional blocks associated with the Sciatica. (Photo 10) *Step should only take about 2 minutes.*

6. Proceed to the 1st Chakra. Visualize the Power Symbol over it, activate it (Photo 11), then embed it into the center of the Chakra. (Photo 12) *Step should only take 15 seconds.*

7. Stay with the 1st Chakra. Visualize the Long Distance Symbol over it, activate it (Photo 13), then embed it into the center of the Chakra. (Photo 14) *Step should only take 15 seconds.*

Note: If you are a 2nd Level, bypass Step 8 and go to Step 9.

8. Stay with the 1st Chakra. Visualize the Master Symbol over it, activate it (Photo 15), then embed it into the center of the Chakra. (Photo 16) *Step should only take 15 seconds.*

9. The Reiki Symbols are now embedded into the 1st Chakra. Next, channel Reiki into the center of the 1st Chakra with the intent for it to flow to the Sciatica. (Photo 17) *Step should only take 5 minutes.*

10. Next, turn on your stomach and proceed to the back 1st Chakra. Channel Reiki into the center of the back 1st Chakra with the intent for it to flow to the Sciatica. (Photo 18) *Step should only take 5 minutes.*

11. The Attunement is complete. Perform the finishing steps outlined in Chapter 10.

(Photo 8) Visualize the Mental/Emotional symbol in front of the 7th Chakra , activate it.

(Photo 9) Embed it into the center of the Chakra. *Step should only take 15 seconds.*

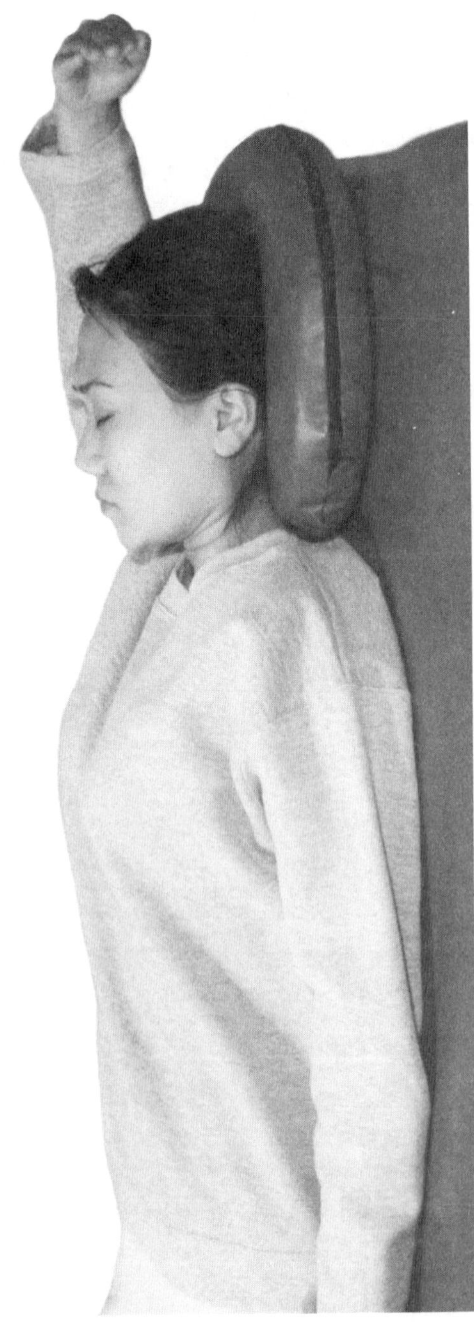

(Photo 10) Channel Reiki into the 7th Chakra with the intent to clear any mental or emotional blocks associated with the Sciatica. *Step should only take about 2 minutes.*

(Photo 11) Proceed to the 1st Chakra. Visualize the Power Symbol over it, activate it.

(Photo 12) Embed it into the center of the Chakra. *Step should only take 15 seconds*

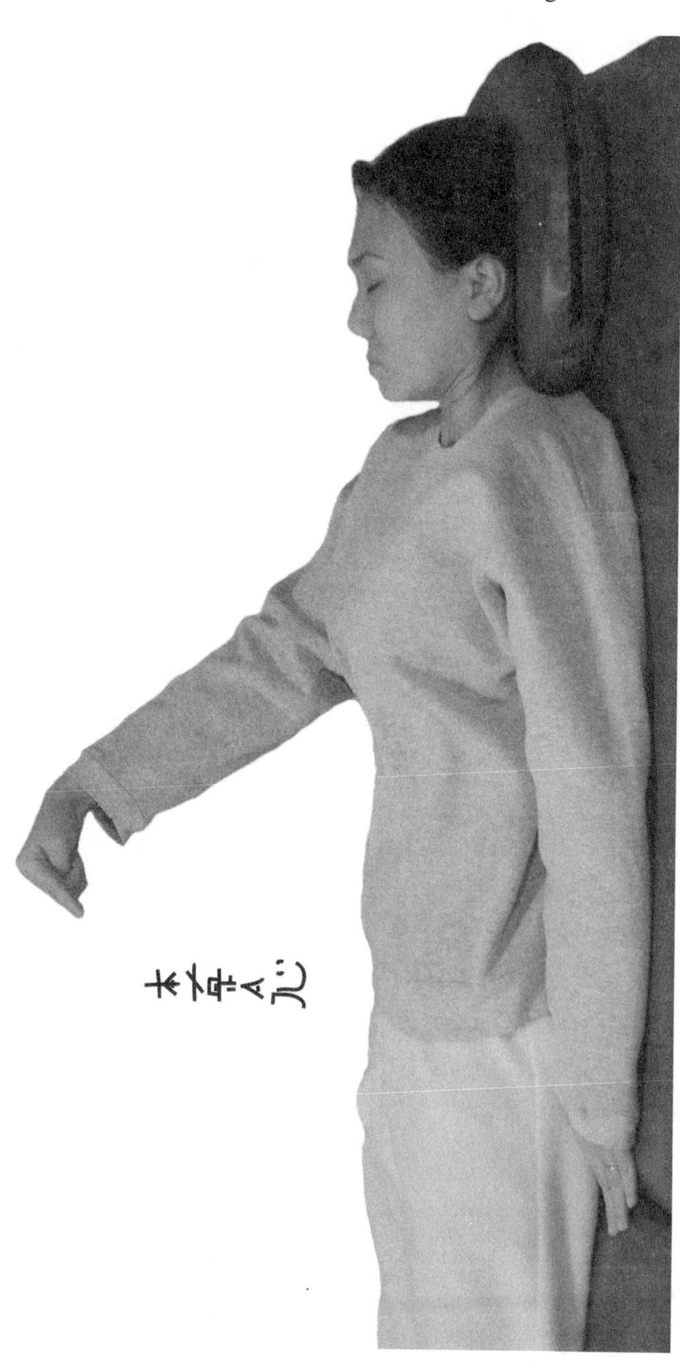

(Photo 13) Stay with the 1st Chakra. Visualize the Long Distance Symbol over it, activate it.

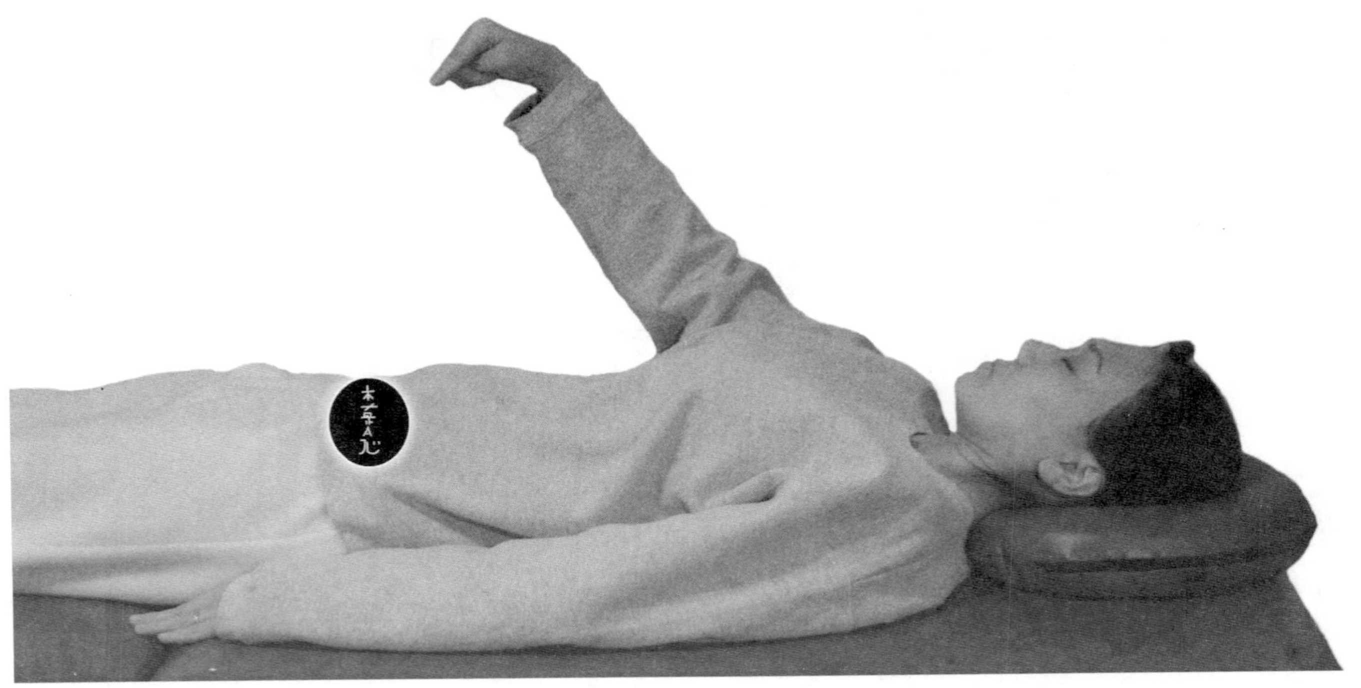

(Photo 14) Embed it into the center of the Chakra. *Step should only take 15 seconds.*

(Photo 15) Stay with the 1st Chakra. Visualize the Master Symbol over it, activate it.

(Photo 16) Embed it into the center of the Chakra. *Step should only take 15 seconds.*

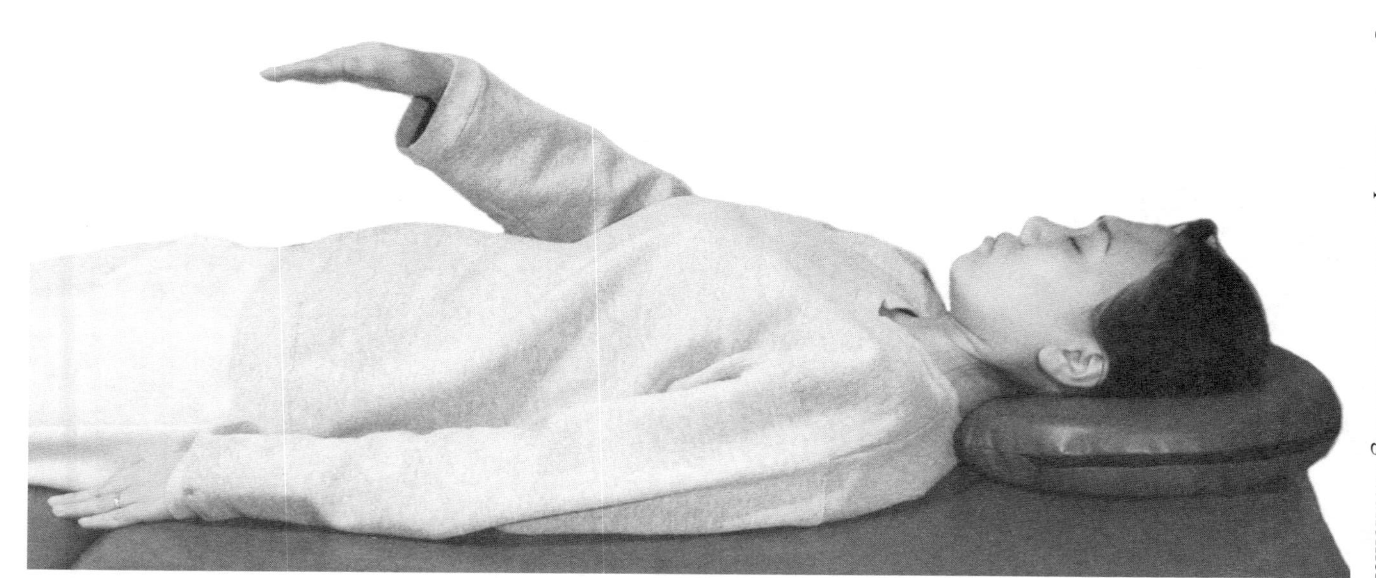

(Photo 17) The Reiki Symbols are now embedded into the 1st Chakra. Next, channel Reiki into the center of the 1st Chakra with the intent for it to flow to the Sciatica. *Step should only take 5 minutes.*

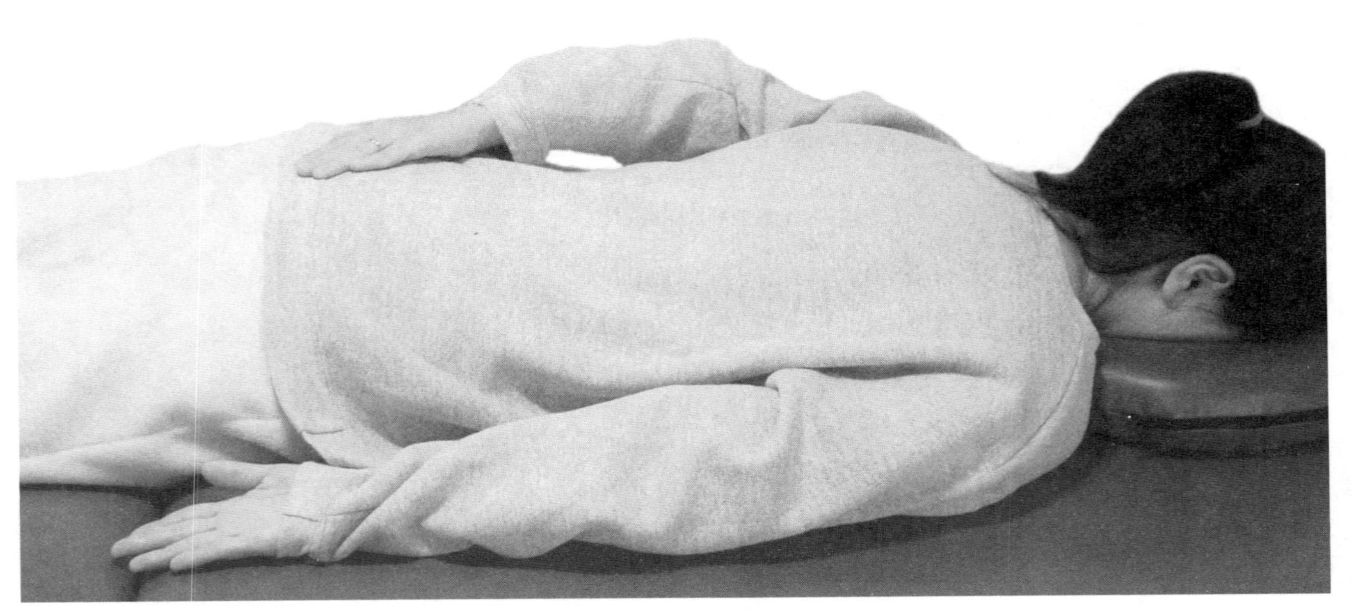

(Photo 18) Next, turn on your stomach and proceed to the back 1st Chakra. Channel Reiki into the center of the back 1st Chakra with the intent for it to flow to the Sciatica. *Step should only take 5 minutes.*

Healing Attunement for Reiki 2nd Level and Master: Performed on Another Person.

1. You have prepared for the Healing Attunement.

2. You are in the correct position to perform the Attunement on another person.

3. State the intent for the Healing Attunement (Sciatica) silently to yourself before you begin. At this time, you can also ask for guidance during the Attunement. *Step should only take a few seconds.*

4. Visualize the Mental/Emotional symbol in front of the 7th Chakra, activate it (Photo 19), then embed it into the center of the Chakra. (Photo 20) *Step should only take 15 seconds.*

5. Channel Reiki into the 7th Chakra with the intent to clear any mental or emotional blocks associated with the Sciatica. (Photo 21) *Step should only take about 2 minutes.*

6. Proceed to the 1st Chakra. Visualize the Power Symbol over it, activate it (Photo 22), then embed it into the center of the Chakra. (Photo 23) *Step should only take 15 seconds.*

7. Stay with the 1st Chakra. Visualize the Long Distance Symbol over it, activate it (Photo 24), then embed it into the center of the Chakra. (Photo 25) *Step should only take 15 seconds.*

Note: If you are a 2nd Level, bypass Step 8 and go to Step 9.

8. Stay with the 1st Chakra. Visualize the Master Symbol over it, activate it (Photo 26), then embed it into the center of the Chakra. (Photo 27) *Step should only take 15 seconds.*

9. The Reiki Symbols are now embedded into the 1st Chakra. Next, channel Reiki into the center of the 1st Chakra with the intent for it to flow to the Sciatica. (Photo 28) *Step should only take 5 minutes.*

10. Next, have the person turn on his or her stomach and proceed to the back 1st Chakra. Channel Reiki into the center of the back 1st Chakra with the intent for it to flow to the Sciatica. (Photo 29) *Step should only take 5 minutes.*

11. The Attunement is complete. Perform the finishing steps outlined in Chapter 10.

(Photo 19) Visualize the Mental/Emotional Symbol in front of the 7th Chakra, activate it.

(Photo 20) Embed it into the center of the Chakra. *Step should only take 15 seconds.*

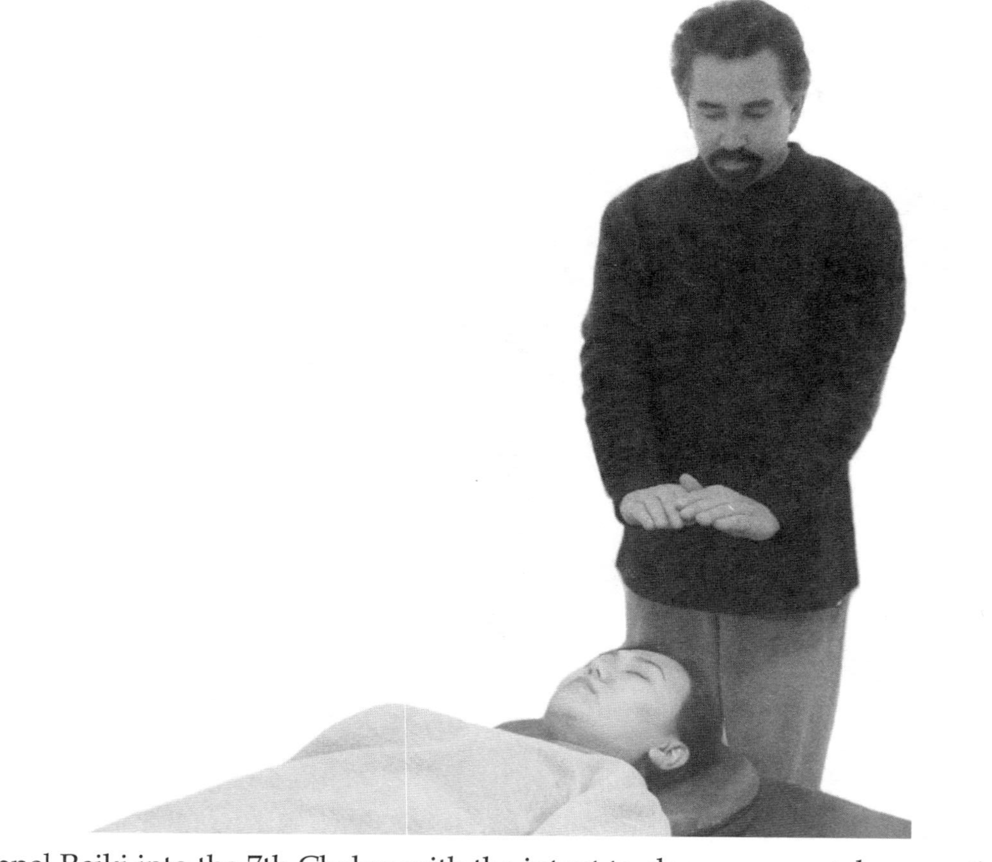

(Photo 21) Channel Reiki into the 7th Chakra with the intent to clear any mental or emotional blocks associated with the Sciatica. *Step should only take about 2 minutes.*

(Photo 22) Proceed to the 1st Chakra. Visualize the Power Symbol over it, activate it.

(Photo 23) Embed it into the center of the Chakra. *Step should only take 15 seconds.*

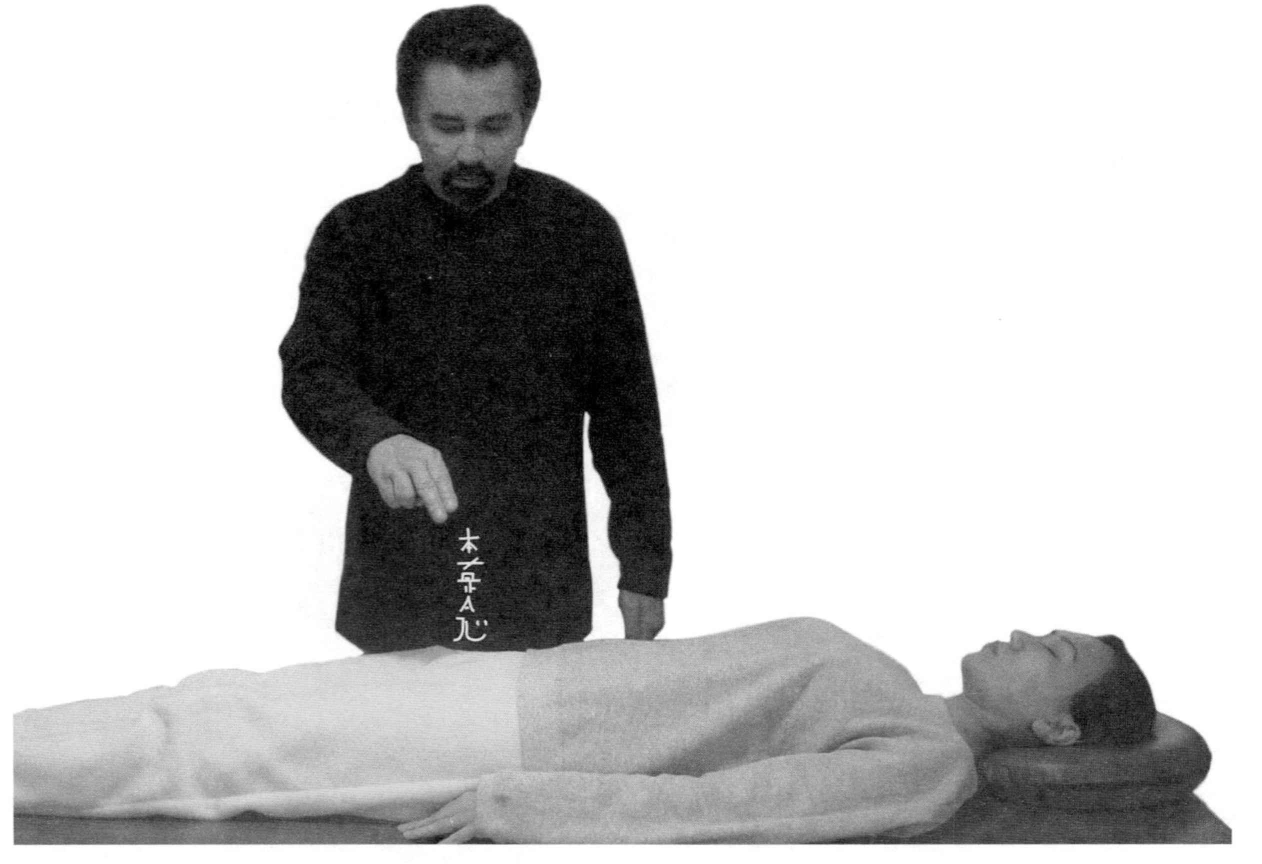

(Photo 24) Stay with the 1st Chakra. Visualize the Long Distance Symbol over it, activate it.

(Photo 25) Embed it into the center of the Chakra. *Step should only take 15 seconds.*

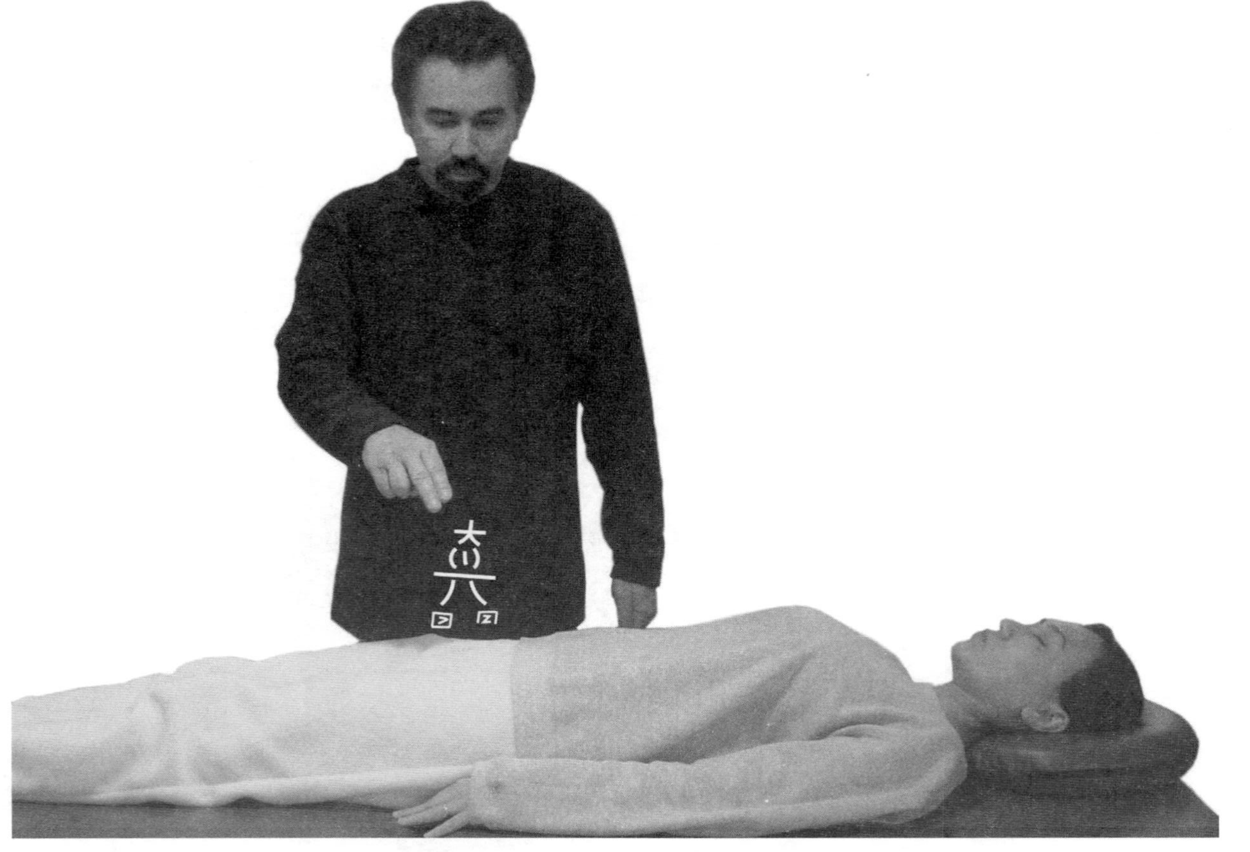

(Photo 26) Stay with the 1st Chakra. Visualize the Master Symbol over it, activate it.

(Photo 27) Embed it into the center of the Chakra. *Step should only take 15 seconds.*

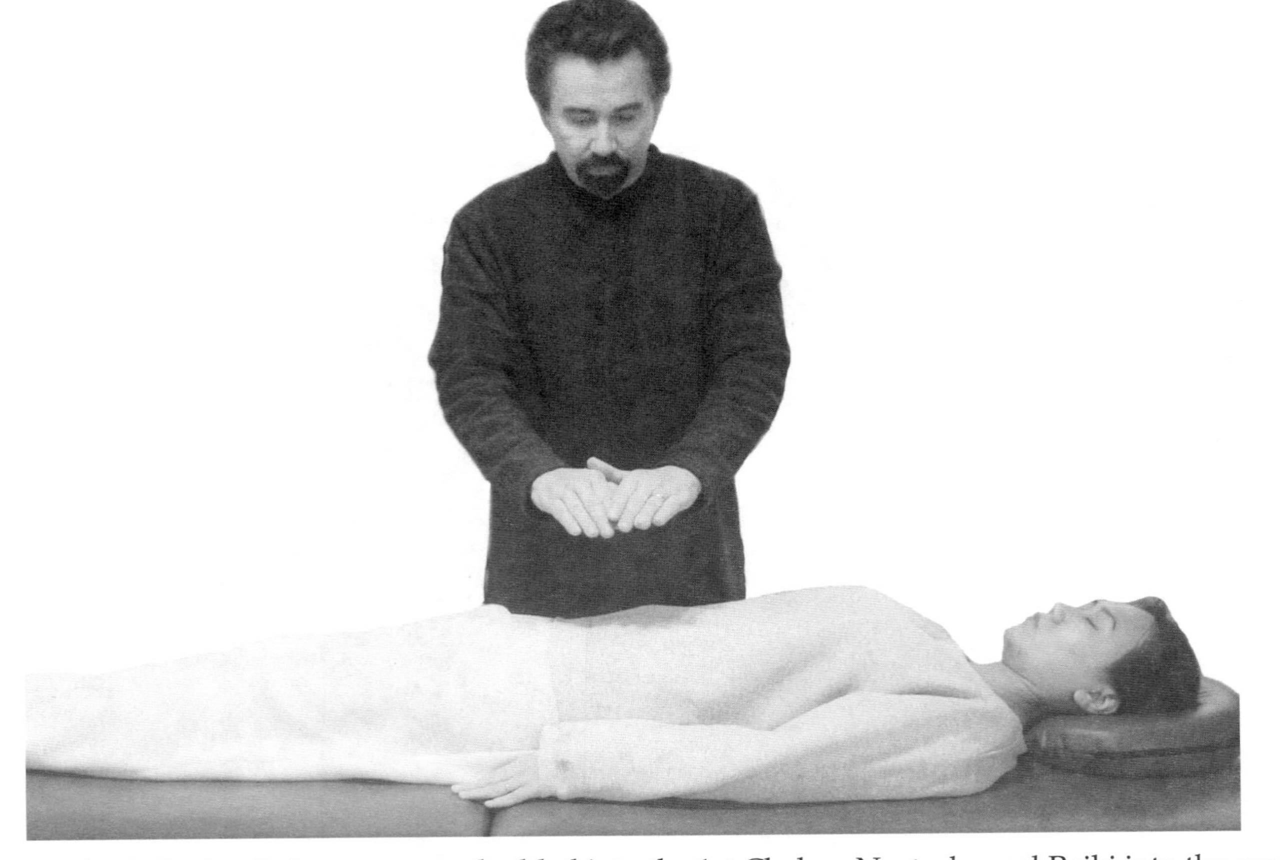

(Photo 28) The Reiki Symbols are now embedded into the 1st Chakra. Next, channel Reiki into the center of the 1st Chakra with the intent for it to flow to the Sciatica. *Step should only take 5 minutes.*

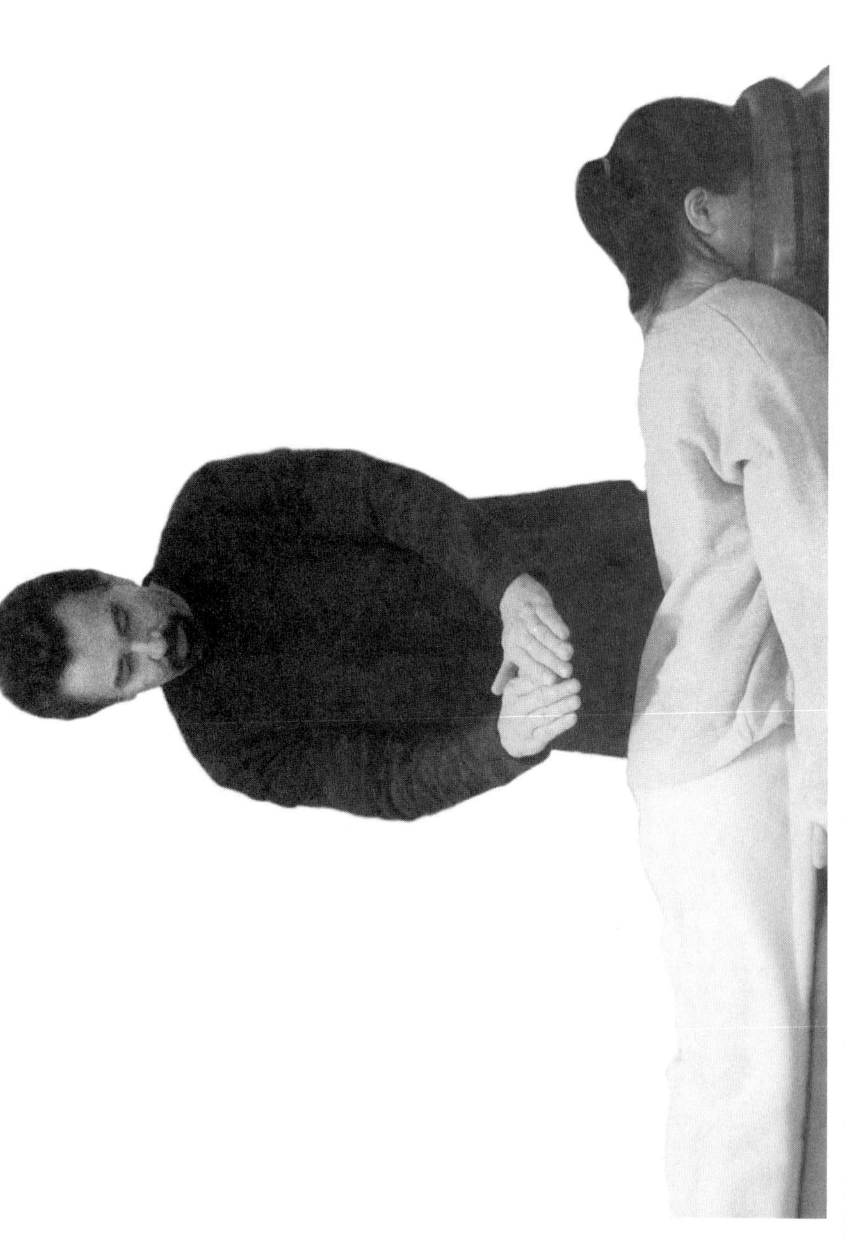

(Photo 29) Next, have the person turn on his or her stomach and proceed to the back 1st Chakra. Channel Reiki into the center of the back 1st Chakra with the intent for it to flow to the Sciatica. *Step should only take 5 minutes.*

"He is a letter to everyone.
You open it. It says, 'Live!'"

-Rumi

Example Two: Reiki Healing Attunement

Example of a Reiki Healing Attunement for Irritable Bowel Syndrome (IBS) performed on yourself using the 2nd Chakra.

Healing Attunement for 1st Level Reiki: Performed on Yourself

1. You have prepared for the Healing Attunement.

2. You are in the correct position to perform the Attunement on yourself.

3. State the intent for the Healing Attunement (IBS) silently to yourself before you begin. At this time, you can also ask for guidance during the Attunement. *Step should only take a few seconds.*

4. Channel Reiki into the 7th Chakra with the intent to clear any mental or emotional blocks associated with the IBS. (Photo 30) *Step should only take about 2 minutes.*

5. Proceed to the 2nd Chakra. Focus and channel Reiki into the center of the Chakra with the intent for it to flow to the IBS. (Photo 31) *Step should only take 5 minutes.*

6. Next, turn on your stomach and proceed to the back 2nd Chakra. Channel Reiki into the center of the back 2nd Chakra with the intent for it to flow to the IBS. (Photo 32) *Step should only take 5 minutes.*

7. The Attunement is complete. Perform the finishing steps outlined in Chapter 10.

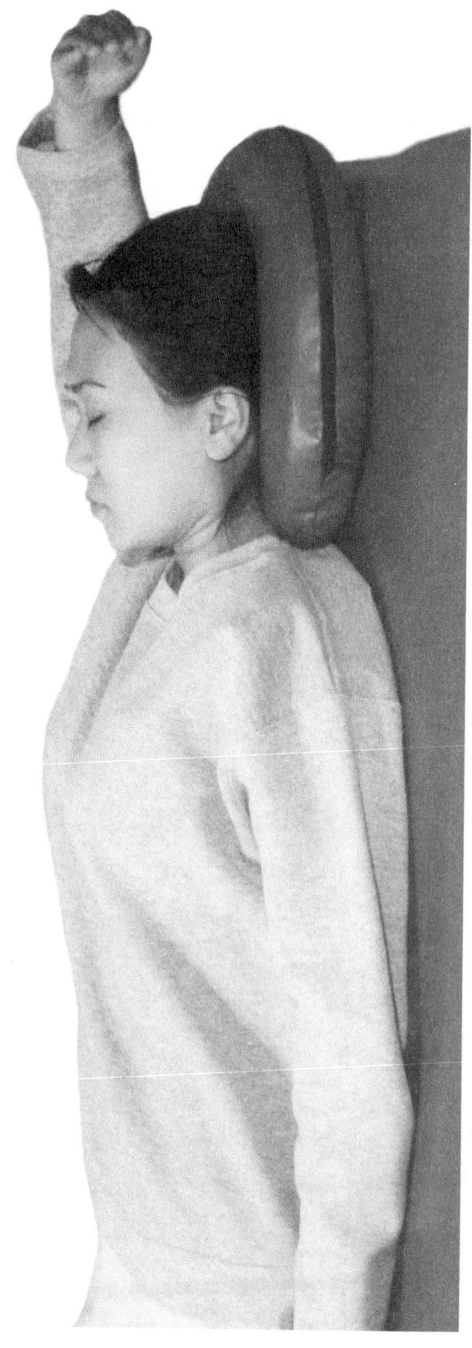

(Photo 30) Channel Reiki into the 7th Chakra with the intent to clear any mental or emotional blocks associated with the IBS. *Step should only take about 2 minutes*

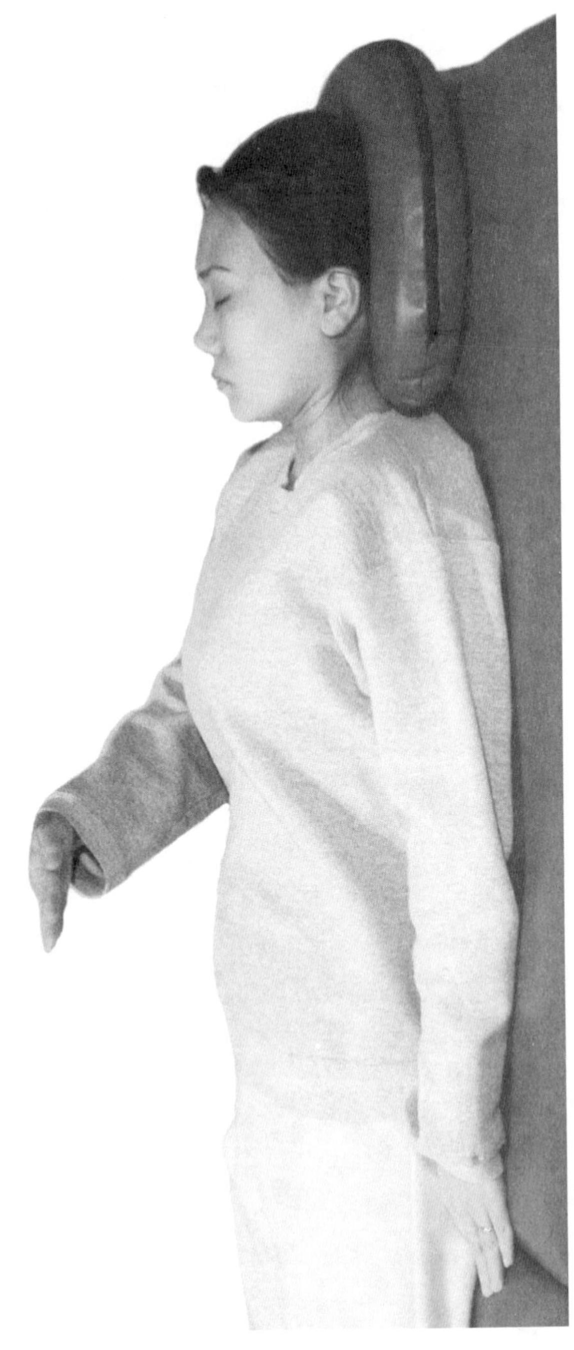

(Photo 31) Proceed to the 2nd Chakra. Focus and channel Reiki into the center of the Chakra with the intent for it to flow to the IBS. *Step should only take 5 minutes.*

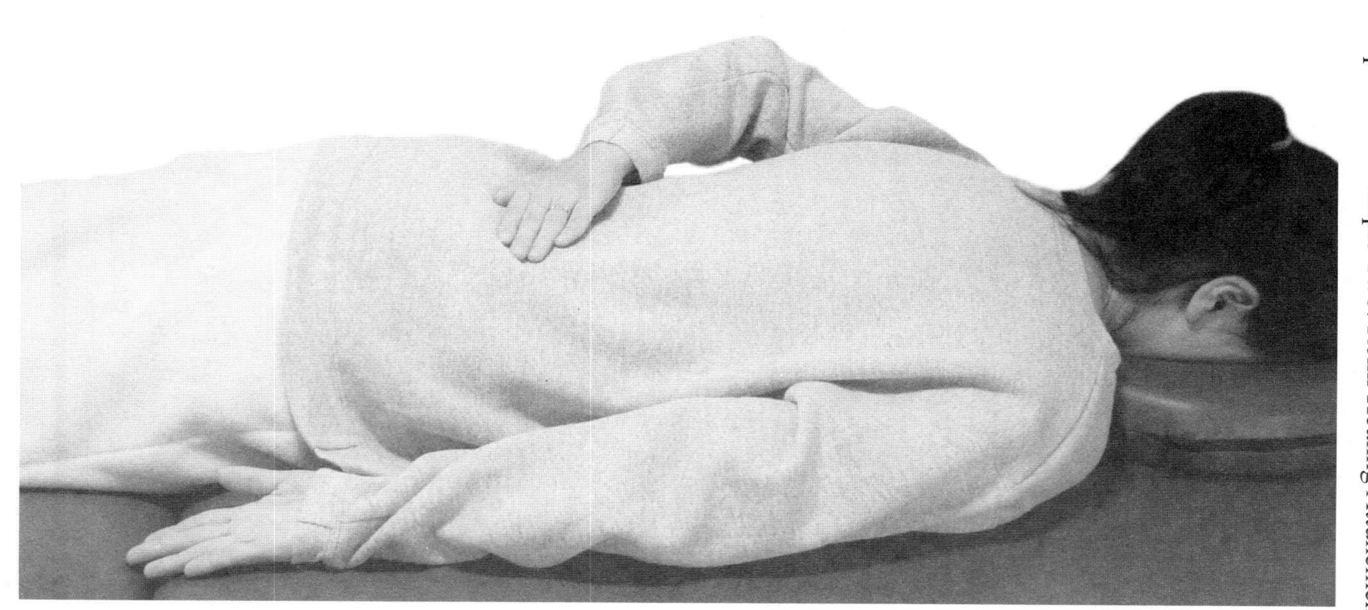

(Photo 32) Next, turn on your stomach and proceed to the back 2nd Chakra. Channel Reiki into the center of the back 2nd Chakra with the intent for it to flow to the IBS. *Step should only take 5 minutes.*

Healing Attunement for Reiki 2nd Level and Master: Performed on Yourself

1. You have prepared for the Healing Attunement.

2. You are in the correct position to perform the Attunement on yourself.

3. State the intent for the Healing Attunement (IBS) silently to yourself before you begin. At this time, you can also ask for guidance during the Attunement. *Step should only take a few seconds.*

4. Visualize the Mental/Emotional Symbol in front of the 7th Chakra, activate it (Photo 33), then embed it into the center of the Chakra. (Photo 34) *Step should only take 15 seconds.*

5. Channel Reiki into the 7th Chakra with the intent to clear any mental or emotional blocks associated with the IBS. (Photo 35) *Step should only take about 2 minutes.*

6. Proceed to the 2nd Chakra. Visualize the Power Symbol over it, activate it (Photo 36), then embed it into the center of the Chakra. (Photo 37) *Step should only take 15 seconds.*

7. Stay with the 2nd Chakra. Visualize the Long Distance Symbol over it, activate it (Photo 38), then embed it into the center of the Chakra. (Photo 39) *Step should only take 15 seconds.*

Note: If you are a 2nd Level, bypass Step 8 and go to Step 9.

8. Stay with the 2nd Chakra. Visualize the Master Symbol over it, activate it (Photo 40), then embed it into the center of the Chakra. (Photo 41) *Step should only take 15 seconds.*

9. The Reiki Symbols are now embedded into the 2nd Chakra. Next, channel Reiki into the center of the 2nd Chakra with the intent for it to flow to the IBS. (Photo 42) *Step should only take 5 minutes.*

10. Next, turn on your stomach and proceed to the back 2nd Chakra. Channel Reiki into the center of the back 2nd Chakra with the intent for it to flow to the IBS. (Photo 43) *Step should only take 5 minutes.*

11. The Attunement is complete. Perform the finishing steps outlined in Chapter 10.

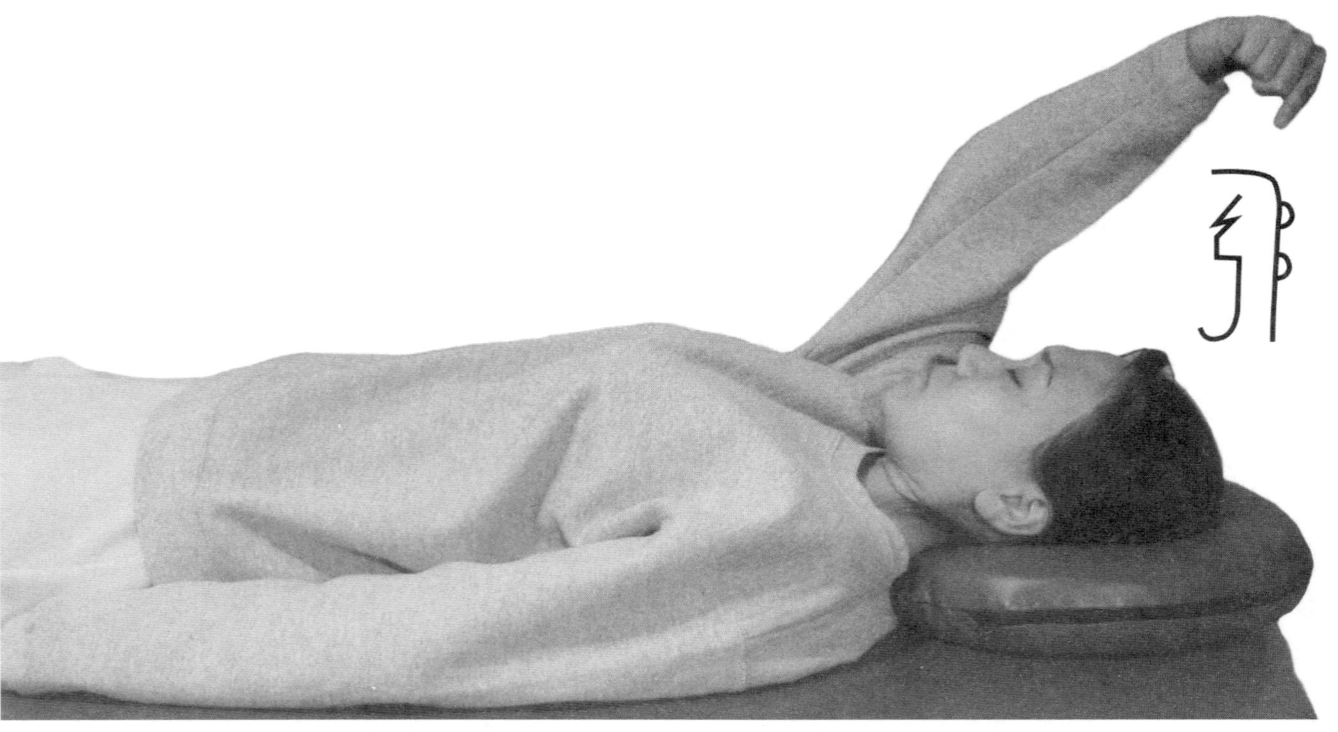

(Photo 33) Visualize the Mental/Emotional Symbol in front of the 7th Chakra, activate it.

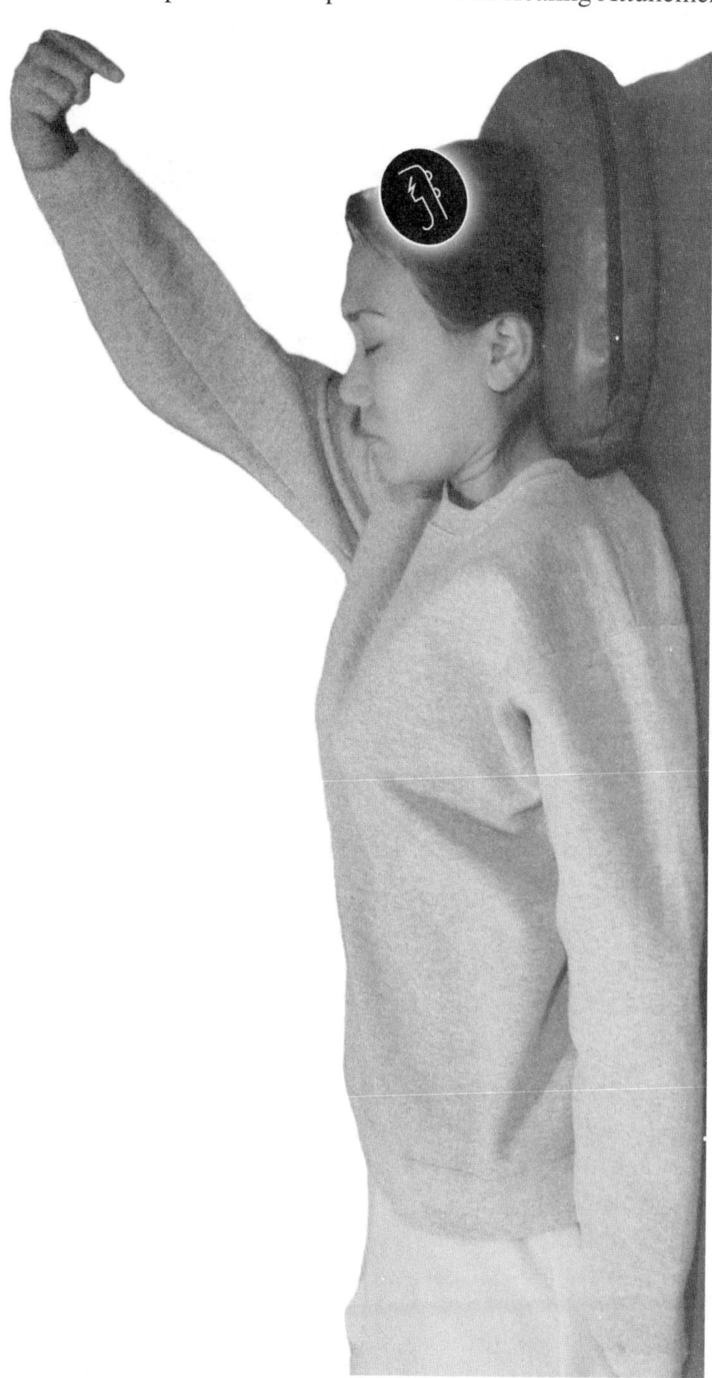

(Photo 34) Embed it into the center of the Chakra. *Step should only take 15 seconds.*

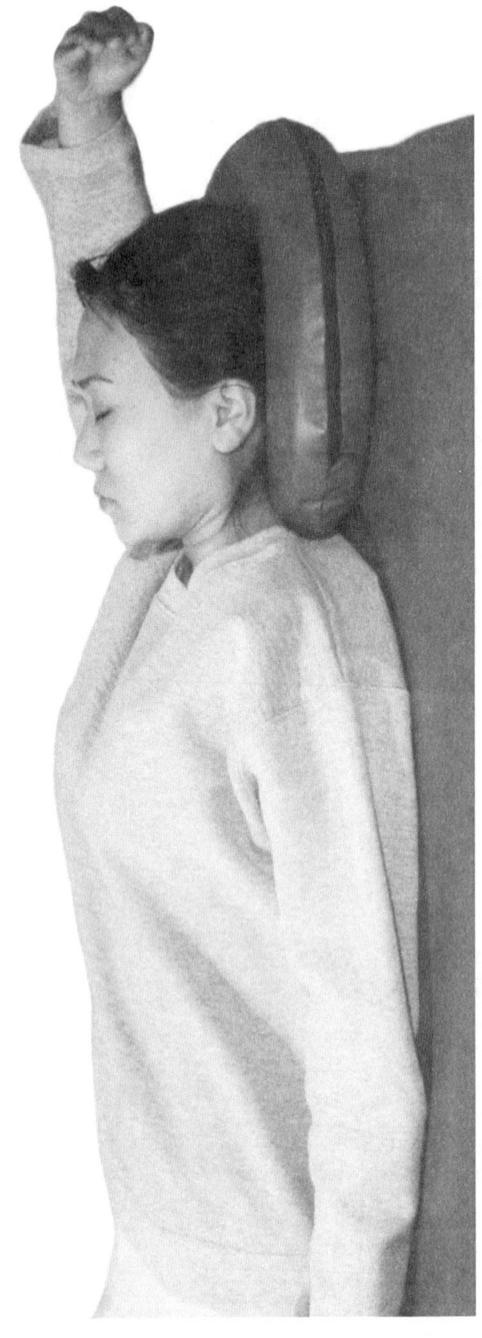

(Photo 35) Channel Reiki into the 7th Chakra with the intent to clear any mental or emotional blocks associated with the IBS. *Step should only take about 2 minutes.*

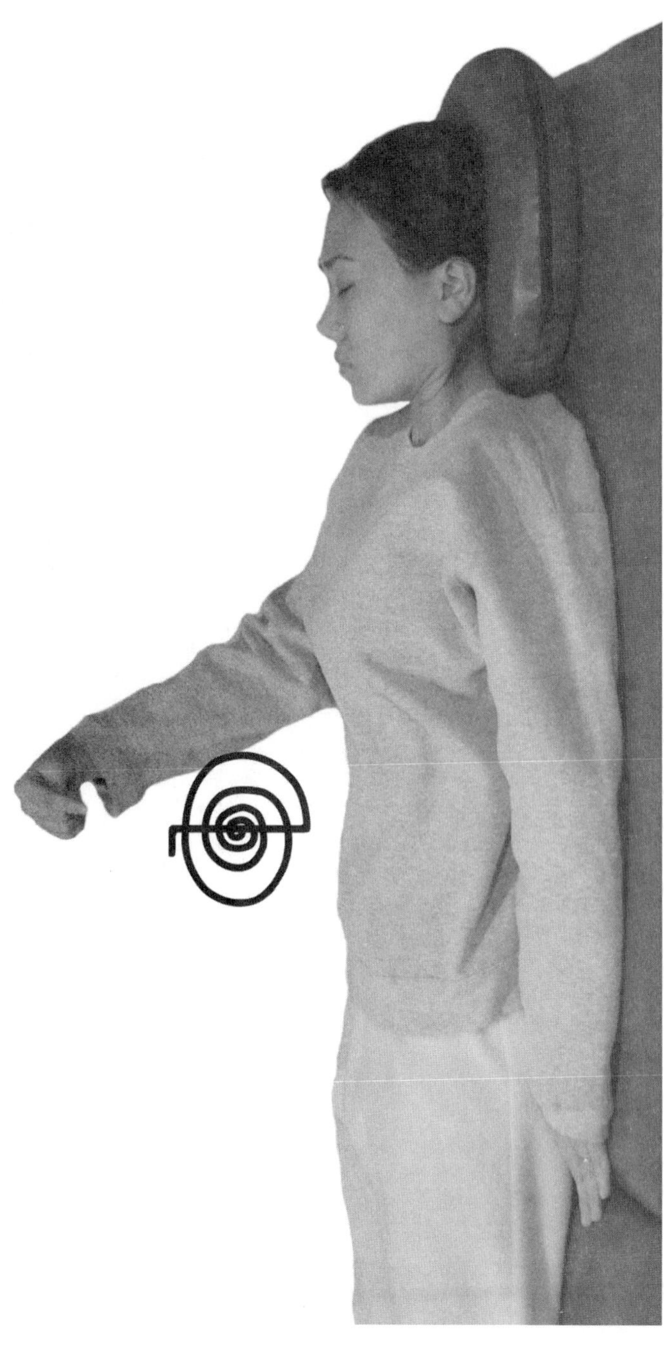

(Photo 36) Proceed to the 2nd Chakra. Visualize the Power Symbol over it, activate it.

(Photo 37) Embed it into the center of the Chakra. *Step should only take 15 seconds*

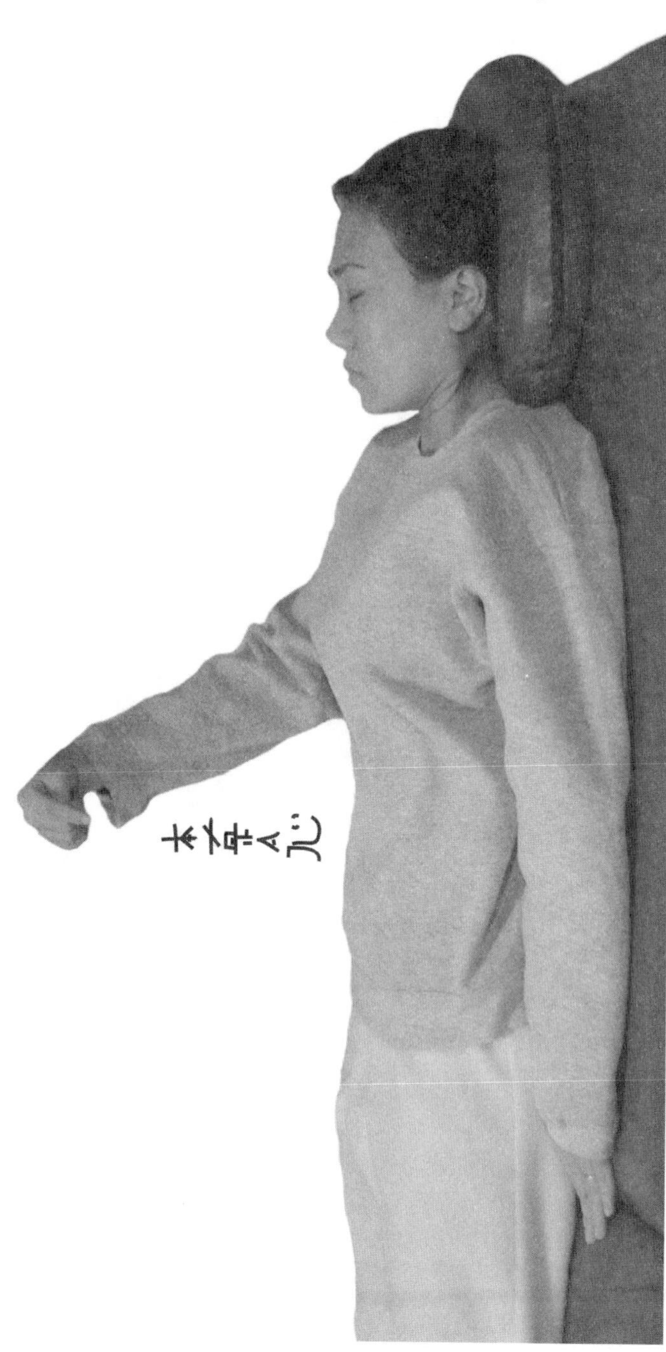

(Photo 38) Stay with the 2nd Chakra. Visualize the Long Distance Symbol over it, activate it.

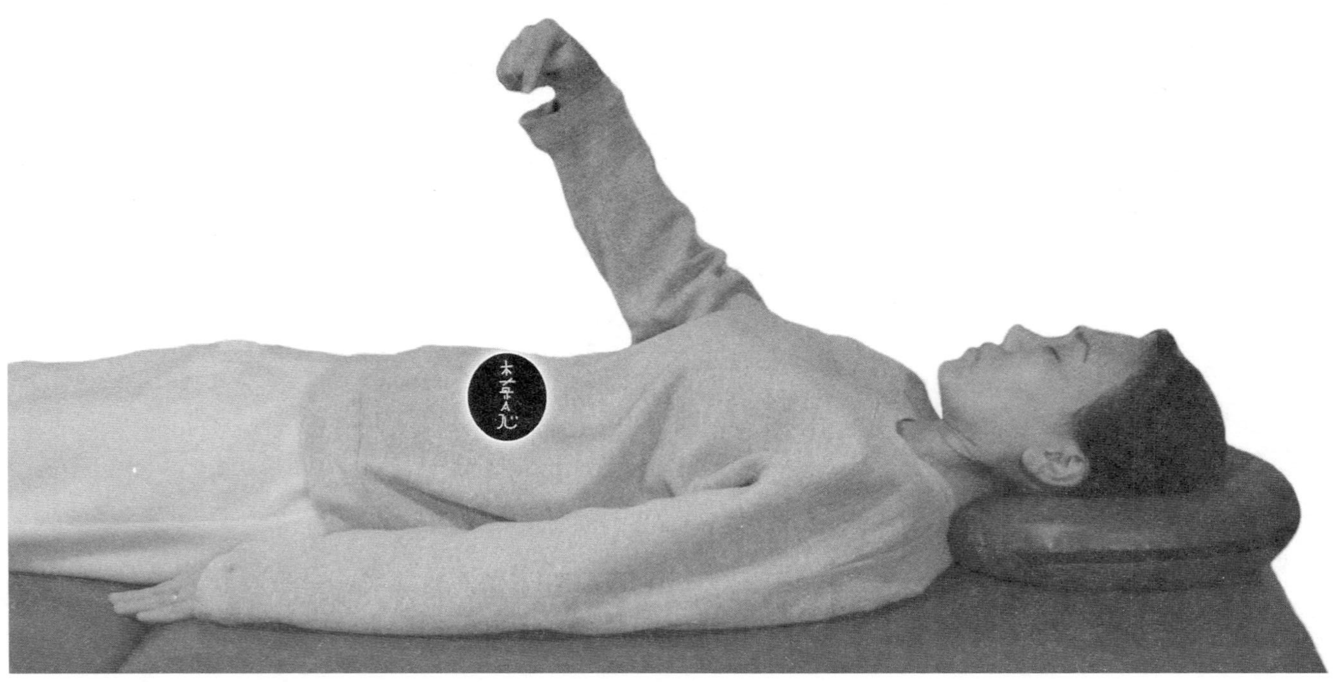

(Photo 39) Embed it into the center of the Chakra. *Step should only take 15 seconds.*

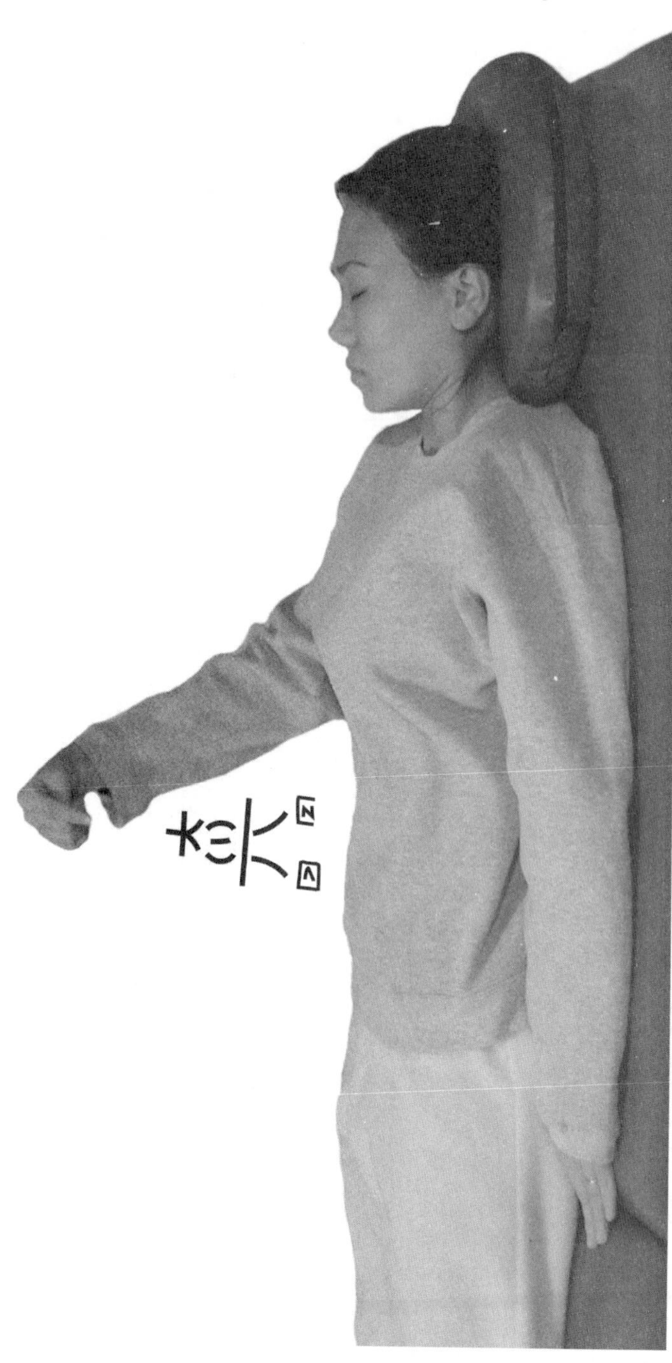

(Photo 40) Stay with the 2nd Chakra. Visualize the Master Symbol over it, activate it.

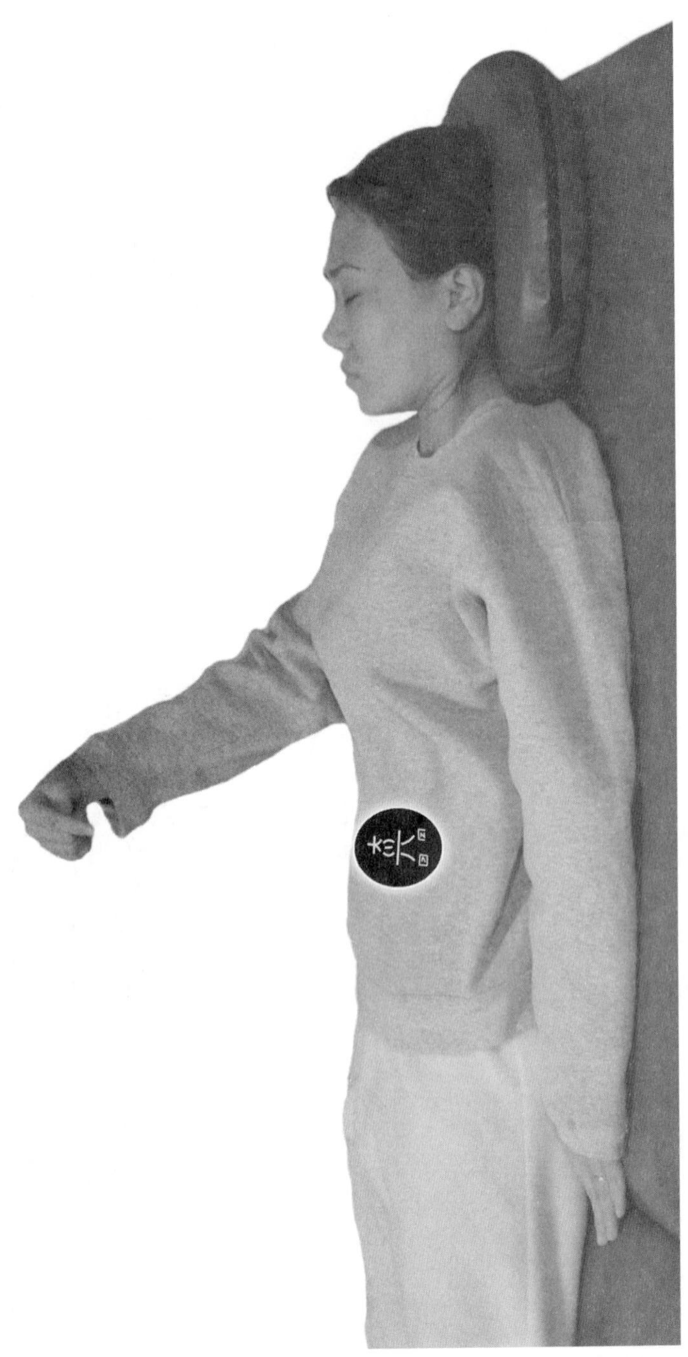

(Photo 41) Embed it into the center of the Chakra. *Step should only take 15 seconds.*

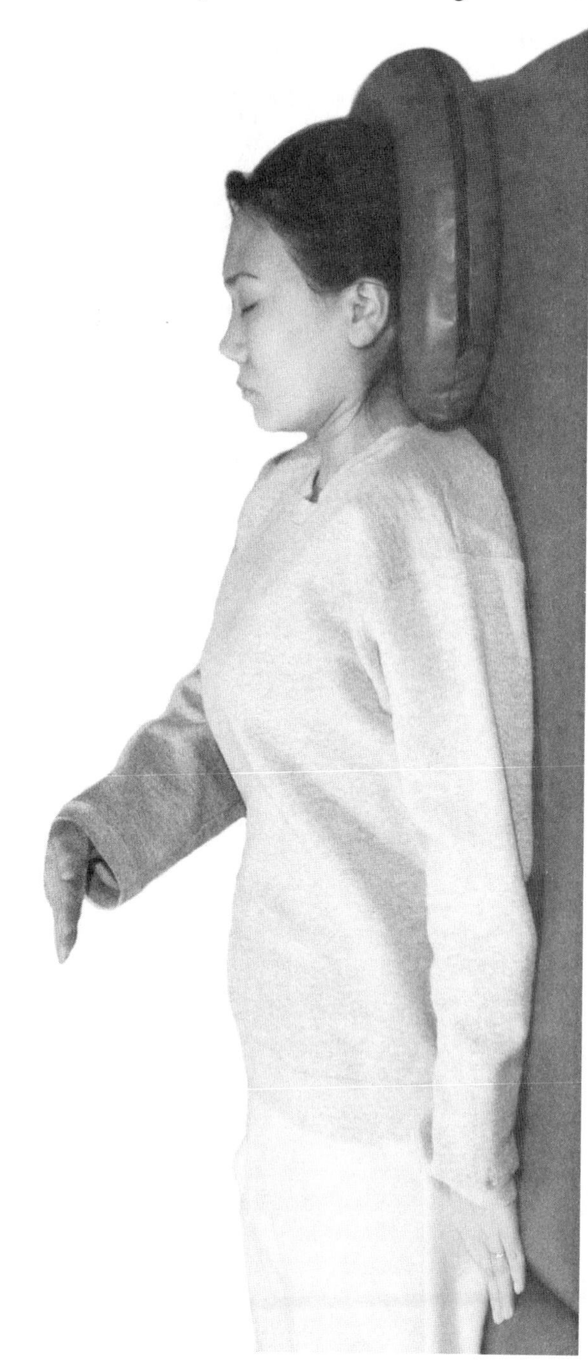

(Photo 42) The Reiki Symbols are now embedded into the 2nd Chakra. Next, channel Reiki into the center of the 2nd Chakra with the intent for it to flow to the IBS. *Step should only take 5 minutes.*

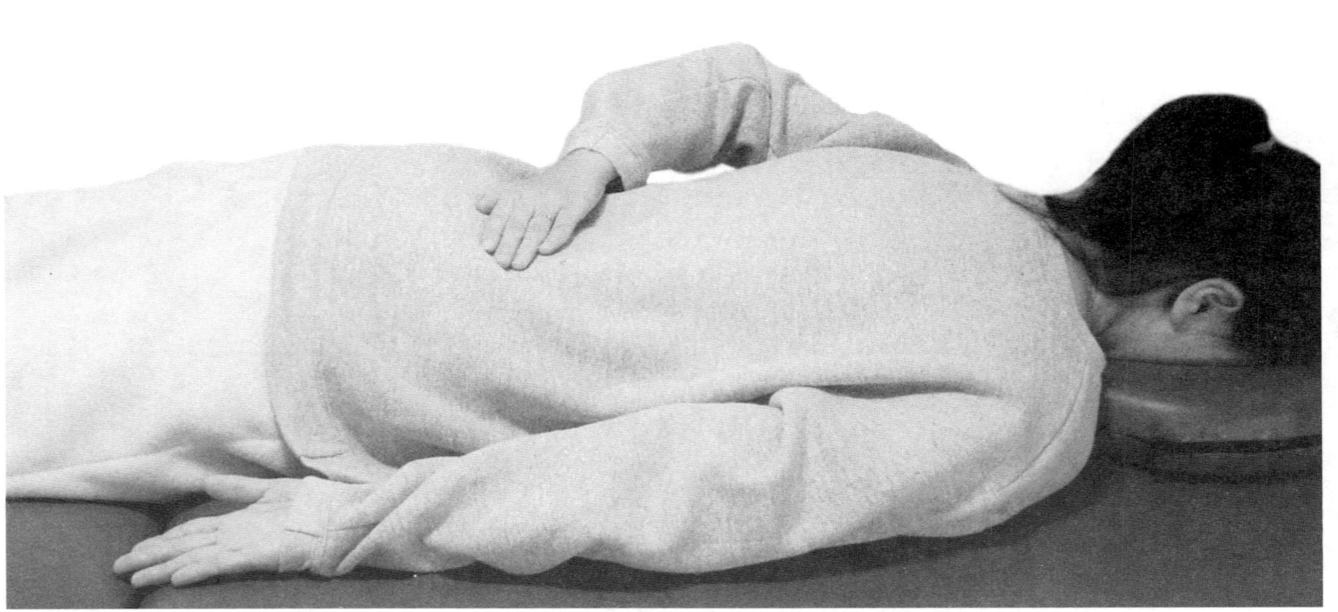

(Photo 43) Next, turn on your stomach and proceed to the back 2nd Chakra. Channel Reiki into the center of the back 2nd Chakra with the intent for it to flow to the IBS. *Step should only take 5 minutes*

“Indeed envy is a defect; worse than any other.”

-Rumi

“Regard a king as someone unconcerned with kingship.”

-Rumi

Example Three: Reiki Healing Attunement

Example of a Reiki Healing Attunement for a Kidney Stone, performed on another person using the 3rd Chakra.

Healing Attunement for 1st Level Reiki: Performed on Another Person

1. You have prepared for the Healing Attunement.

2. You are in the correct position to perform the Attunement on another person.

3. State the intent for the Healing Attunement (Kidney Stone) silently to yourself before you begin. At this time, you can also ask for guidance during the Attunement. *Step should only take a few seconds.*

4. Channel Reiki into the 7th Chakra with the intent to clear any mental or emotional blocks associated with the Kidney Stone. (Photo 44) *Step should only take about 2 minutes.*

5. Proceed to the 3rd Chakra. Focus and channel Reiki into the center of the Chakra with the intent for it to flow to the Kidney Stone. (Photo 45) *Step should only take 5 minutes.*

6. Next, have the person turn on his or her stomach and proceed to the back 3rd Chakra. Channel Reiki into the center of the back 3rd Chakra with the intent for it to flow to the Kidney Stone. (Photo 46) *Step should only take 5 minutes.*

7. The Attunement is complete. Perform the finishing steps outlined in Chapter 10.

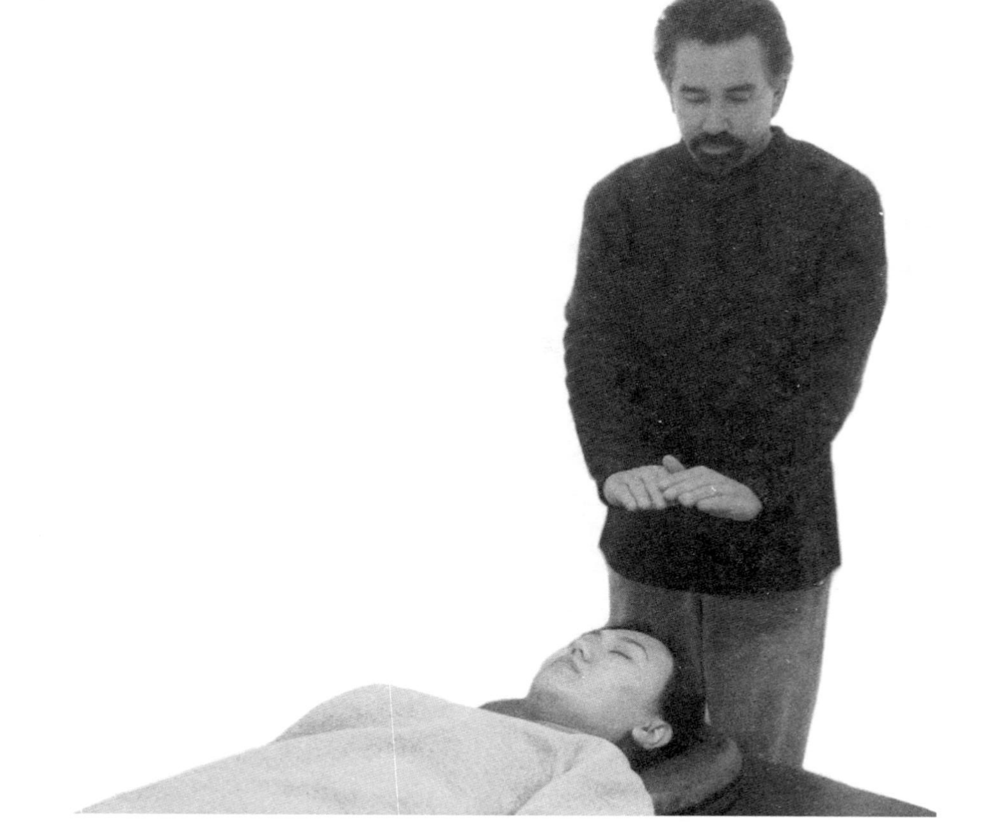

(Photo 44) Channel Reiki into the 7th Chakra with the intent to clear any mental or emotional blocks associated with the Kidney Stone. *Step should only take about 2 minutes.*

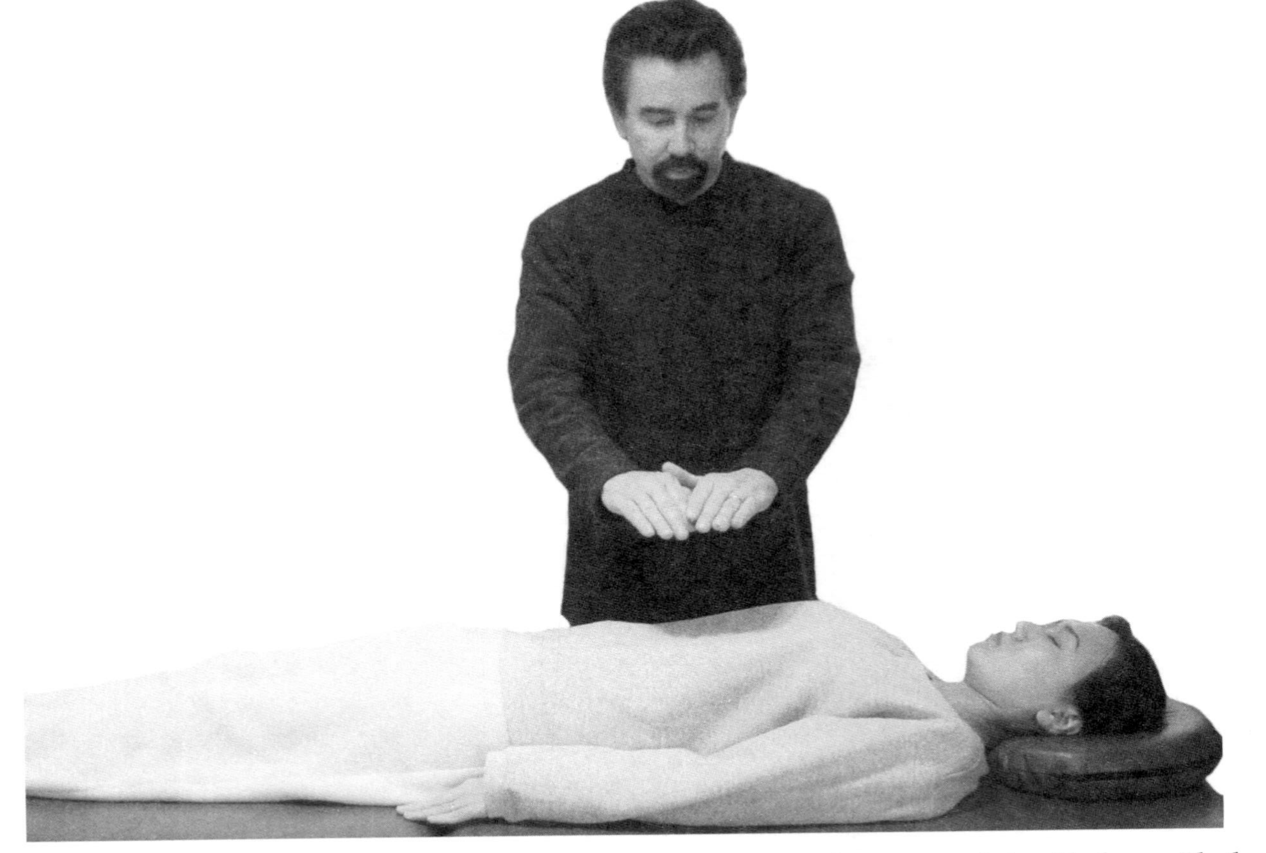

(Photo 45) Proceed to the 3rd Chakra. Focus and channel Reiki into the center of the Chakra with the intent for it to flow to the Kidney Stone. *Step should only take 5 minutes.*

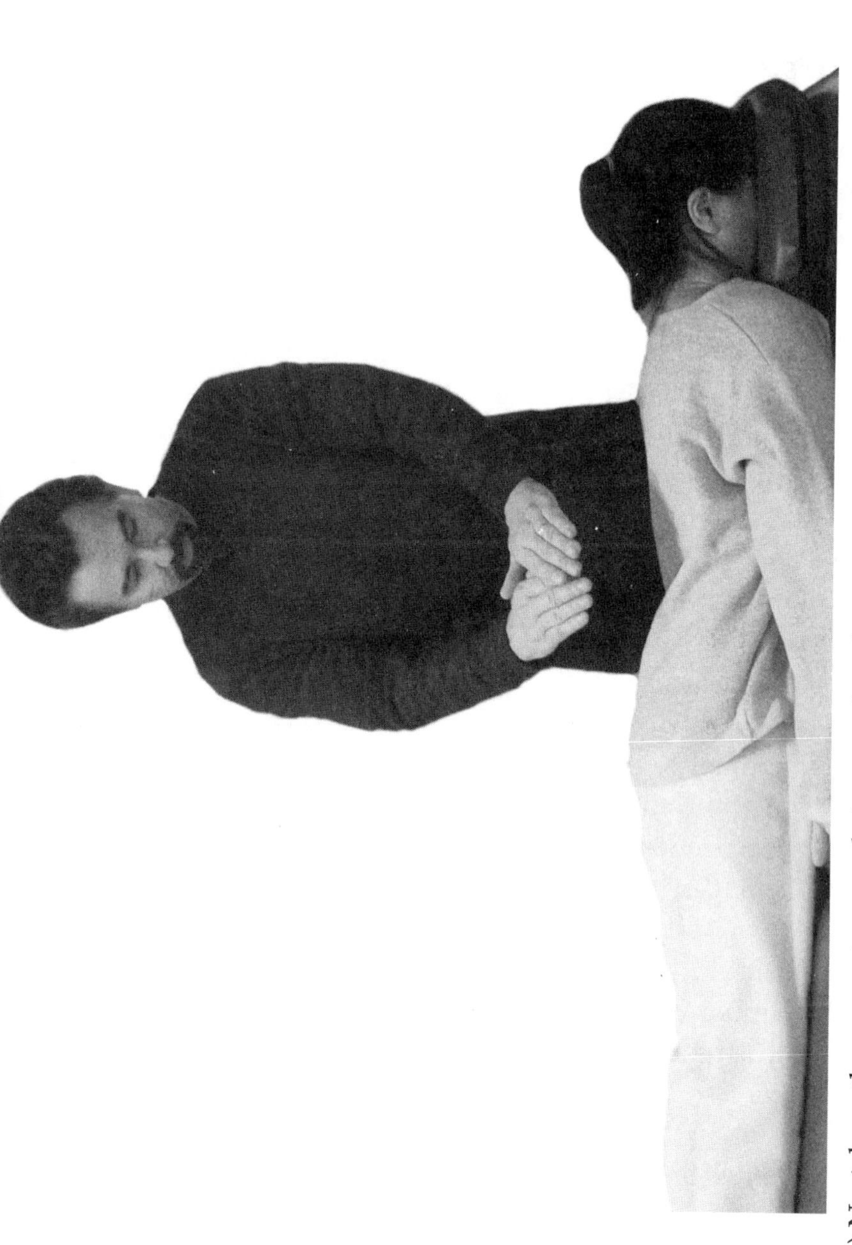

(Photo 46) Next, have the person turn on their stomach and proceed to the back 3rd Chakra. Channel Reiki into the center of the back 3rd Chakra with the intent for it to flow to the Kidney Stone. *Step should only take 5 minutes.*

Healing Attunement for Reiki 2nd Level and Master: Performed on Another Person.

1. You have prepared for the Healing Attunement.

2. You are in the correct position to perform the Attunement on another person.

3. State the intent for the Healing Attunement (Kidney Stone) silently to yourself before you begin. At this time, you can also ask for guidance during the Attunement. *Step should only take a few seconds.*

4. Visualize the Mental/Emotional Symbol in front of the 7th Chakra, activate it (Photo 47), then embed it into the center of the Chakra. (Photo 48) *Step should only take 15 seconds.*

5. Channel Reiki into the 7th Chakra with the intent to clear any mental or emotional blocks associated with the Kidney Stone. (Photo 49) *Step should only take about 2 minutes.*

6. Proceed to the 3rd Chakra. Visualize the Power Symbol over it, activate it (Photo 50), then embed it into the center of the Chakra. (Photo 51) *Step should only take 15 seconds.*

7. Stay with the 3rd Chakra. Visualize the Long Distance Symbol over it, activate it (Photo 52), then embed it into the center of the Chakra. (Photo 53) *Step should only take 15 seconds.*

Note: If you are a 2nd Level, bypass Step 8 and go to Step 9.

8. Stay with the 3rd Chakra. Visualize the Master Symbol over it, activate it (Photo 54), then embed it into the center of the Chakra. (Photo 55) *Step should only take 15 seconds.*

9. The Reiki Symbols are now embedded into the 3rd Chakra. Next, channel Reiki into the center of the 3rd Chakra with the intent for it to flow to the Kidney Stone. (Photo 56) *Step should only take 5 minutes.*

10. Next, have the person turn on his or her stomach and proceed to the back 3rd Chakra. Channel Reiki into the center of the back 3rd Chakra with the intent for it to flow to the Kidney Stone. (Photo 57) *Step should only take 5 minutes.*

11. The Attunement is complete. Perform the finishing steps outlined in Chapter 10.

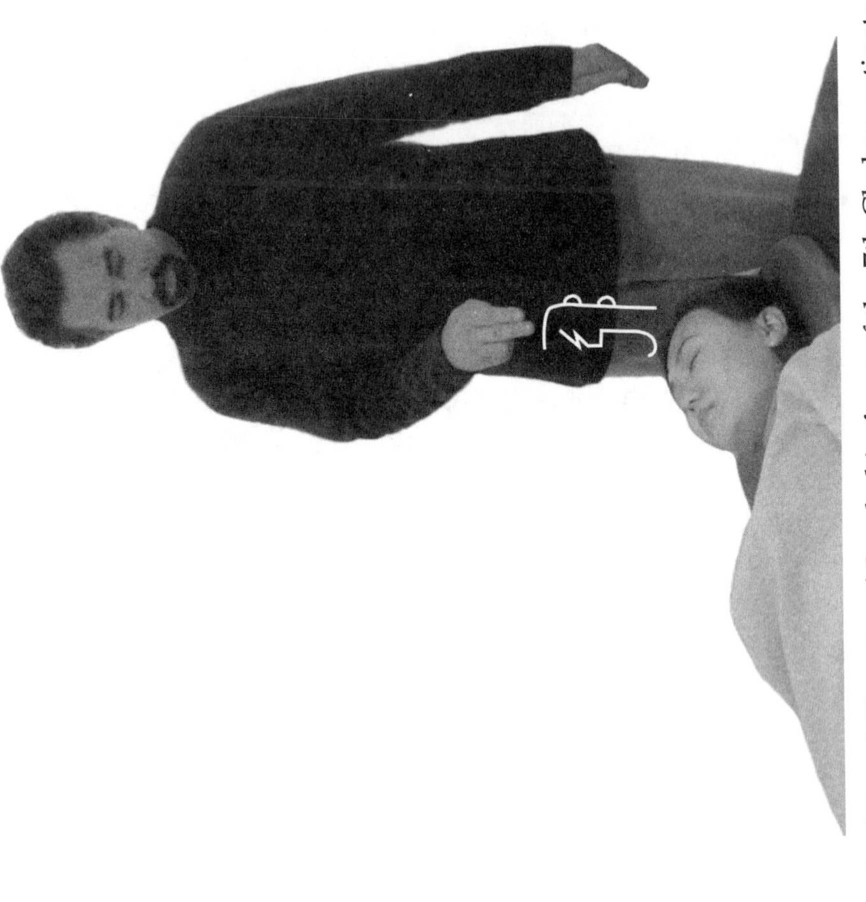

(Photo 47) Visualize the Mental/Emotional Symbol in front of the 7th Chakra, activate it.

(Photo 48) Embed it into the center of the Chakra. *Step should only take 15 seconds.*

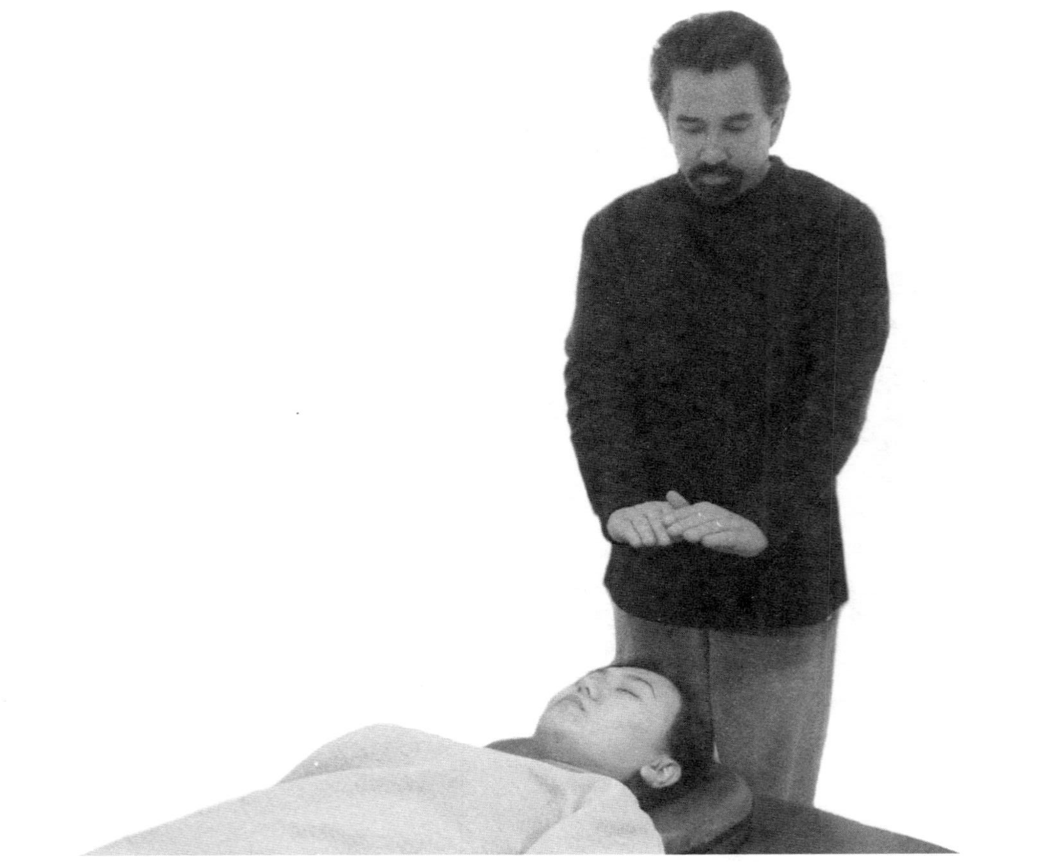

(Photo 49) Channel Reiki into the 7th Chakra with the intent to clear any mental or emotional blocks associated with the Kidney Stone. *Step should only take about 2 minutes.*

(Photo 50) Proceed to the 3rd Chakra. Visualize the Power Symbol over it, activate it.

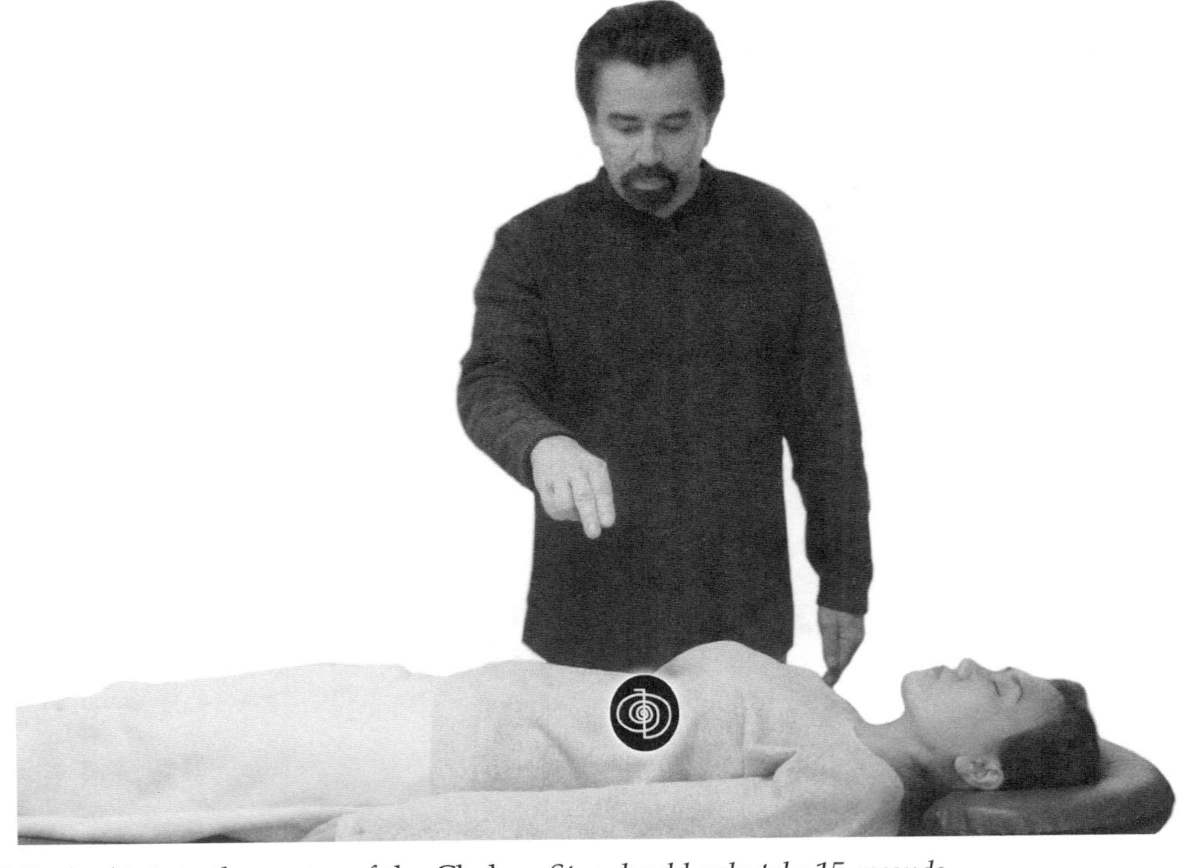

(Photo 51) Embed it into the center of the Chakra. *Step should only take 15 seconds.*

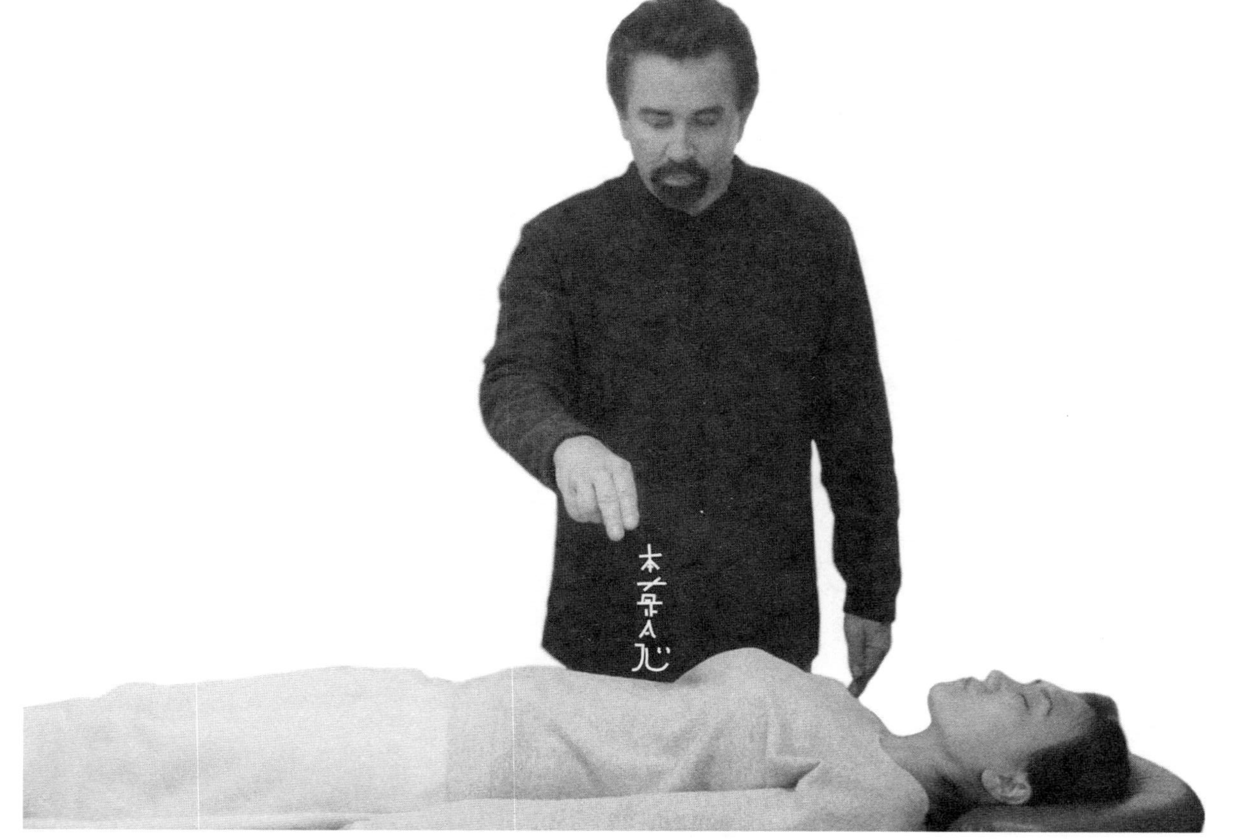

(Photo 52) Stay with the 3rd Chakra. Visualize the Long Distance Symbol over it, activate it.

(Photo 53) Embed it into the center of the Chakra. *Step should only take 15 seconds.*

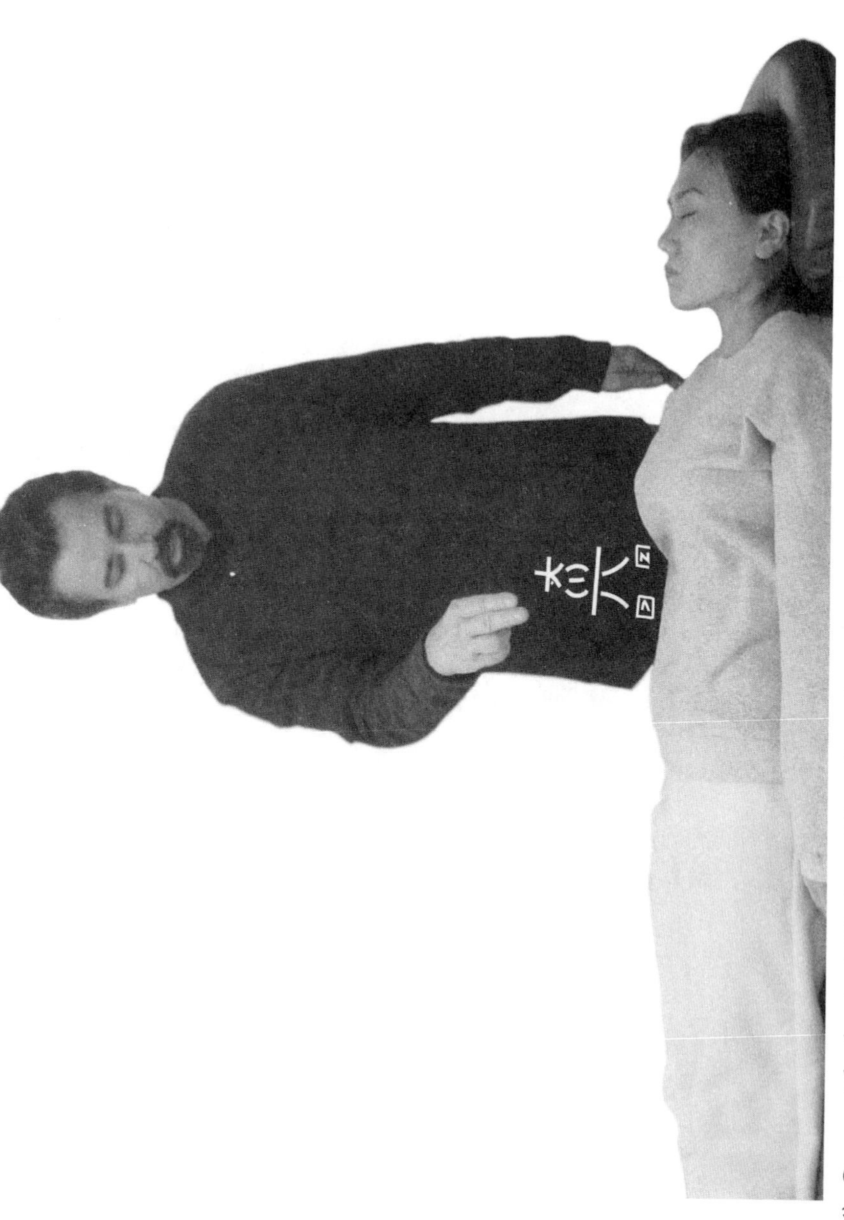

(Photo 54) Stay with the 3rd Chakra. Visualize the Master Symbol over it, activate it.

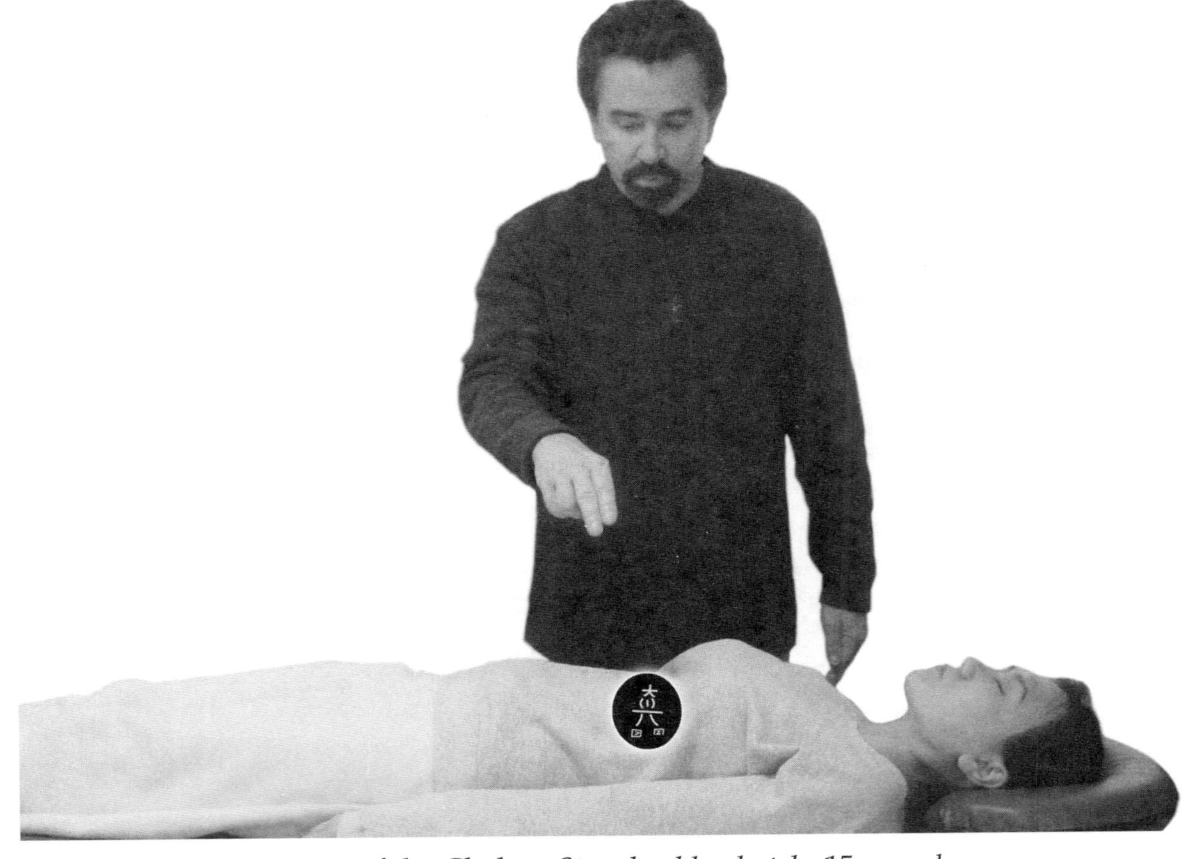

(Photo 55) Embed it into the center of the Chakra. *Step should only take 15 seconds.*

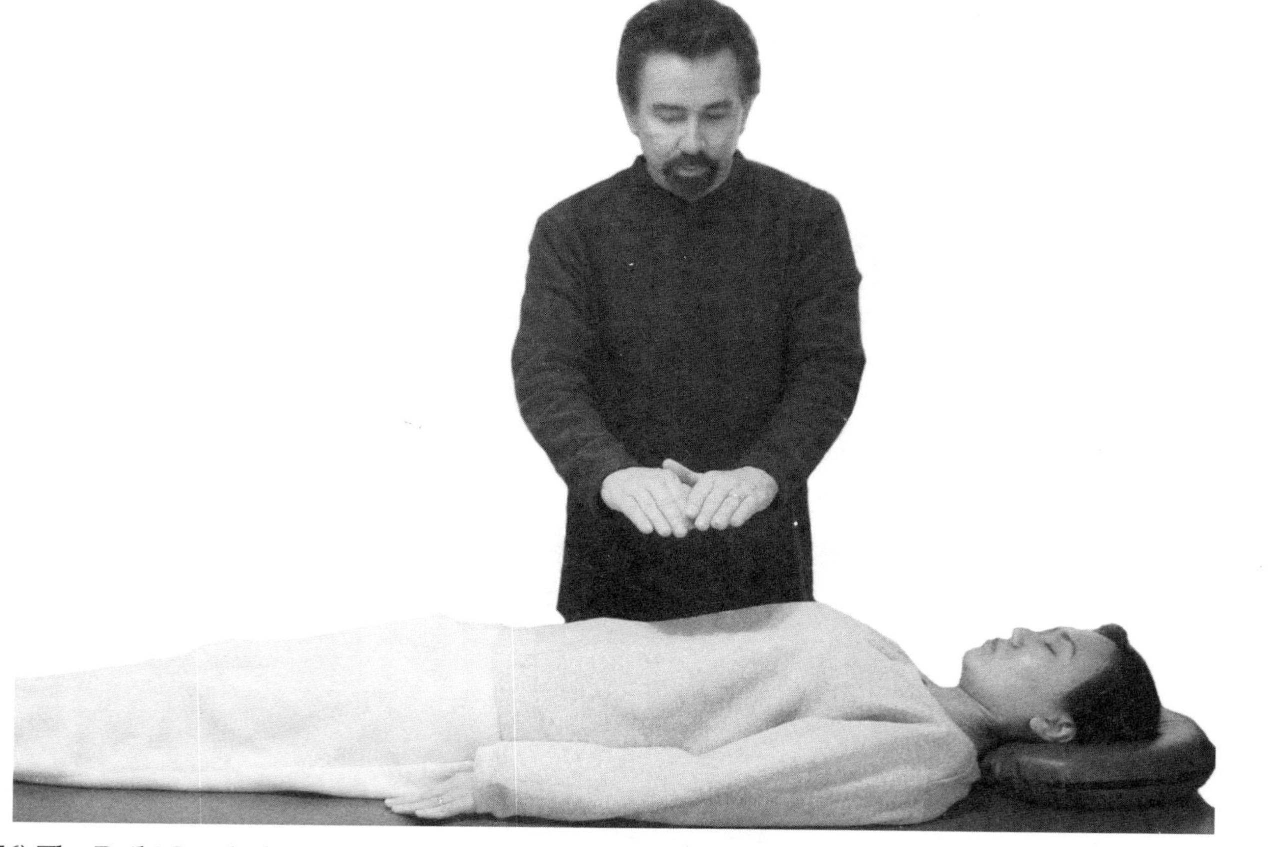

(Photo 56) The Reiki Symbols are now embedded into the 3rd Chakra. Next, channel Reiki into the center of the 3rd Chakra with the intent for it to flow to the Kidney Stone. *Step should only take 5 minutes.*

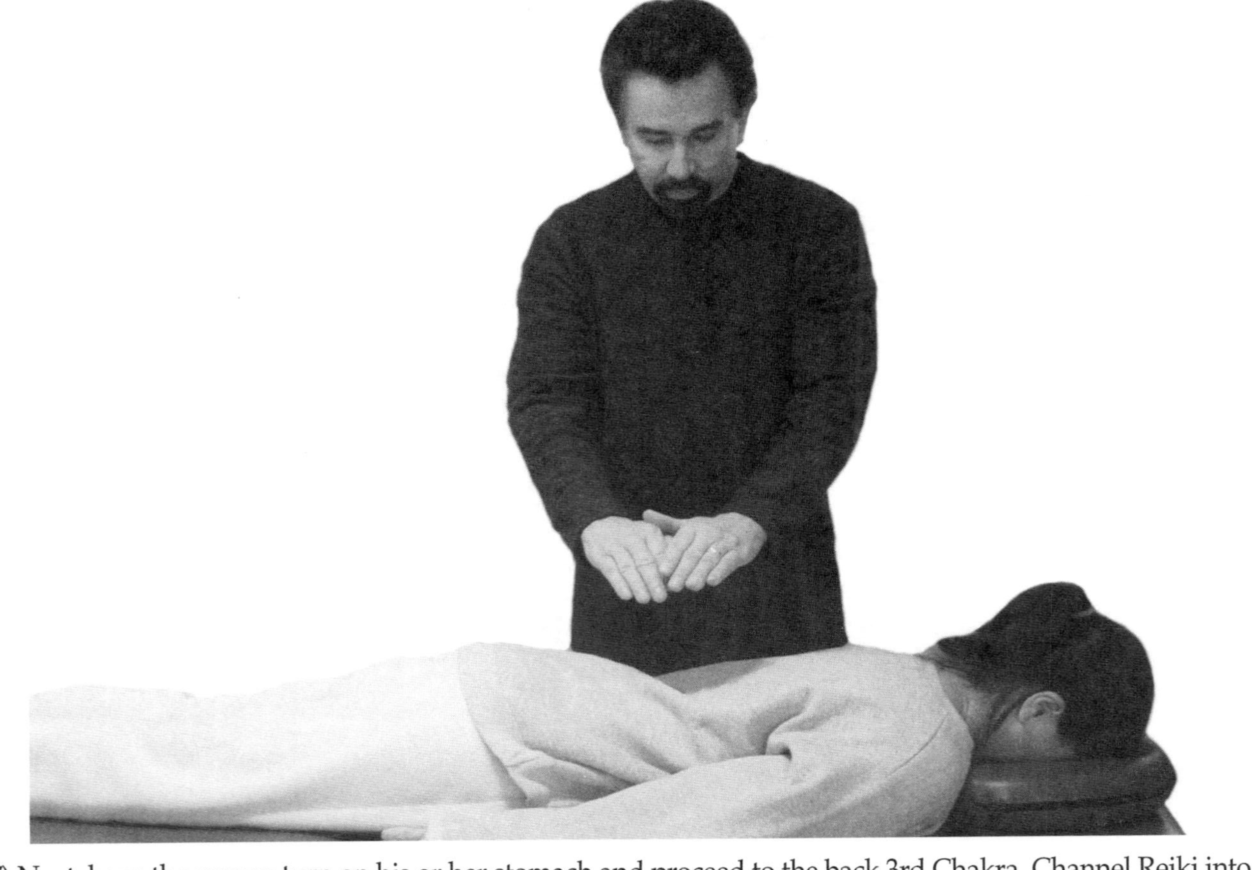

(Photo 57) Next, have the person turn on his or her stomach and proceed to the back 3rd Chakra. Channel Reiki into the center of the back 3rd Chakra with the intent for it to flow to the Kidney Stone. *Step should only take 5 minutes.*

“The sword of reality is the saint’s protection.”

-Rumi

"You think the shadow is the substance."
-Rumi

Example Four: Reiki Healing Attunement

Example of a Reiki Healing Attunement for Asthma, performed on yourself using the 4th Chakra.

Healing Attunement for 1st Level Reiki: Performed on Yourself

1. You have prepared for the Healing Attunement.

2. You are in the correct position to perform the Attunement on yourself.

3. State the intent for the Healing Attunement (Asthma) silently to yourself before you begin. At this time, you can also ask for guidance during the Attunement. *Step should only take a few seconds.*

4. Channel Reiki into the 7th Chakra with the intent to clear any mental or emotional blocks associated with the Asthma. (Photo 58) *Step should only take about 2 minutes.*

5. Proceed to the 4th Chakra. Focus and channel Reiki into the center of the Chakra with the intent for it to flow to the Asthma. (Photo 59) *Step should only take 5 minutes.*

6. Next, turn on your stomach and proceed to the back 4th Chakra. Channel Reiki into the center of the back 4th Chakra with the intent for it to flow to the Asthma. (Photo 60) *Step should only take 5 minutes.*

7. The Attunement is complete. Perform the finishing steps outlined in Chapter 10.

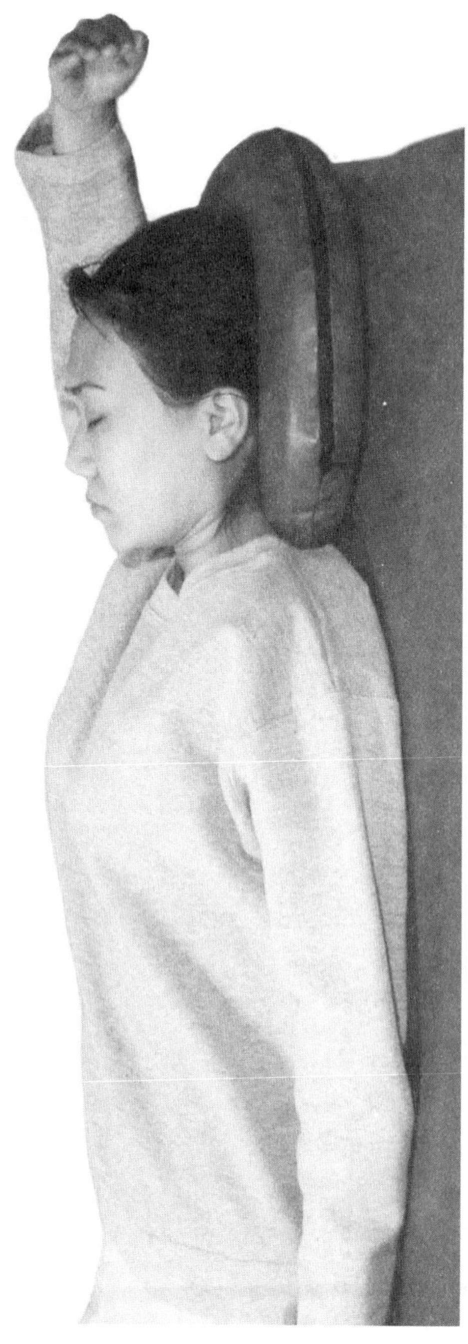

(Photo 58) Channel Reiki into the 7th Chakra with the intent to clear any mental or emotional blocks associated with the Asthma. *Step should only take about 2 minutes.*

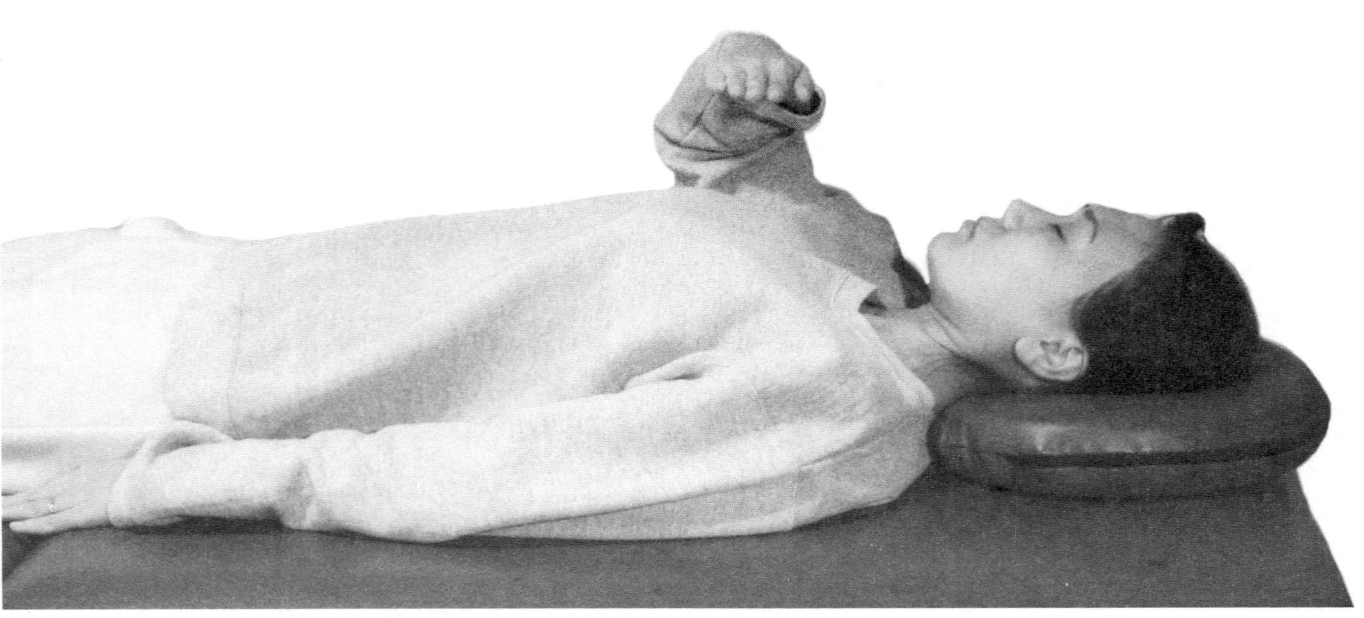

(Photo 59) Proceed to the 4th Chakra. Focus and channel Reiki into the center of the Chakra with the intent for it to flow to the Asthma. *Step should only take 5 minutes.*

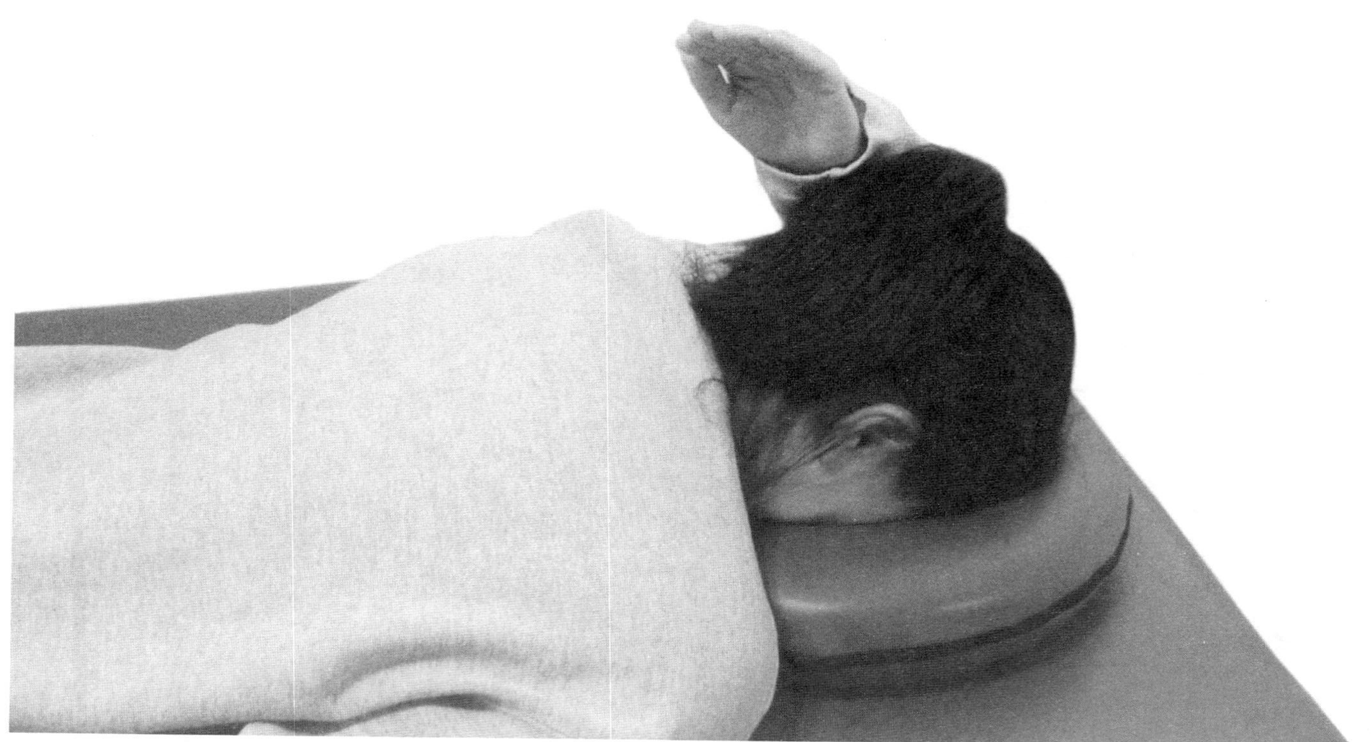

(Photo 60) Next, turn on your stomach and proceed to the back 4th Chakra. Channel Reiki into the center of the back 4th Chakra with the intent for it to flow to the Asthma. *Step should only take 5 minutes.*

Healing Attunement for Reiki 2nd Level and Master: Performed on Yourself

1. You have prepared for the Healing Attunement.

2. You are in the correct position to perform the Attunement on yourself.

3. State the intent for the Healing Attunement (Asthma) silently to yourself before you begin. At this time, you can also ask for guidance during the Attunement. *Step should only take a few seconds.*

4. Visualize the Mental/Emotional Symbol in front of the 7th Chakra, activate it (Photo 61), then embed it into the center of the Chakra. (Photo 62) *Step should only take 15 seconds.*

5. Channel Reiki into the 7th Chakra with the intent to clear any mental or emotional blocks associated with the Asthma. (Photo 63) *Step should only take about 2 minutes.*

6. Proceed to the 4th Chakra. Visualize the Power Symbol over it, activate it (Photo 64), then embed it into the center of the Chakra. (Photo 65) *Step should only take 15 seconds.*

7. Stay with the 4th Chakra. Visualize the Long Distance Symbol over it, activate it (Photo 66), then embed it into the center of the Chakra. (Photo 67) *Step should only take 15 seconds.*

Note: If you are a 2nd Level, bypass Step 8 and go to Step 9.

8. Stay with the 4th Chakra. Visualize the Master Symbol over it, activate it (Photo 68), then embed it into the center of the Chakra. (Photo 69) *Step should only take 15 seconds.*

9. The Reiki Symbols are now embedded into the 4th Chakra. Next, channel Reiki into the center of the 4th Chakra with the intent for it to flow to the Asthma. (Photo 70) *Step should only take 5 minutes.*

10. Next, turn on your stomach and proceed to the back 4th Chakra. Channel Reiki into the center of the back 4th Chakra with the intent for it to flow to the Asthma. (Photo 71) *Step should only take 5 minutes.*

11. The Attunement is complete. Perform the finishing steps outlined in Chapter 10.

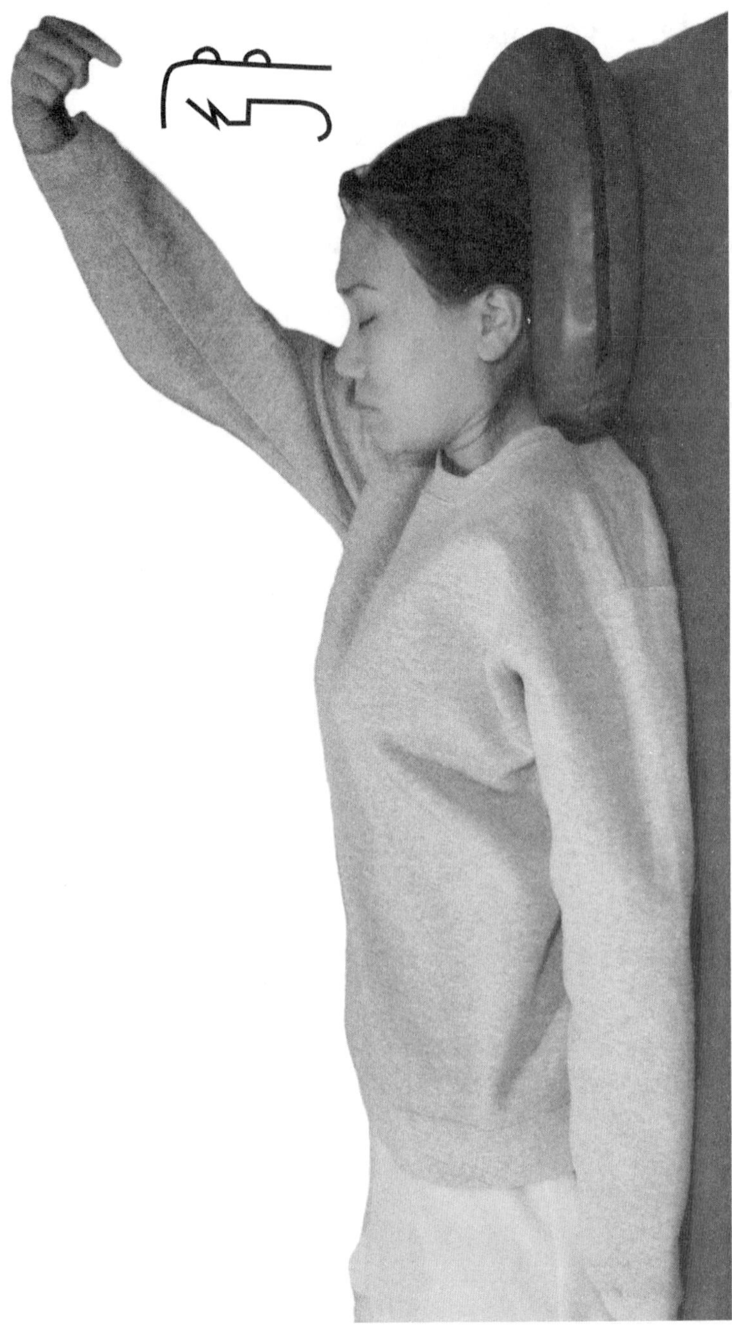

(Photo 61) Visualize the Mental/Emotional Symbol in front of the 7th Chakra , activate it.

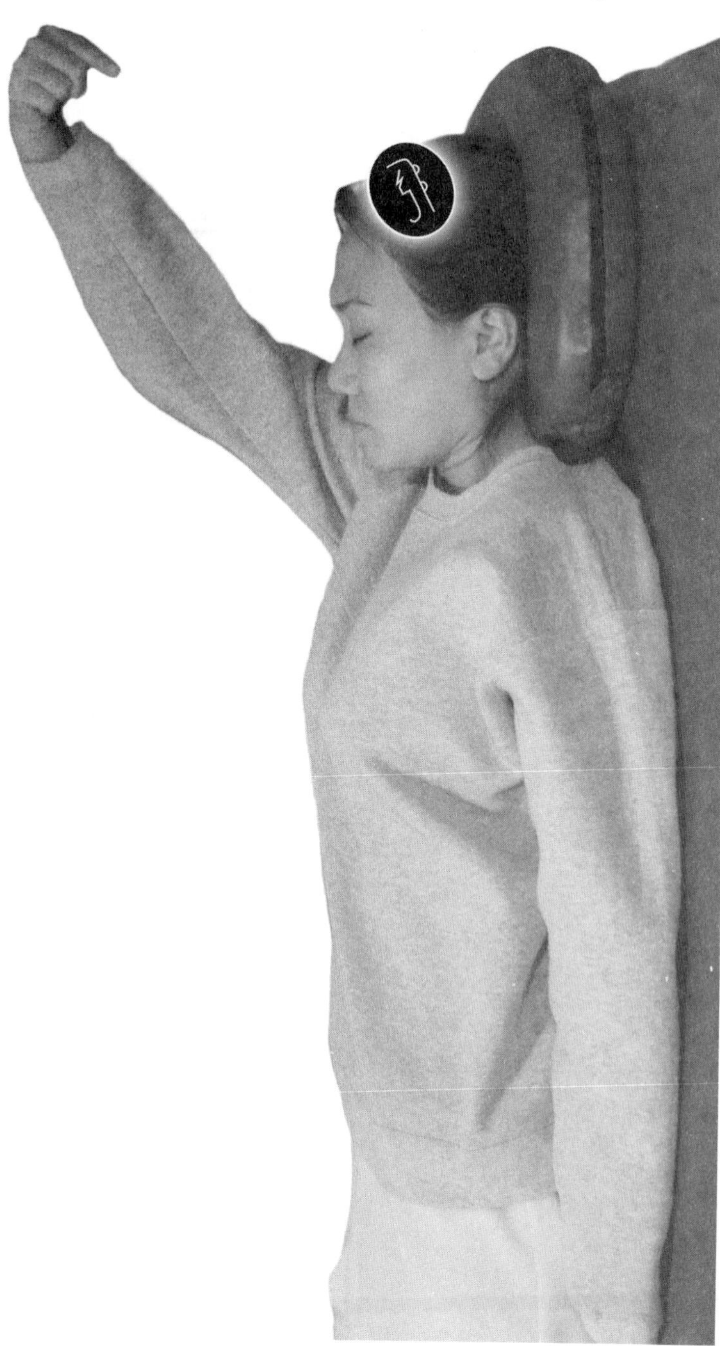

(Photo 62) Embed it into the center of the Chakra. *Step should only take 15 seconds.*

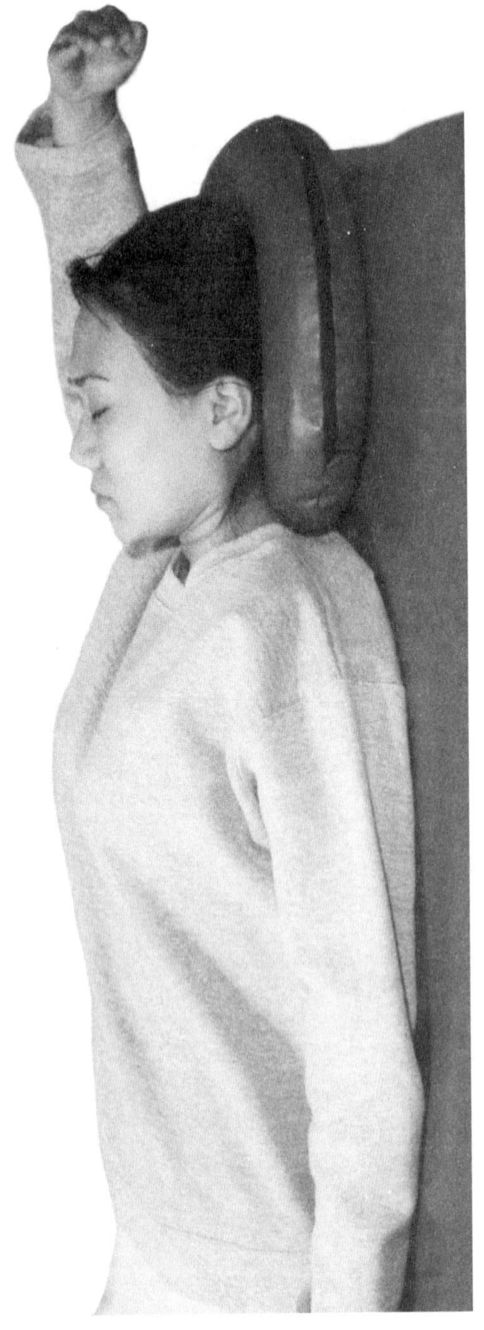

(Photo 63) Channel Reiki into the 7th Chakra with the intent to clear any mental or emotional blocks associated with the Asthma. *Step should only take about 2 minutes.*

(Photo 64) Proceed to the 4th Chakra. Visualize the Power Symbol over it, activate it.

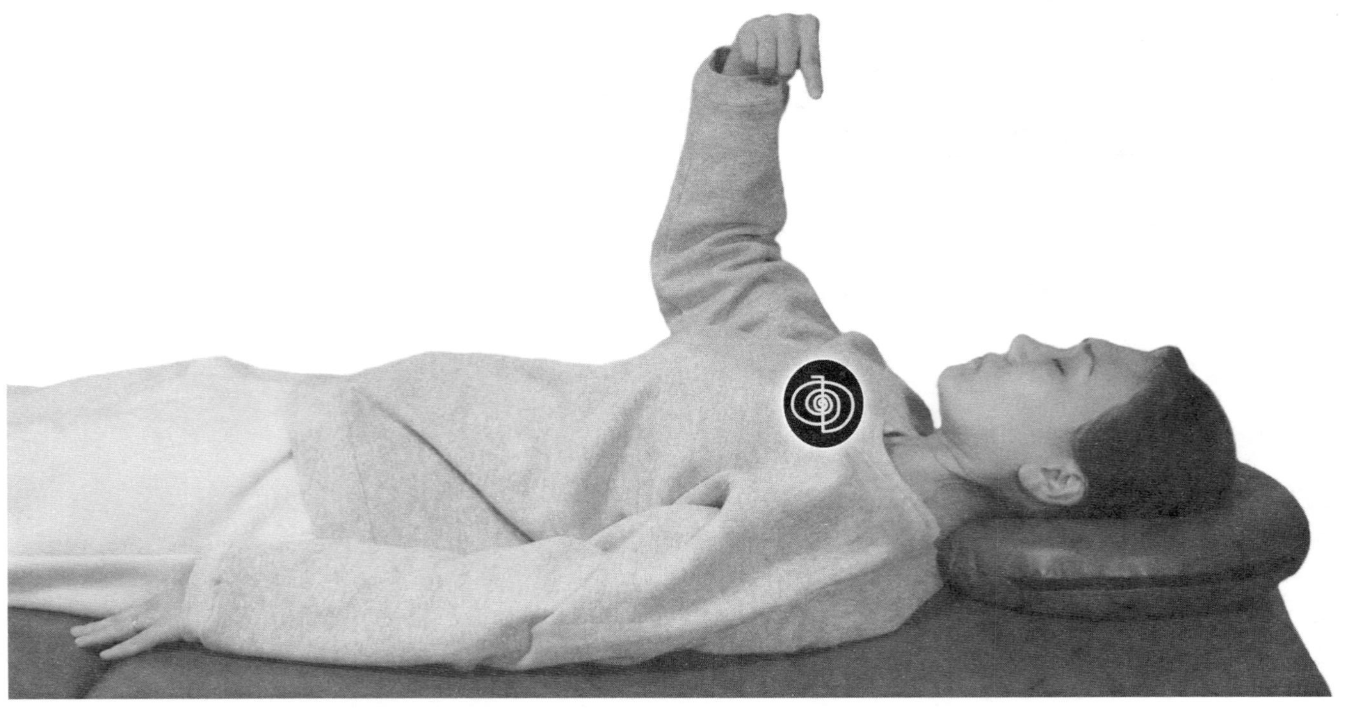

(Photo 65) Embed it into the center of the Chakra. *Step should only take 15 seconds.*

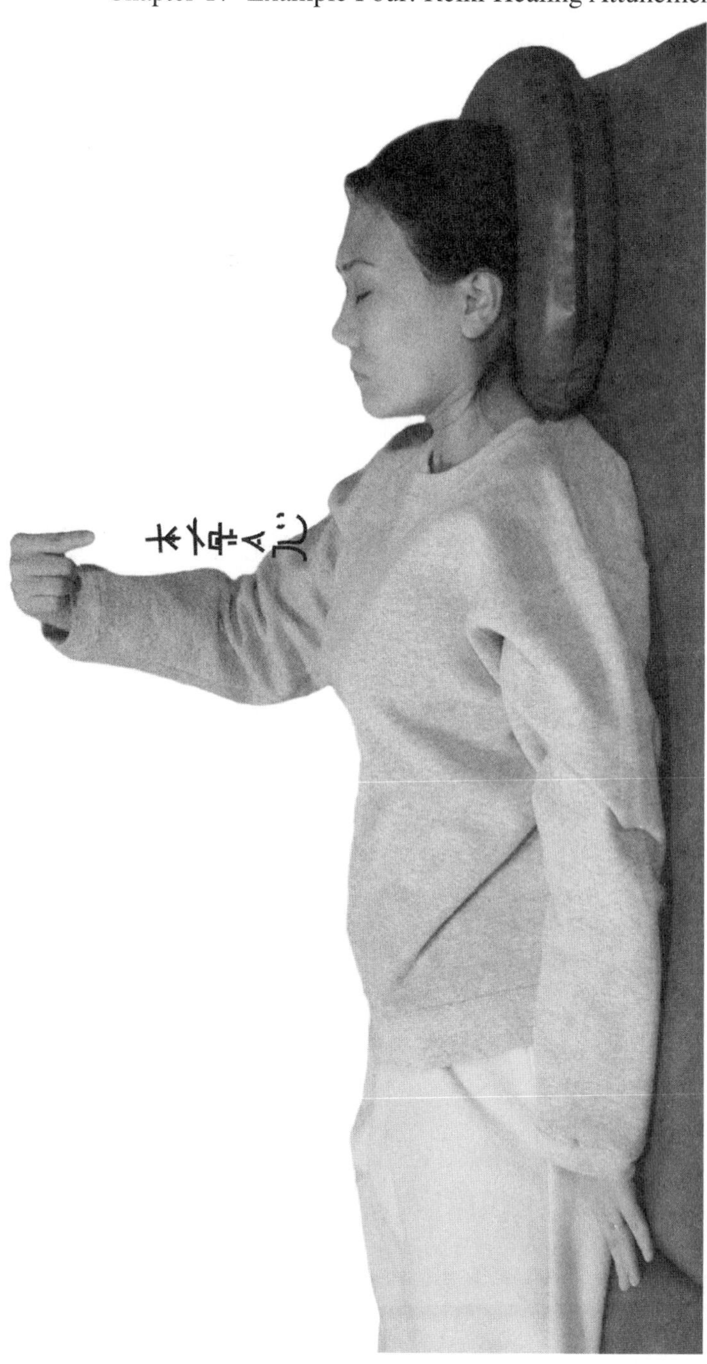

(Photo 66) Stay with the 4th Chakra. Visualize the Long Distance Symbol over it, activate it.

(Photo 67) Embed it into the center of the Chakra. *Step should only take 15 seconds.*

(Photo 68) Stay with the 4th Chakra. Visualize the Master Symbol over it, activate it.

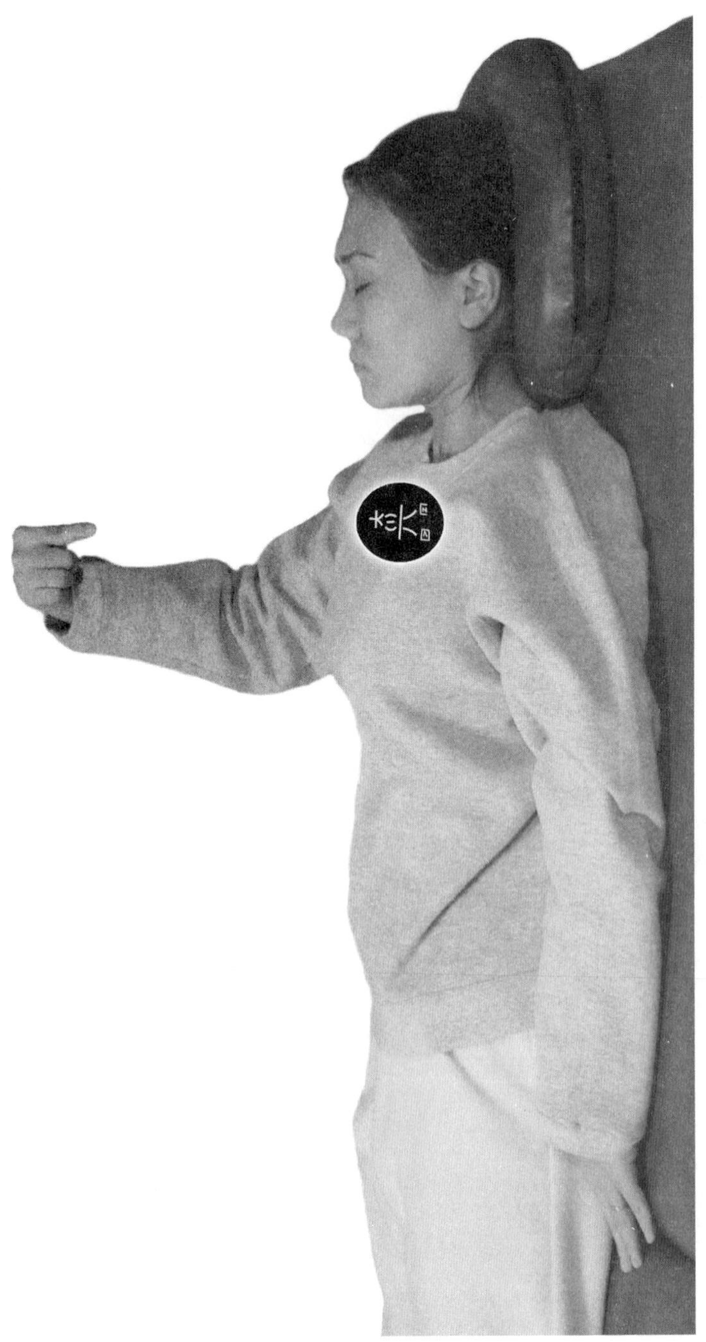

(Photo 69) Embed it into the center of the Chakra. *Step should only take 15 seconds.*

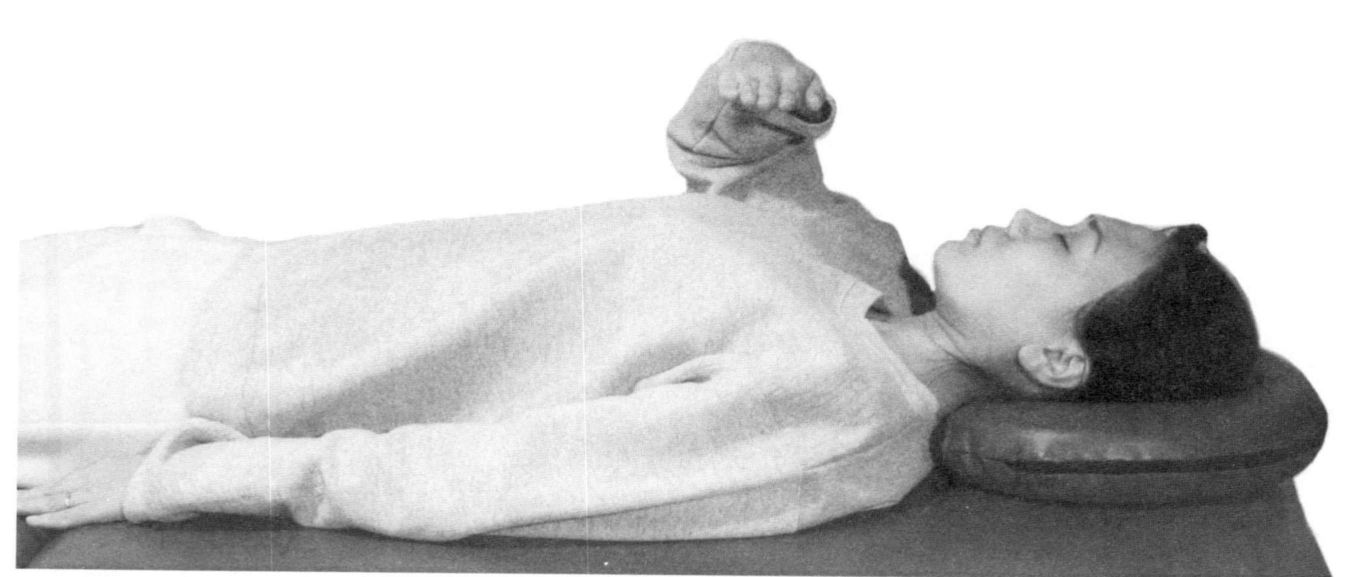

(Photo 70) The Reiki Symbols are now embedded into the 4th Chakra. Next, channel Reiki into the center of the 4th Chakra with the intent for it to flow to the Asthma. *Step should only take 5 minutes.*

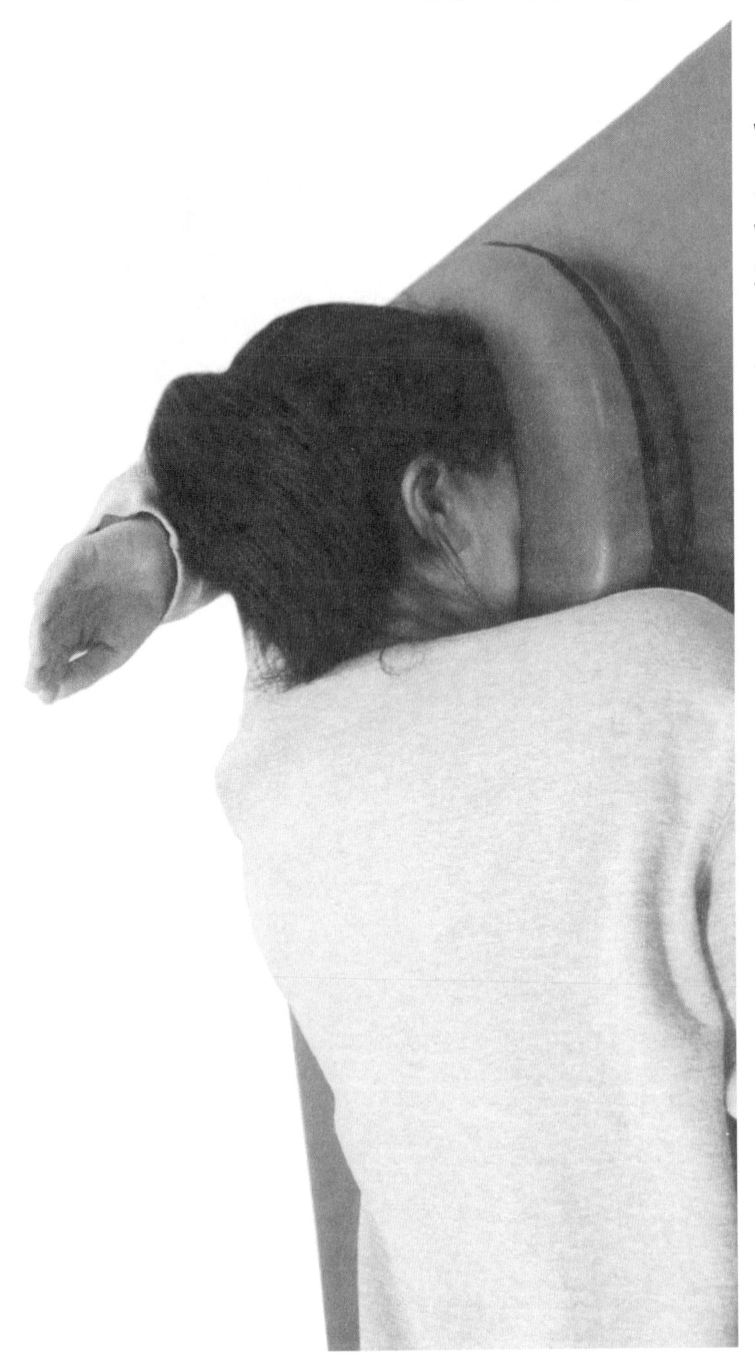

(Photo 71) Next, turn on your stomach and proceed to the back 4th Chakra. Channel Reiki into the center of the back 4th Chakra with the intent for it to flow to the Asthma. *Step should only take 5 minutes.*

"...one cannot lodge in 'if'."

-Rumi

“Burdens are the foundations of ease and bitter things the forerunners of pleasure.”

-Rumi

Example Five:
Reiki Healing Attunement

Example of a Reiki Healing Attunement for Strep Throat, performed on another person using the 5th Chakra.

Healing Attunement for 1st Level Reiki: Performed on Another Person

1. You have prepared for the Healing Attunement.

2. You are in the correct position to perform the Attunement on another person.

3. State the intent for the Healing Attunement (Strep Throat) silently to yourself before you begin. At this time, you can also ask for guidance during the Attunement. *Step should only take a few seconds.*

4. Channel Reiki into the 7th Chakra with the intent to clear any mental or emotional blocks associated with the Strep Throat. (Photo 72) *Step should only take about 2 minutes.*

5. Proceed to the 5th Chakra. Focus and channel Reiki into the center of the Chakra with the intent for it to flow to the Strep Throat. (Photo 73) *Step should only take 5 minutes.*

6. Next, have the person turn on his or her stomach and proceed to the back 5th Chakra. Channel Reiki into the center of the back 5th Chakra with the intent for it to flow to the Strep Throat. (Photo 74) *Step should only take 5 minutes.*

7. The Attunement is complete. Perform the finishing steps outlined in Chapter 10.

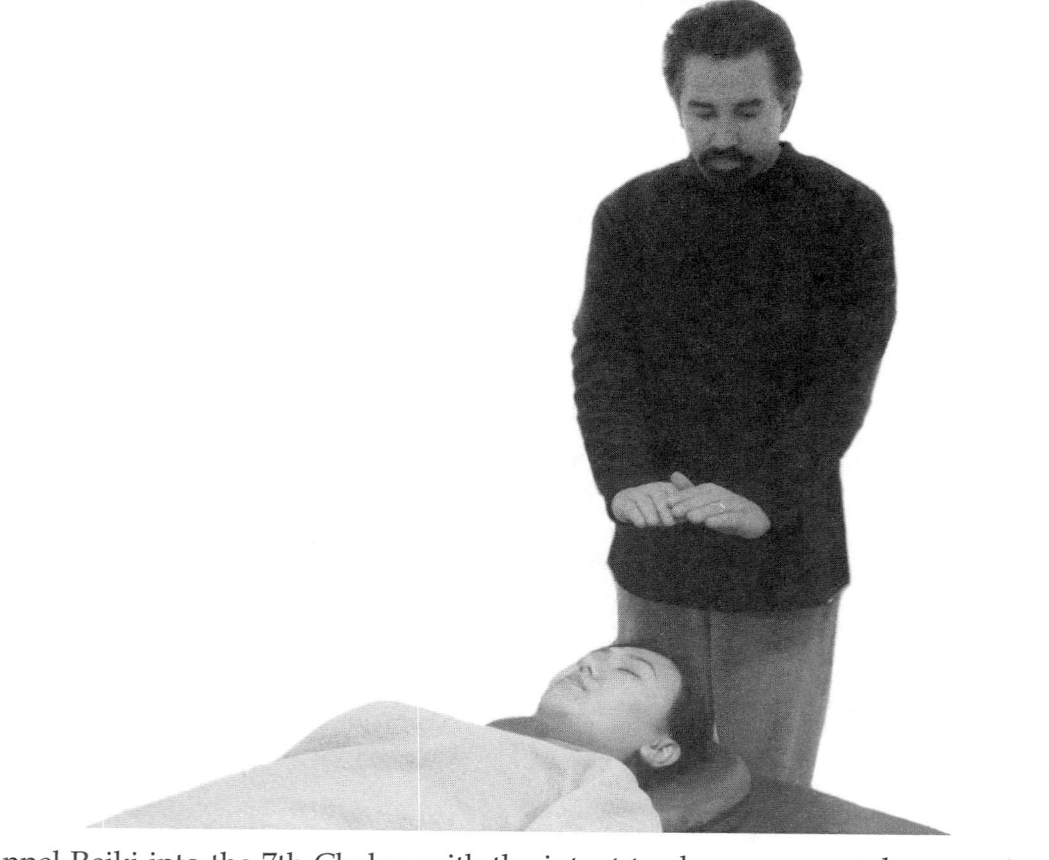

(Photo 72) Channel Reiki into the 7th Chakra with the intent to clear any mental or emotional blocks associated with the Strep Throat. *Step should only take about 2 minutes.*

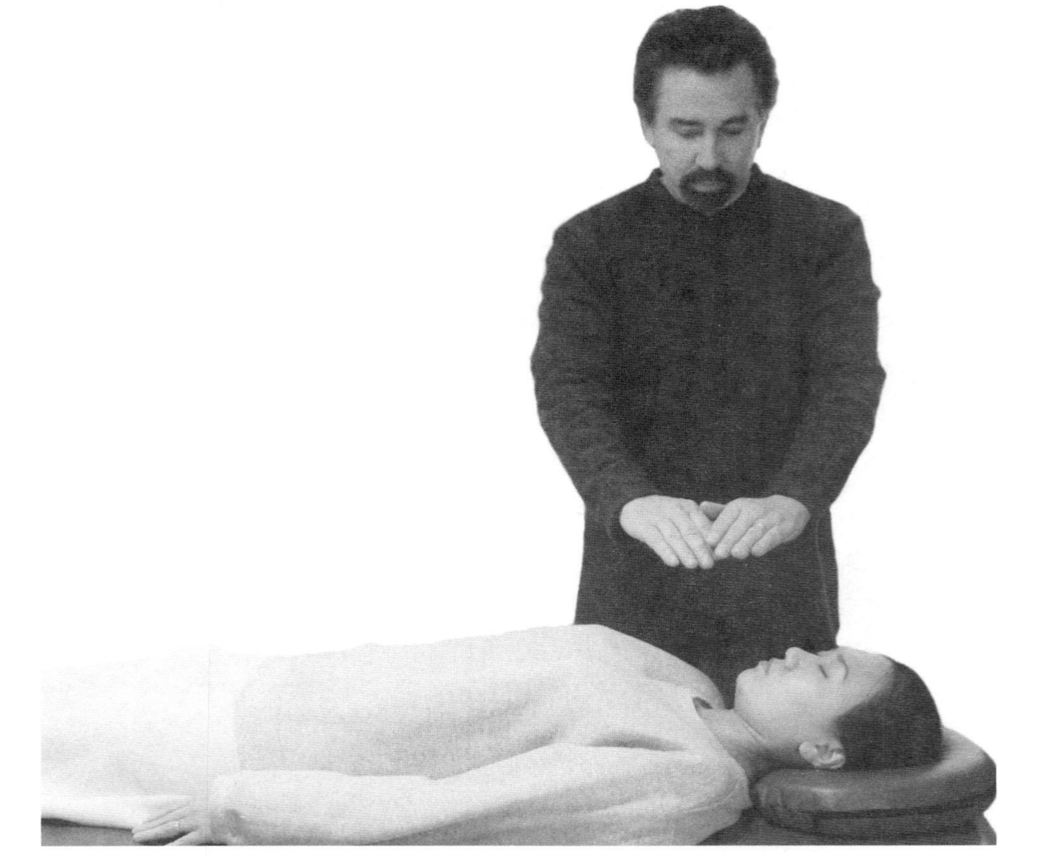

(Photo 73) Proceed to the 5th Chakra. Focus and channel Reiki into the center of the Chakra with the intent for it to flow to the Strep Throat. *Step should only take 5 minutes*

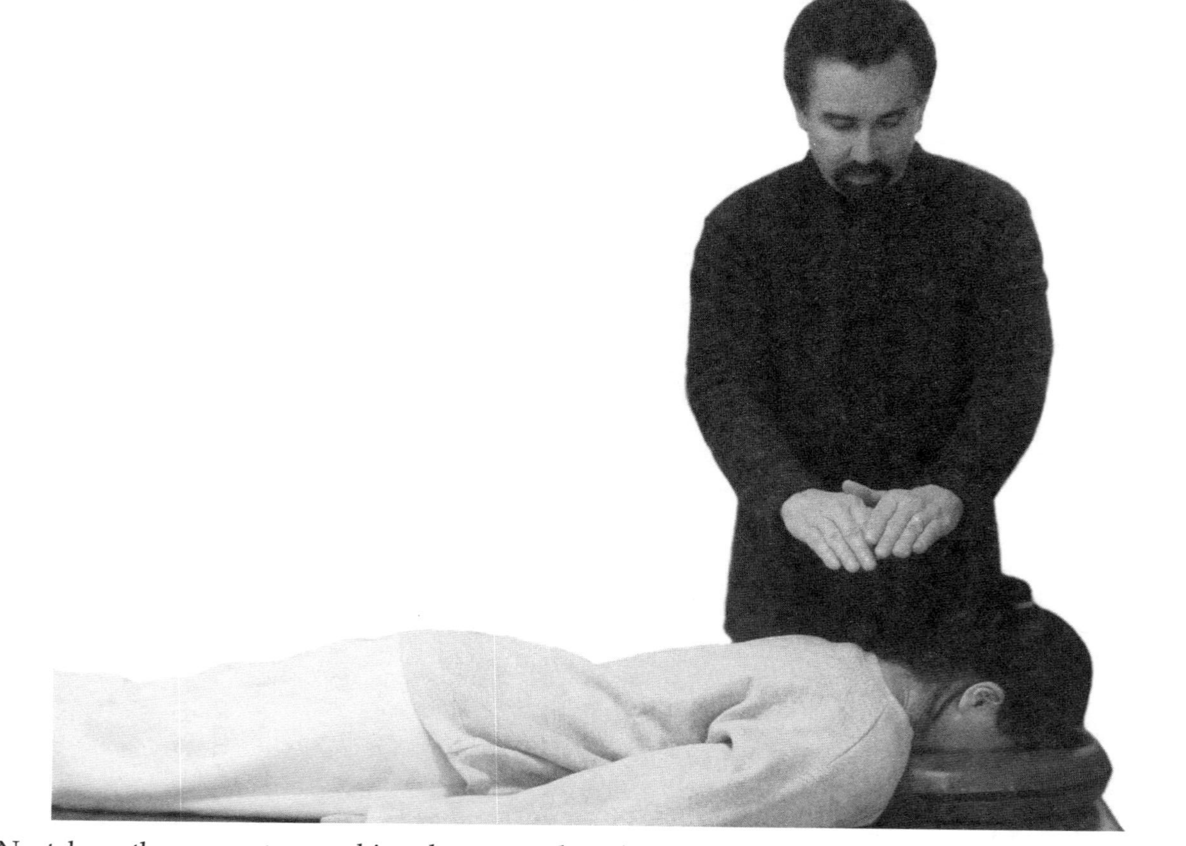

(Photo 74) Next, have the person turn on his or her stomach and proceed to the back 5th Chakra. Channel Reiki into the center of the back 5th Chakra with the intent for it to flow to the Strep Throat. *Step should only take 5 minutes.*

Healing Attunement for Reiki 2nd Level and Master: Performed on Another Person.

1. You have prepared for the Healing Attunement.

2. You are in the correct position to perform the Attunement on another person.

3. State the intent for the Healing Attunement (Strep Throat) silently to yourself before you begin. At this time, you can also ask for guidance during the Attunement. *Step should only take a few seconds.*

4. Visualize the Mental/Emotional Symbol in front of the 7th Chakra, activate it (Photo 75), then embed it into the center of the Chakra. (Photo 76) *Step should only take 15 seconds.*

5. Channel Reiki into the 7th Chakra with the intent to clear any mental or emotional blocks associated with the Strep Throat. (Photo 77) *Step should only take about 2 minutes.*

6. Proceed to the 5th Chakra. Visualize the Power Symbol over it, activate it (Photo 78),then embed it into the center of the Chakra. (Photo 79) *Step should only take 15 seconds.*

7. Stay with the 5th Chakra. Visualize the Long Distance Symbol over it, activate it (Photo 80), then embed it into the center of the Chakra. (Photo 81) *Step should only take 15 seconds.*

Note: If you are a 2nd Level, bypass Step 8 and go to Step 9.

8. Stay with the 5th Chakra. Visualize the Master Symbol over it, activate it (Photo 82), then embed it into the center of the Chakra. (Photo 83) *Step should only take 15 seconds.*

9. The Reiki Symbols are now embedded into the 5th Chakra. Next, channel Reiki into the center of the 5th Chakra with the intent for it to flow to the Strep Throat. (Photo 84) *Step should only take 5 minutes.*

10. Next, have the person turn on their stomach and proceed to the back 5th Chakra. Channel Reiki into the center of the back 5th Chakra with the intent for it to flow to the Strep Throat. (Photo 85) *Step should only take 5 minutes.*

11. The Attunement is complete. Perform the finishing steps outlined in Chapter 10.

(Photo 75) Visualize the Mental/Emotional symbol in front of the 7th Chakra, activate it.

(Photo 76) Embed it into the center of the Chakra. *Step should only take 15 seconds.*

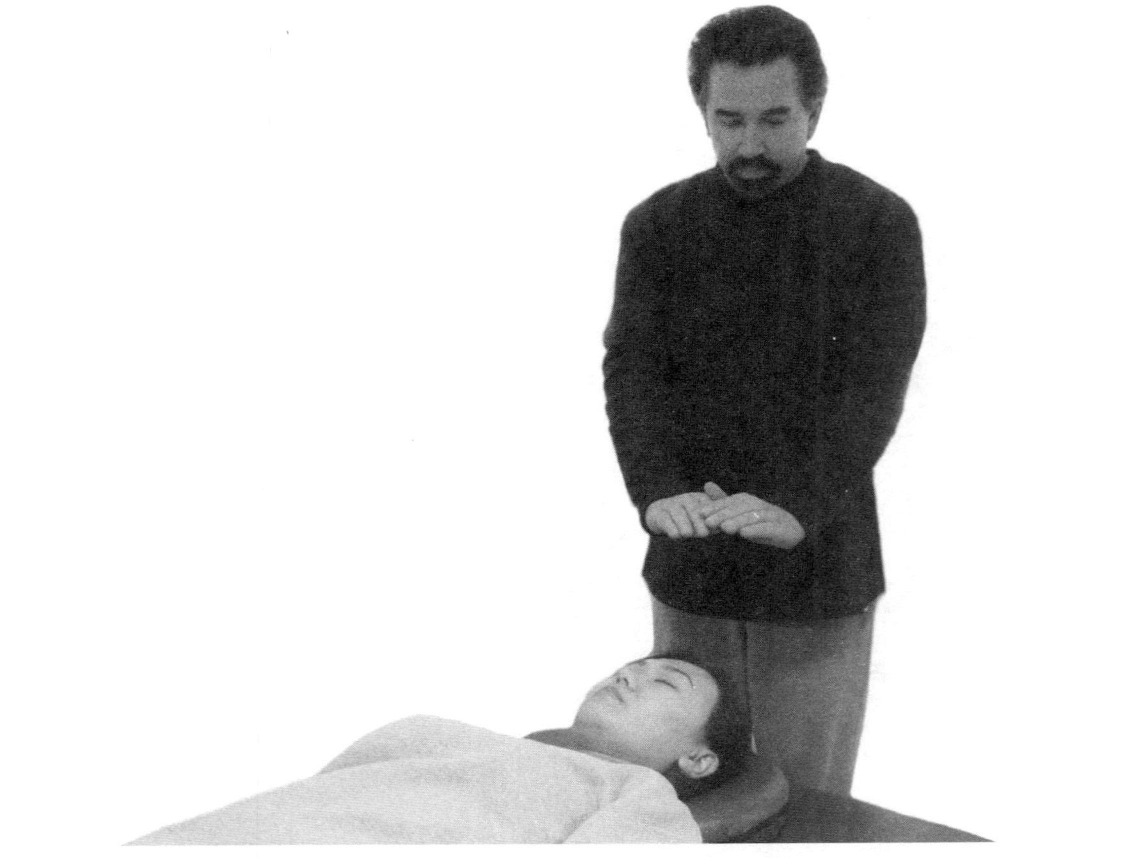

(Photo 77) Channel Reiki into the 7th Chakra with the intent to clear any mental or emotional blocks associated with the Strep Throat. *Step should only take about 2 minutes.*

(Photo 78) Proceed to the 5th Chakra. Visualize the Power Symbol over it, activate it.

(Photo 79) Embed it into the center of the Chakra. *Step should only take 15 seconds.*

(Photo 80) Stay with the 5th Chakra. Visualize the Long Distance Symbol over it, activate it.

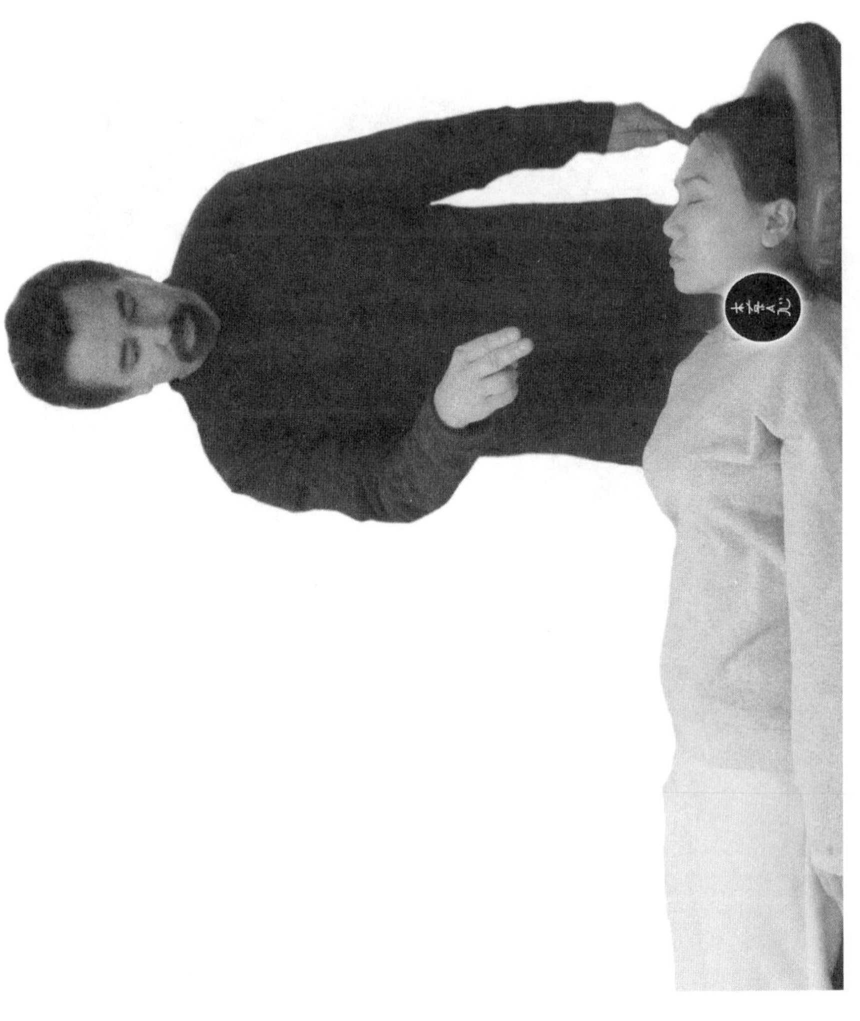

(Photo 81) Embed it into the center of the Chakra. *Step should only take 15 seconds.*

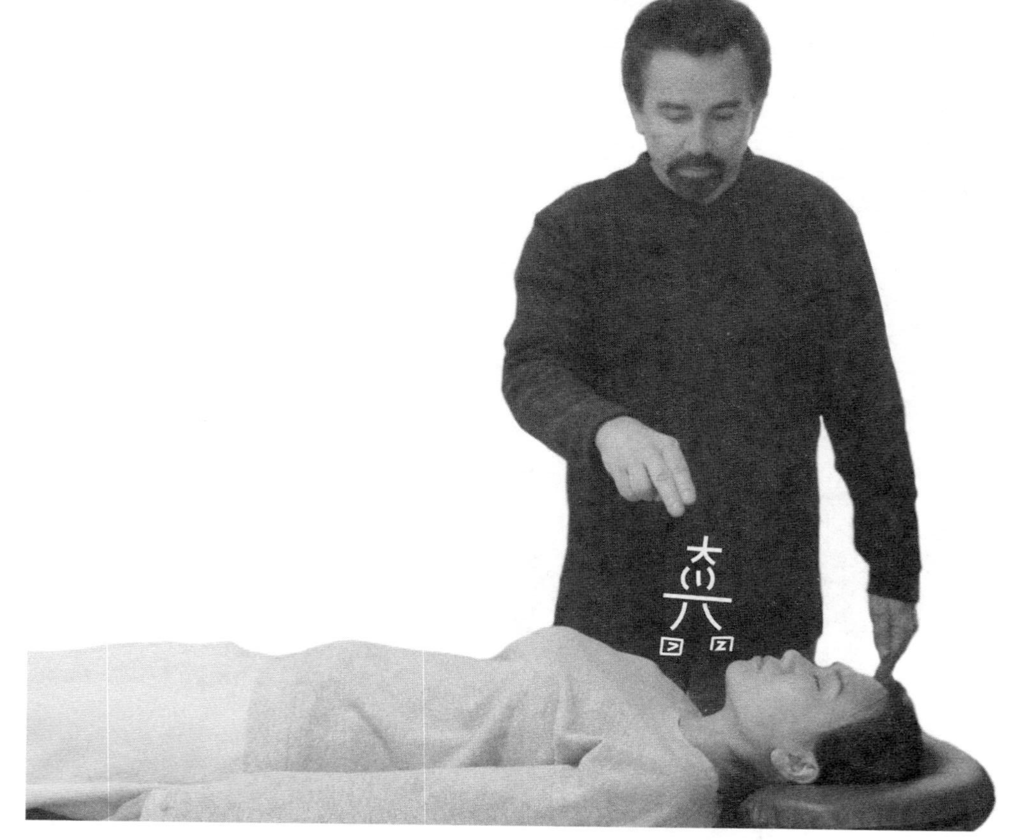

(Photo 82) Stay with the 5th Chakra. Visualize the Master Symbol over it, activate it.

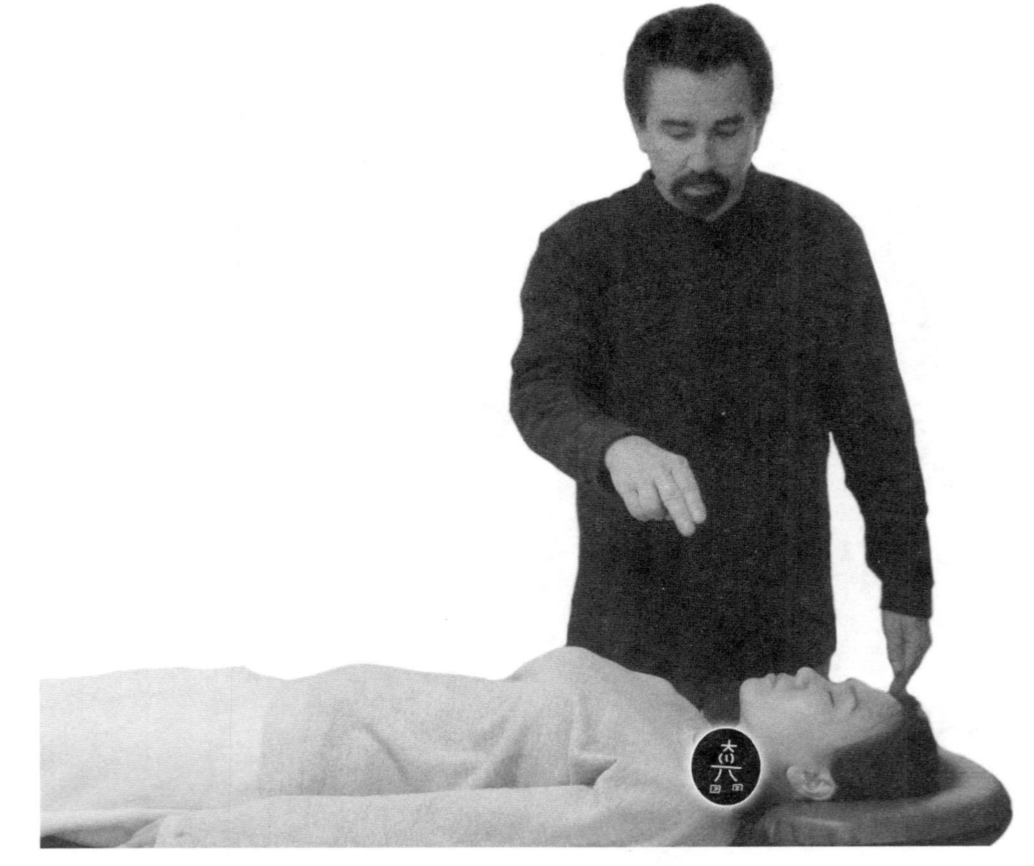

(Photo 83) Embed it into the center of the Chakra. *Step should only take 15 seconds.*

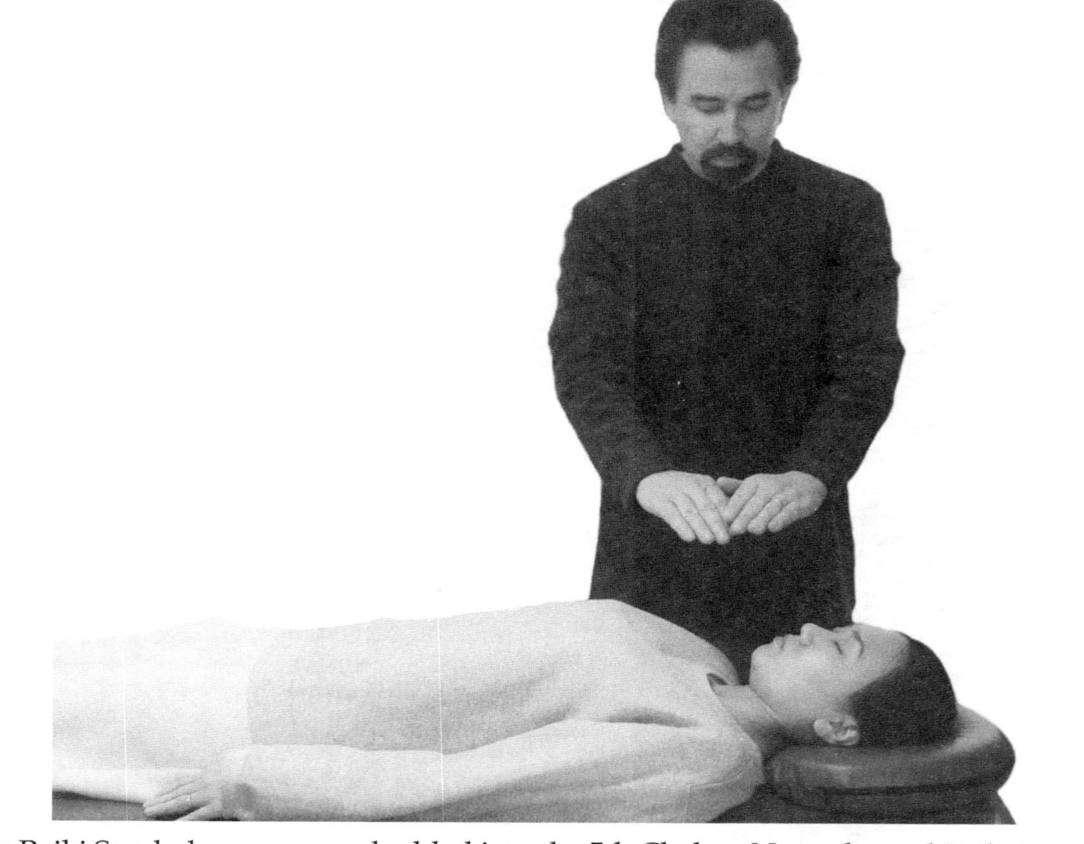

(Photo 84) The Reiki Symbols are now embedded into the 5th Chakra. Next, channel Reiki into the center of the 5th Chakra with the intent for it to flow to the Strep Throat. *Step should only take 5 minutes.*

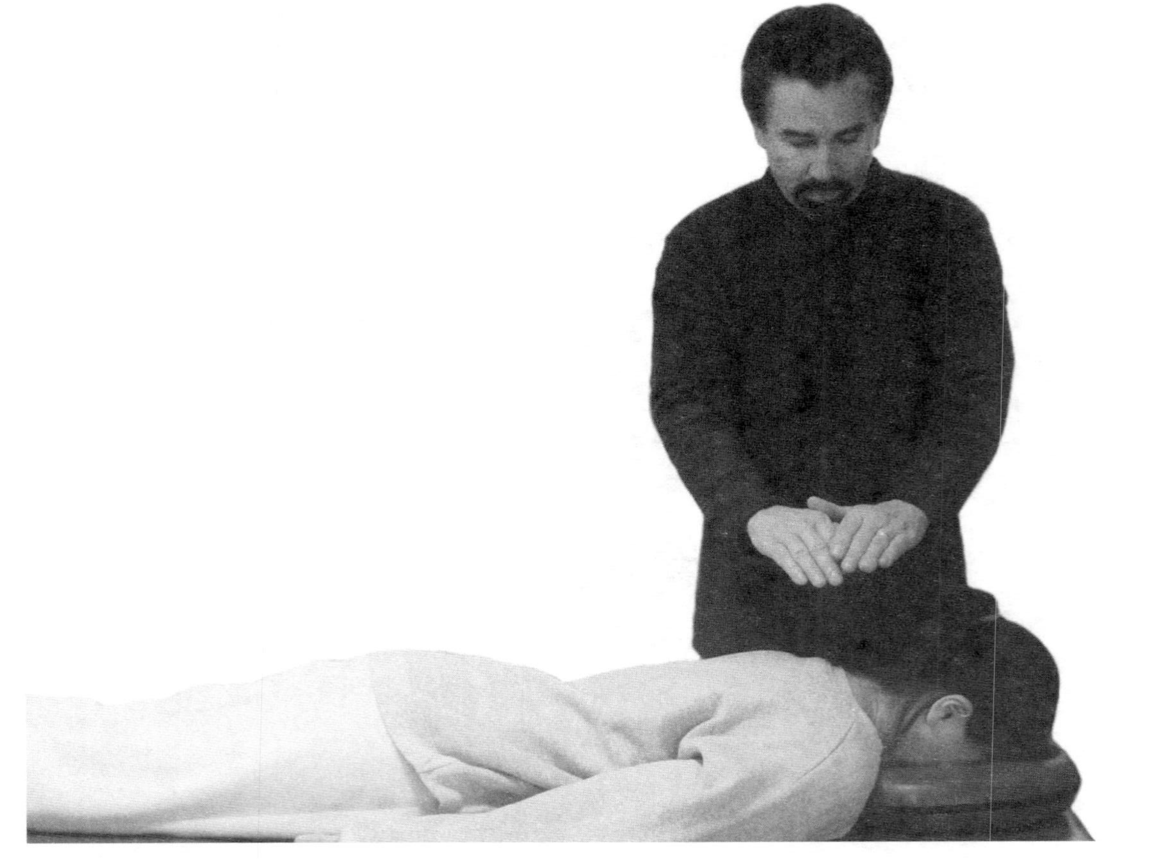

(Photo 85) Next, have the person turn on his or her stomach and proceed to the back 5th Chakra. Channel Reiki into the center of the back 5th Chakra with the intent for it to flow to the Strep Throat. *Step should only take 5 minutes*

**"I am burning. If anyone lacks tinder,
let him set his rubbish ablaze with my fire."**

-Rumi

"If you are irritated by every rub, how will you be polished?"

-Rumi

Example Six: Reiki Healing Attunement

Example of a Reiki Healing Attunement for Sinusitis, performed on yourself using the 6th Chakra.

Healing Attunement for 1st Level Reiki: Performed On Yourself

1. You have prepared for the Healing Attunement.

2. You are in the correct position to perform the Attunement on yourself.

3. State the intent for the Healing Attunement (Sinusitis) silently to yourself before you begin. At this time, you can also ask for guidance during the Attunement. *Step should only take a few seconds.*

4. Channel Reiki into the 7th Chakra with the intent to clear any mental or emotional blocks associated with the Sinusitis. (Photo 86) *Step should only take about 2 minutes.*

5. Proceed to the 6th Chakra. Focus and channel Reiki into the center of the Chakra with the intent for it to flow to the Sinusitis. (Photo 87) *Step should only take 5 minutes.*

6. Next, turn on your stomach and proceed to the back 6th Chakra. Channel Reiki into the center of the back 6th Chakra with the intent for it to flow to the Sinusitis. (Photo 88) *Step should only take 5 minutes.*

7. The Attunement is complete. Perform the finishing steps outlined in Chapter 10.

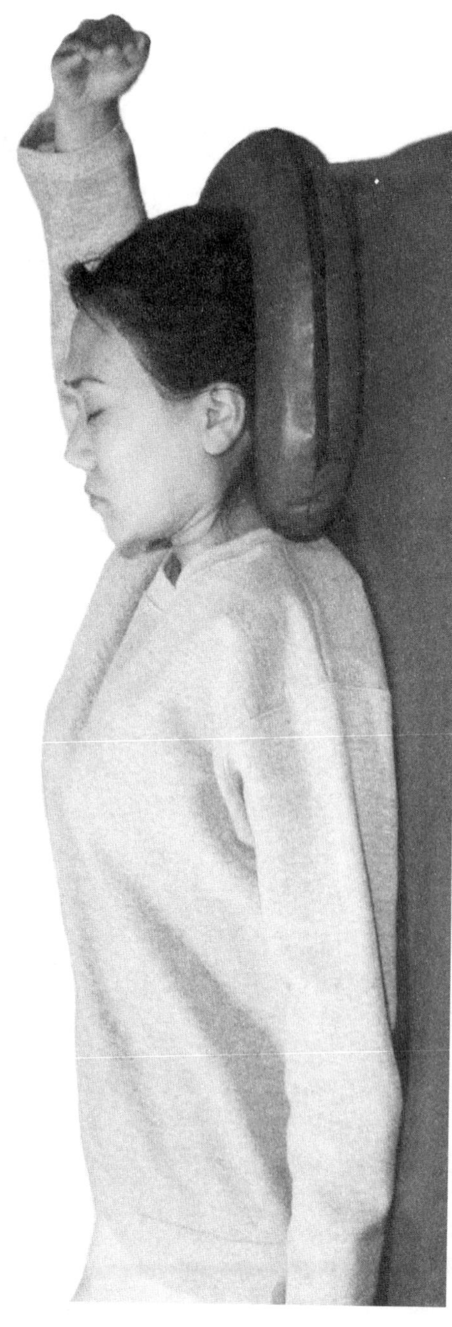

(Photo 86) Channel Reiki into the 7th Chakra with the intent to clear any mental or emotional blocks associated with the Sinusitis. *Step should only take about 2 minutes.*

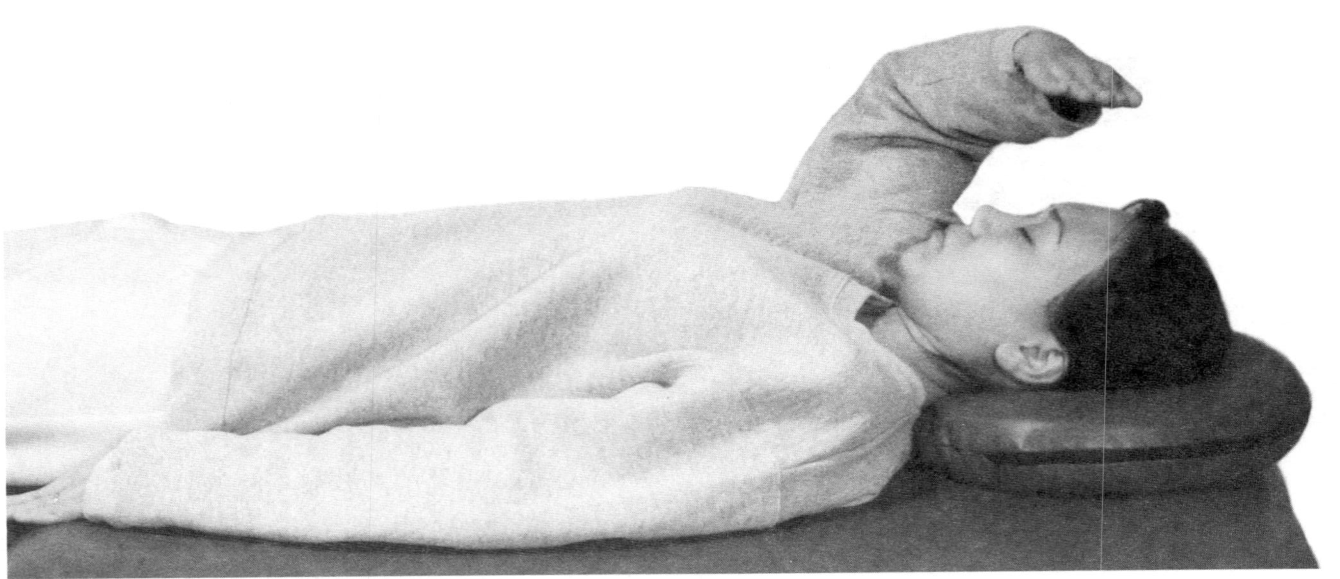

(Photo 87) Proceed to the 6th Chakra. Focus and channel Reiki into the center of the Chakra with the intent for it to flow to the Sinusitis. *Step should only take 5 minutes*

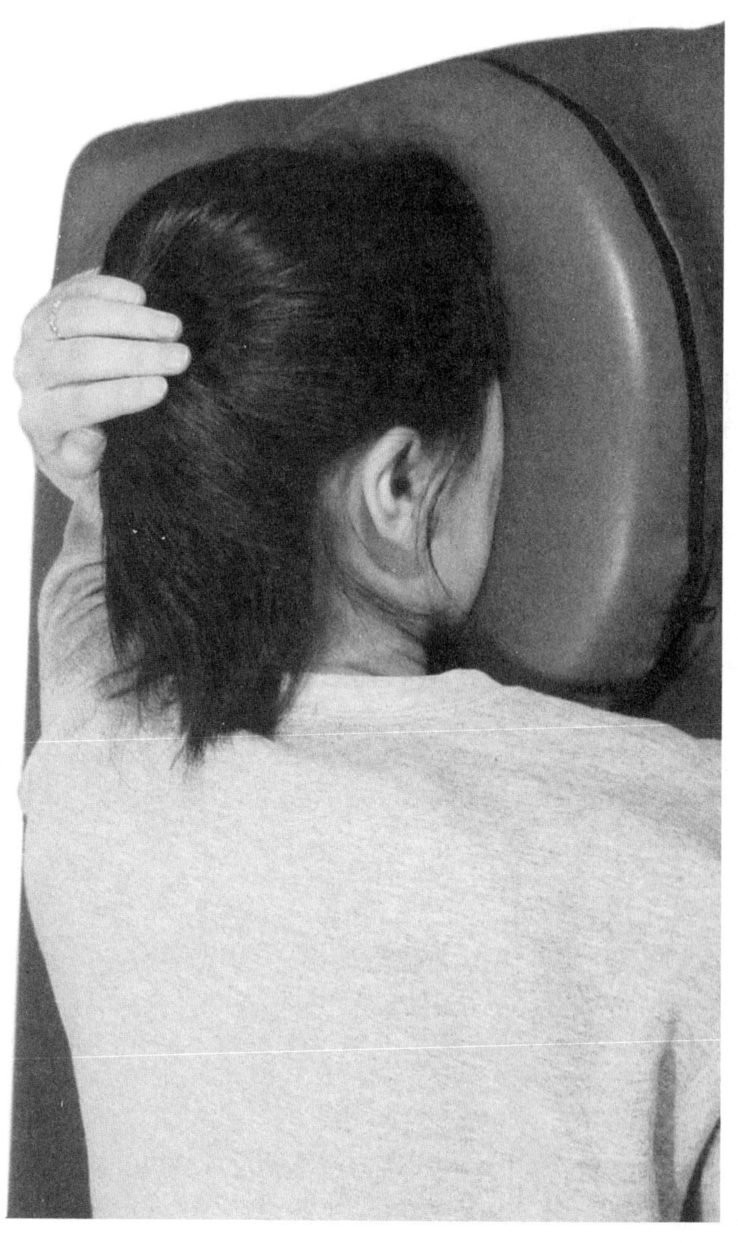

(Photo 88) Next, turn on your stomach and proceed to the back 6th Chakra. Channel Reiki into the center of the back 6th Chakra with the intent for it to flow to the Sinusitis. *Step should only take 5 minutes.*

Healing Attunement for Reiki 2nd Level and Master: Performed on Yourself

1. You have prepared for the Healing Attunement.

2. You are in the correct position to perform the Attunement on yourself.

3. State the intent for the Healing Attunement (Sinusitis) silently to yourself before you begin. At this time, you can also ask for guidance during the Attunement. *Step should only take a few seconds.*

4. Visualize the Mental/Emotional Symbol in front of the 7th Chakra, activate it (Photo 89), then embed it into the center of the Chakra. (Photo 90) *Step should only take 15 seconds.*

5. Channel Reiki into the 7th Chakra with the intent to clear any mental or emotional blocks associated with the Sinusitis. (Photo 91) *Step should only take about 2 minutes.*

6. Proceed to the 6th Chakra. Visualize the Power Symbol over it, activate it (Photo 92), then embed it into the center of the Chakra. (Photo 93) *Step should only take 15 seconds.*

7. Stay with the 6th Chakra. Visualize the Long Distance Symbol over it, activate it (Photo 94), then embed it into the center of the Chakra. (Photo 95) *Step should only take 15 seconds.*

Note: If you are a 2nd Level, bypass Step 8 and go to Step 9.

8. Stay with the 6th Chakra. Visualize the Master Symbol over it, activate it (Photo 96), then embed it into the center of the Chakra. (Photo 97) *Step should only take 15 seconds.*

9. The Reiki Symbols are now embedded into the 6th Chakra. Next, channel Reiki into the center of the 6th Chakra with the intent for it to flow to the Sinusitis. (Photo 98) *Step should only take 5 minutes.*

10. Next, turn on your stomach and proceed to the back 6th Chakra. Channel Reiki into the center of the back 6th Chakra with the intent for it to flow to the Sinusitis. (Photo 99) *Step should only take 5 minutes.*

11. The Attunement is complete. Perform the finishing steps outlined in Chapter 10.

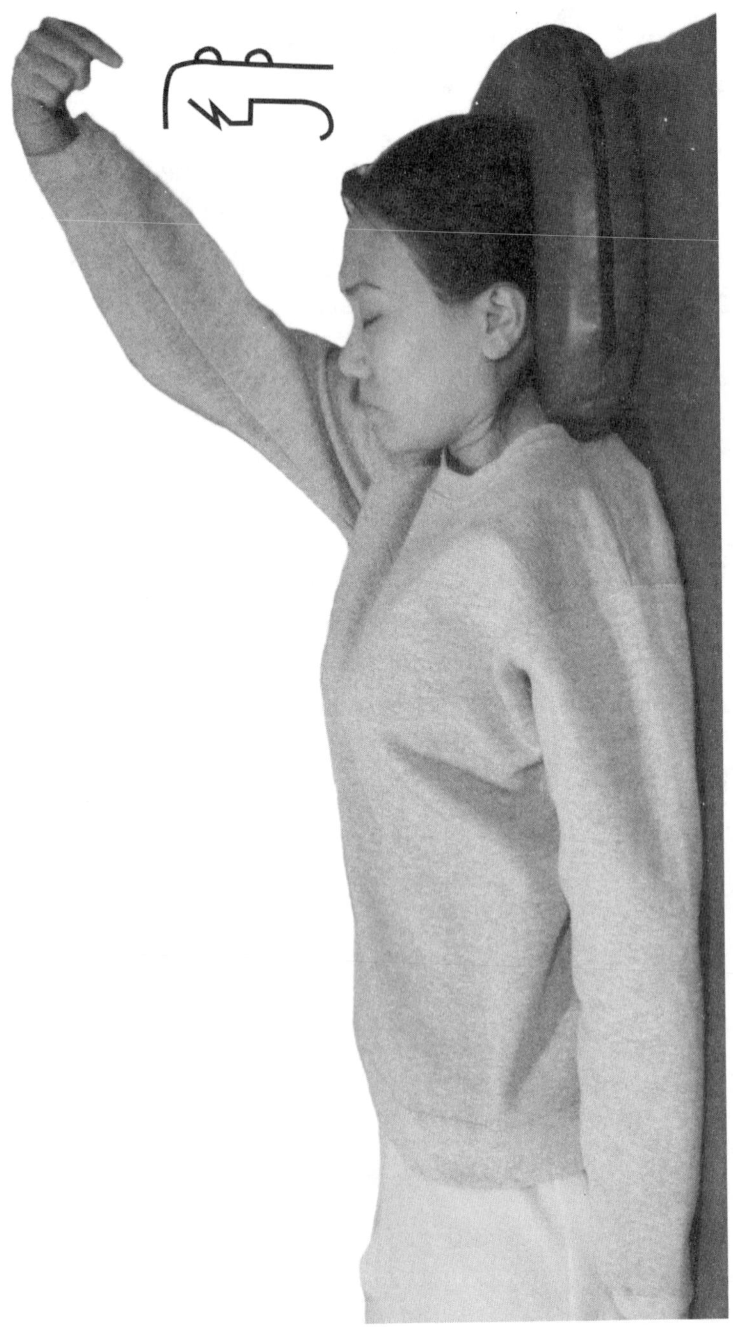

(Photo 89) Visualize the Mental/Emotional Symbol in front of the 7th Chakra , activate it.

(Photo 90) Embed it into the center of the Chakra. *Step should only take 15 seconds.*

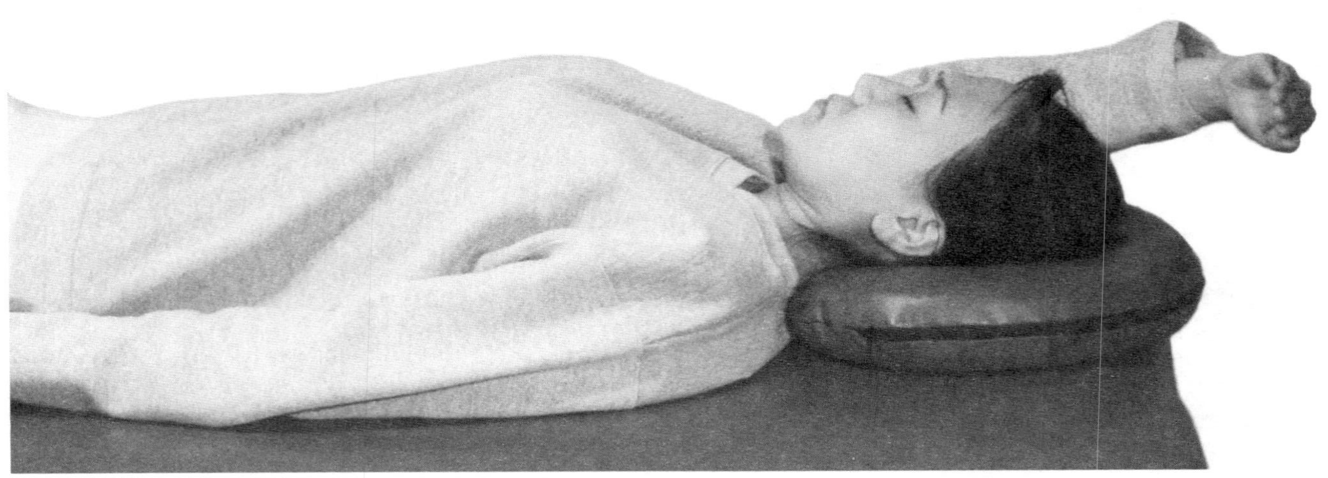

(Photo 91) Channel Reiki into the 7th Chakra with the intent to clear any mental or emotional blocks associated with the Sinusitis. *Step should only take about 2 minutes.*

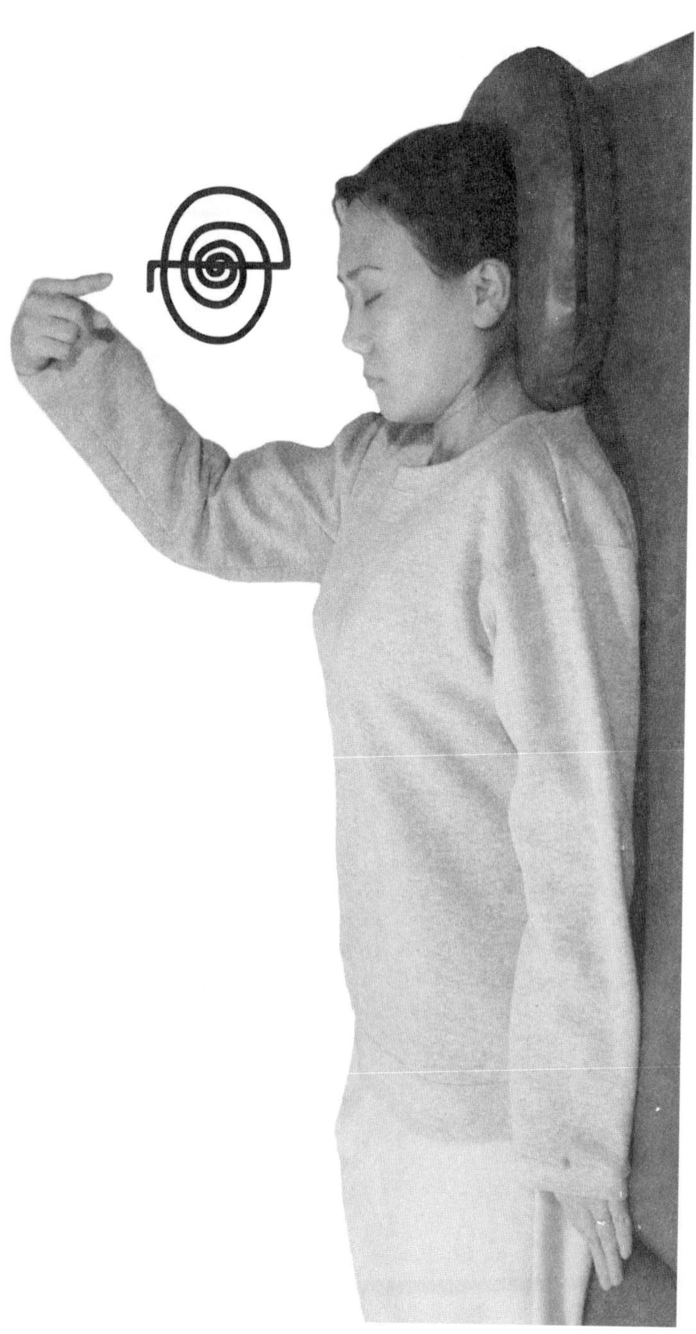

(Photo 92) Proceed to the 6th Chakra. Visualize the Power Symbol over it, activate it.

(Photo 93) Embed it into the center of the Chakra. *Step should only take 15 seconds*

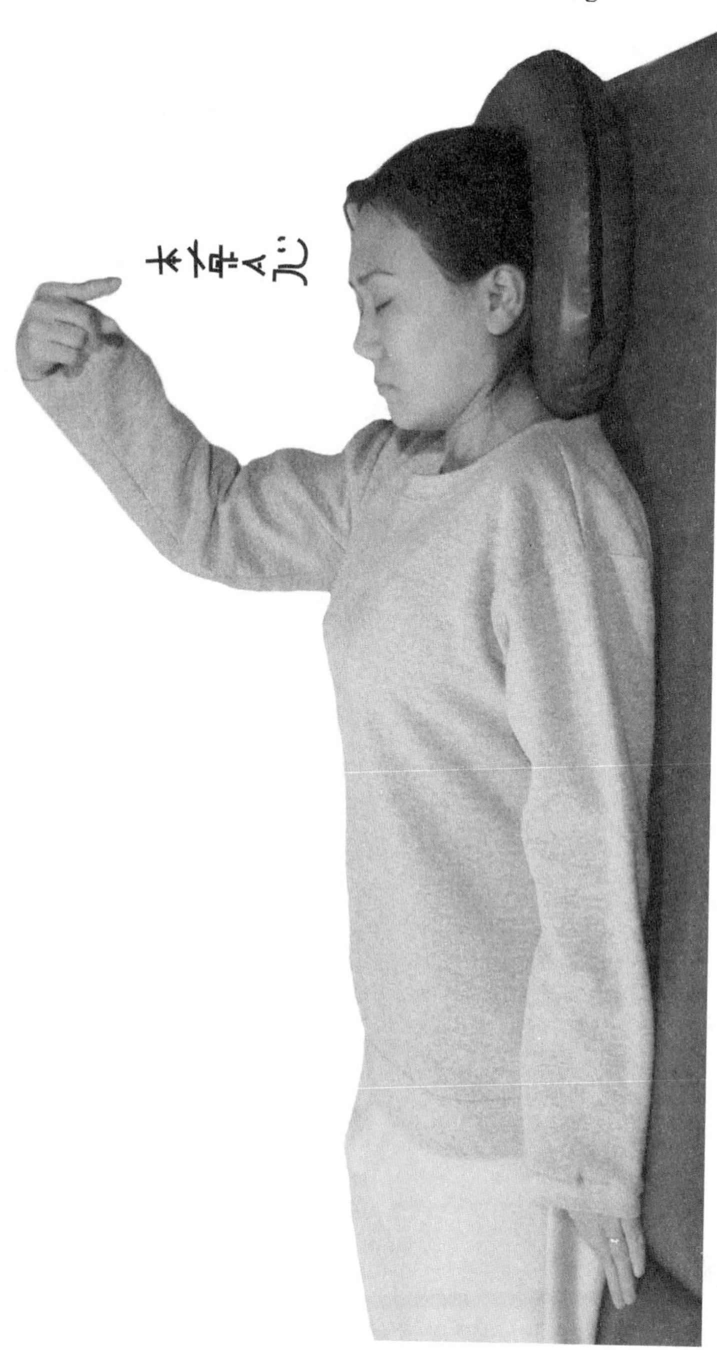

(Photo 94) Stay with the 6th Chakra. Visualize the Long Distance Symbol over it, activate it.

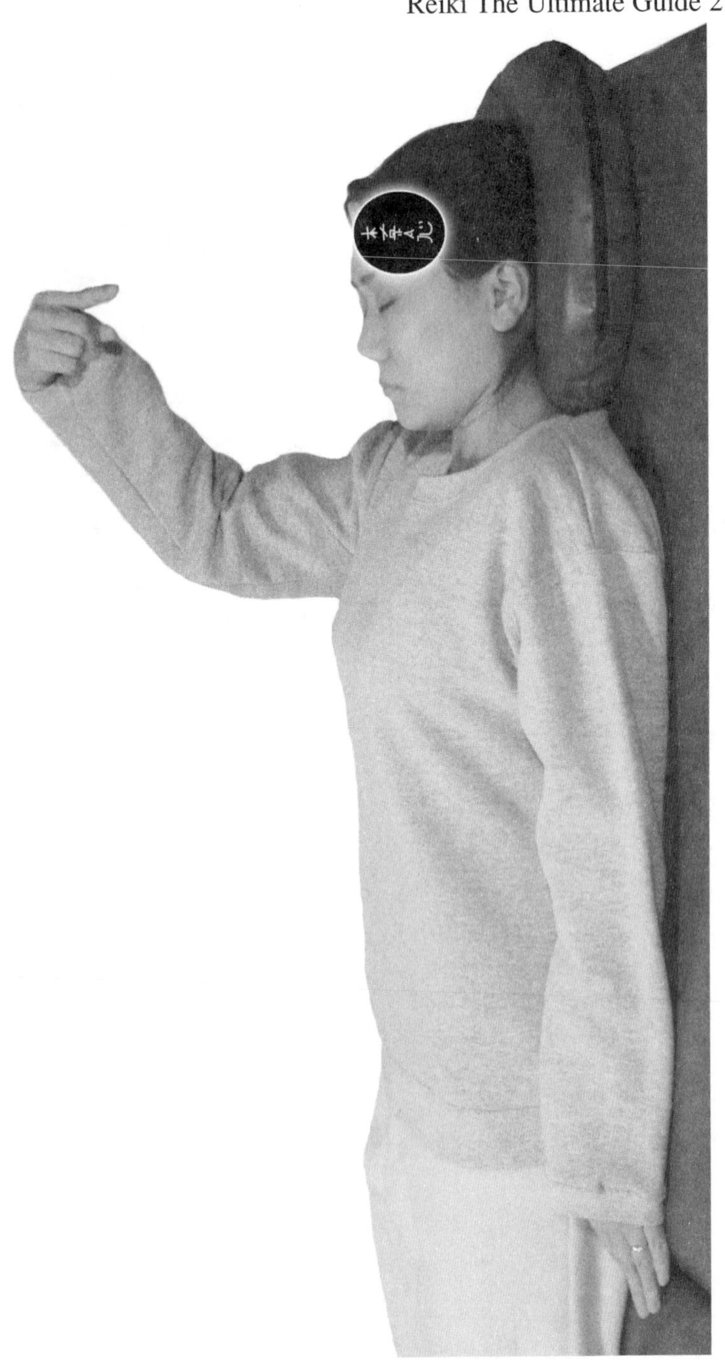

(Photo 95) Embed it into the center of the Chakra. *Step should only take 15 seconds.*

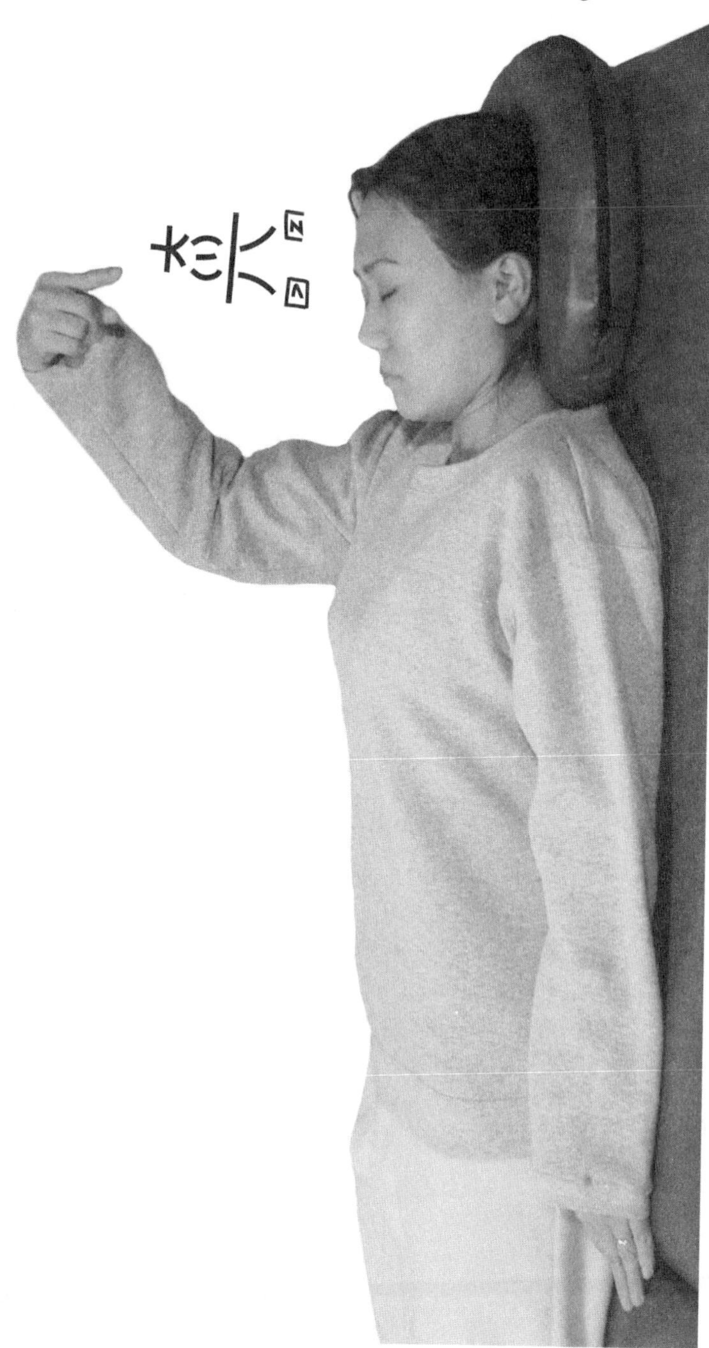

(Photo 96) Stay with the 6th Chakra. Visualize the Master Symbol over it, activate it.

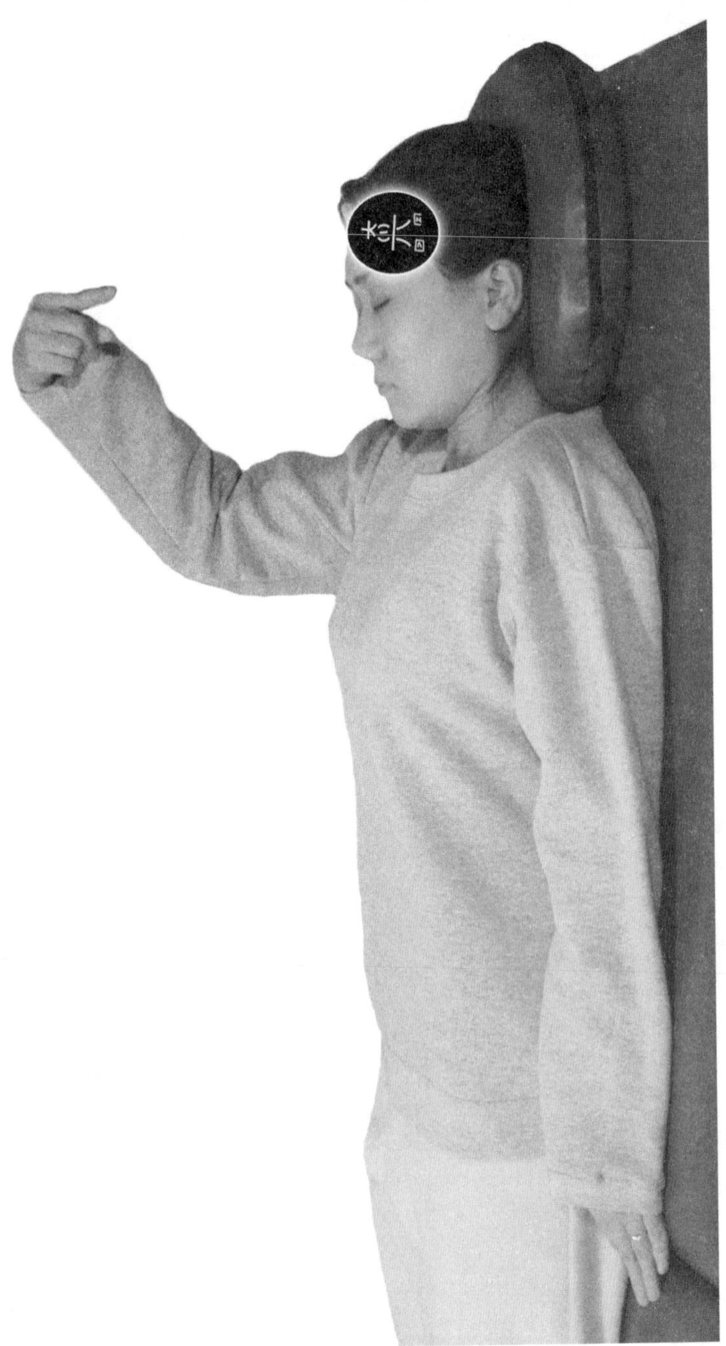

(Photo 97) Embed it into the center of the Chakra. *Step should only take 15 seconds.*

(Photo 98) The Reiki Symbols are now embedded into the 6th Chakra. Next, channel Reiki into the center of the 6th Chakra with the intent for it to flow to the Sinusitis. *Step should only take 5 minutes.*

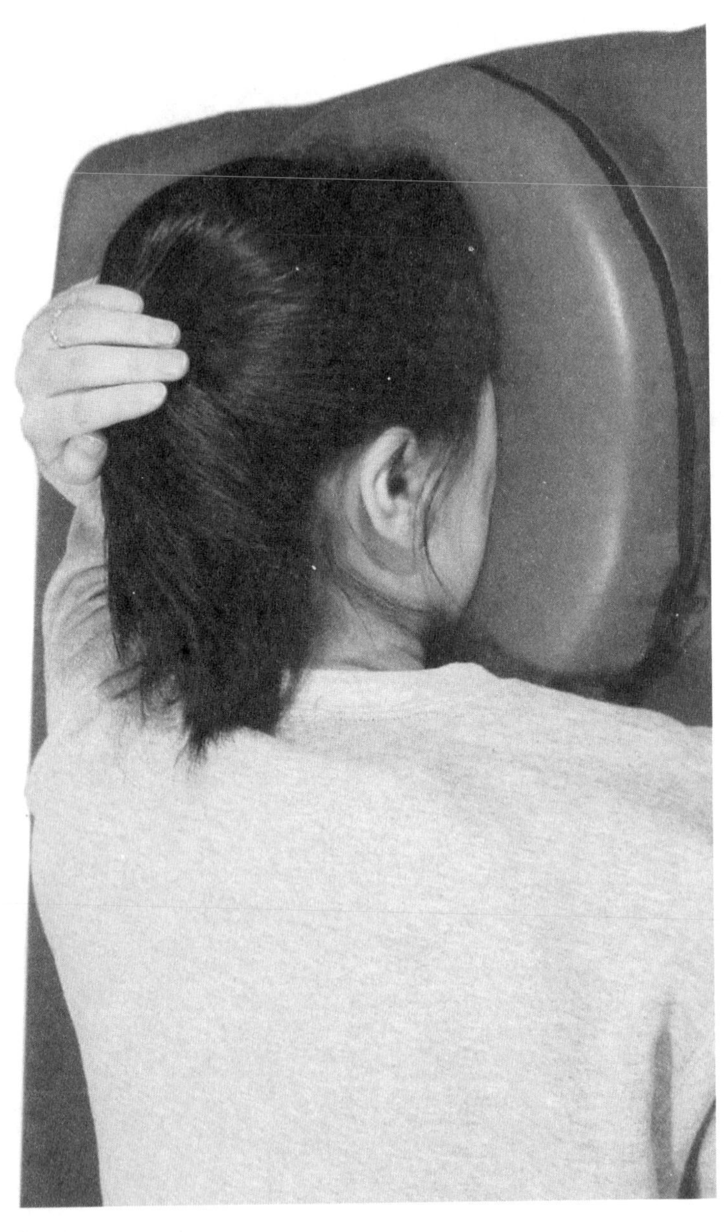

(Photo 99) Next, turn on your stomach and proceed to the back 6th Chakra. Channel Reiki into the center of the back 6th Chakra with the intent for it to flow to the Sinusitis. *Step should only take 5 minutes.*

"It is God's kindness to terrify you in order to lead you to safety."

-Rumi

"Don't allow your animal nature to rule your reason."

-Rumi

Example Seven: Reiki Healing Attunement

Example of a Reiki Healing Attunement for a Migraine Headache, performed on another person using the 7th Chakra.

Note: as mentioned several times before, when working with the 7th Chakra in a Healing Attunement, there is **not** a back Chakra step.

Healing Attunement for 1st Level Reiki: Performed on Another Person

1. You have prepared for the Healing Attunement.

2. You are in the correct position to perform the Attunement on another person.

3. State the intent for the Healing Attunement (Migraine Headache) silently to yourself before you begin. At this time, you can also ask for guidance during the Attunement. *Step should only take a few seconds.*

4. Channel Reiki into the 7th Chakra with the intent to clear any mental or emotional blocks associated with the Migraine Headache. (Photo 100) *Step should only take about 2 minutes.*

5. Stay at the 7th Chakra. Focus and channel Reiki into the center of the Chakra with the intent for it to flow to the Migraine Headache. (Photo 101) *Step should only take 5 minutes.*

6. The Attunement is complete. Perform the finishing steps outlined in Chapter 10.

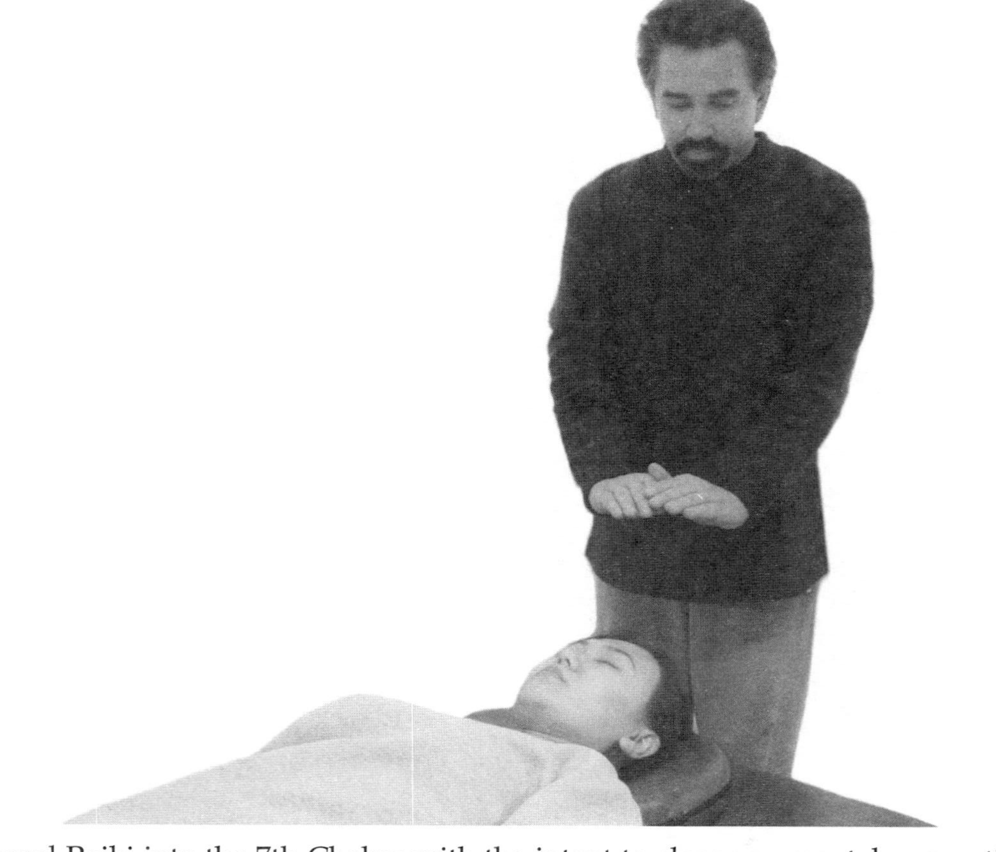

(Photo 100) Channel Reiki into the 7th Chakra with the intent to clear any mental or emotional blocks associated with the Migraine Headache. *Step should only take about 2 minutes.*

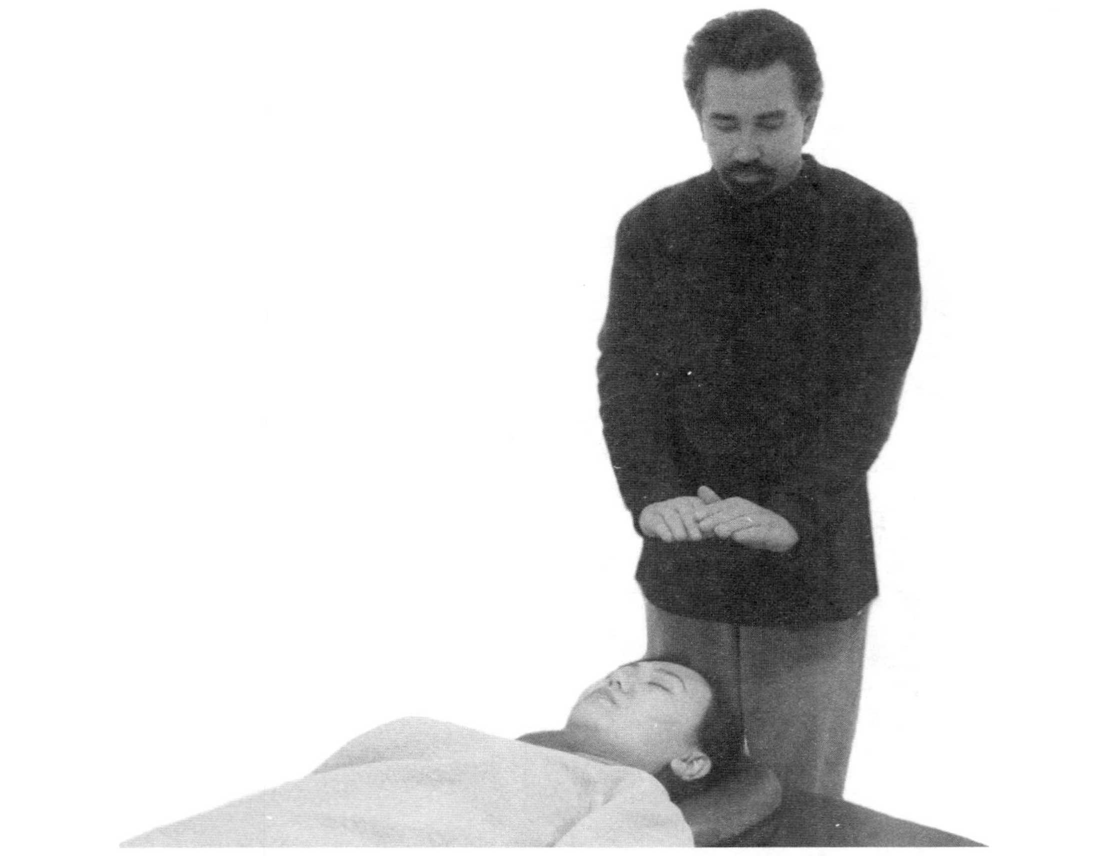

(Photo 101) Stay at the 7th Chakra. Focus and channel Reiki into the center of the Chakra with the intent for it to flow to the Migraine Headache. *Step should only take 5 minutes*

Healing Attunement for Reiki 2nd Level and Master: Performed on Another Person.

1. You have prepared for the Healing Attunement.

2. You are in the correct position to perform the Attunement on another person.

3. State the intent for the Healing Attunement (Migraine Headache) silently to yourself before you begin. At this time, you can also ask for guidance during the Attunement. *Step should only take a few seconds.*

4. Visualize the Mental/Emotional Symbol in front of the 7th Chakra, activate it (Photo 102), then embed it into the center of the Chakra. (Photo 103) *Step should only take 15 seconds.*

5. Channel Reiki into the 7th Chakra with the intent to clear any mental or emotional blocks associated with the Migraine Headache. (Photo 104) *Step should only take about 2 minutes.*

6. Stay at the 7th Chakra. Visualize the Power Symbol over it, activate it (Photo 105), then embed it into the center of the Chakra. (Photo 106) *Step should only take 15 seconds.*

7. Stay with the 7th Chakra. Visualize the Long Distance Symbol over it, activate it (Photo 107), then embed it into the center of the Chakra. (Photo 108) *Step should only take 15 seconds.*

Note: If you are a 2nd Level, bypass Step 8 and go to Step 9.

8. Stay with the 7th Chakra. Visualize the Master Symbol over it, activate it (Photo 109), then embed it into the center of the Chakra. (Photo 110) *Step should only take 15 seconds.*

9. The Reiki Symbols are now embedded into the 7th Chakra. Next, channel Reiki into the center of the 7th Chakra with the intent for it to flow to the Migraine Headache. (Photo 111) *Step should only take 5 minutes.*

10. The Attunement is complete. Perform the finishing steps outlined in Chapter 10.

(Photo 102) Visualize the Mental/Emotional Symbol in front of the 7th Chakra, activate it.

(Photo 103) Embed it into the center of the Chakra. *Step should only take 15 seconds.*

(Photo 104) Channel Reiki into the 7th Chakra with the intent to clear any mental or emotional blocks associated with the Migraine Headache. *Step should only take about 2 minutes.*

(Photo 105) Stay at the 7th Chakra. Visualize the Power Symbol over it, activate it.

(Photo 106) Embed it into the center of the Chakra. *Step should only take 15 seconds.*

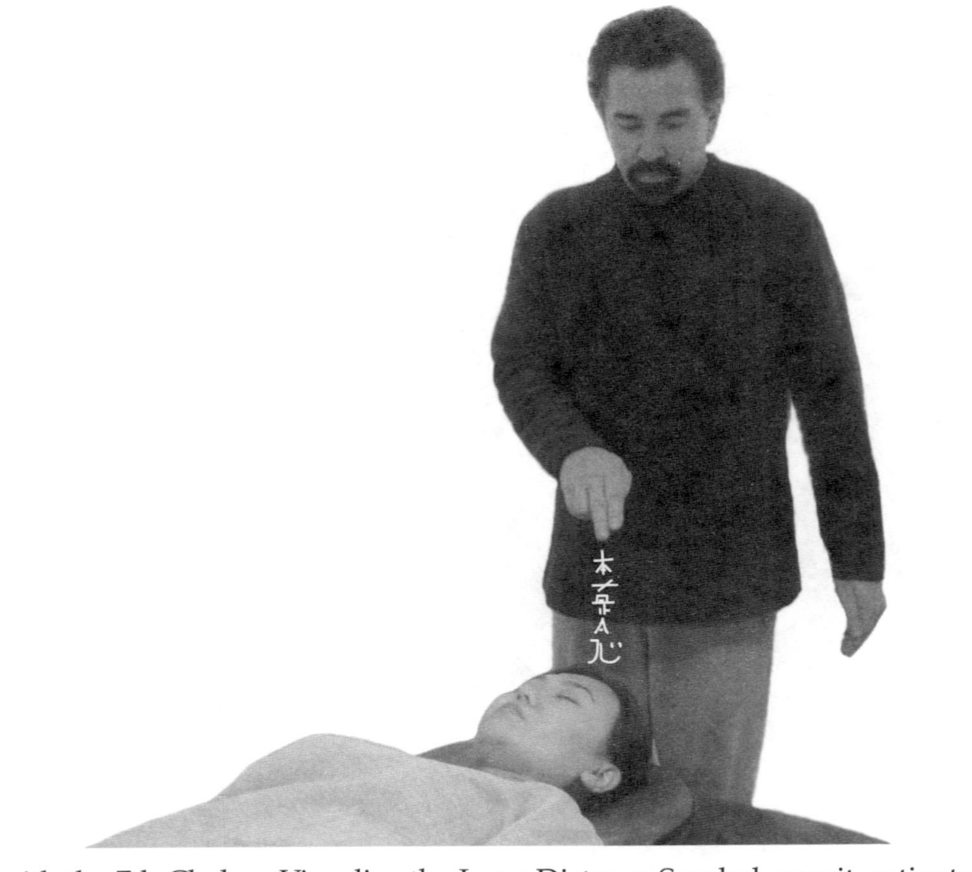

(Photo 107) Stay with the 7th Chakra. Visualize the Long Distance Symbol over it, activate it.

(Photo 108) Embed it into the center of the Chakra. *Step should only take 15 seconds.*

(Photo 109) Stay with the 7th Chakra. Visualize the Master Symbol over it, activate it.

(Photo 110) Embed it into the center of the Chakra. *Step should only take 15 seconds.*

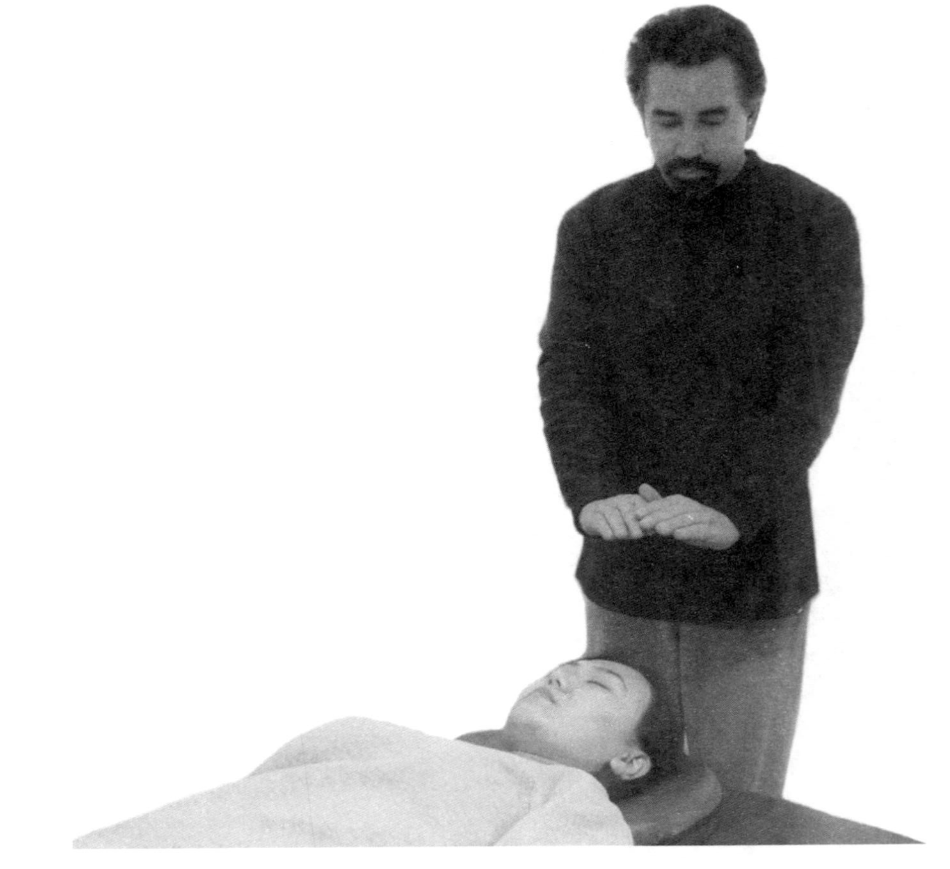

(Photo 111) The Reiki Symbols are now embedded into the 7th Chakra. Next, channel Reiki into the center of the 7th Chakra with the intent for it to flow to the Migraine Headache. *Step should only take 5 minutes.*

"Conventional opinion is the ruin of our souls."

-Rumi

"It may be that the satisfaction I need depends on my going away, so that when I've gone and come back, I'll find it at home."

-Rumi

Clearing and Balancing Chakras

To stay in good physical health, you want to keep your Chakras cleared and balanced. This can be done as a Healing session by itself, or some Healers do it before they perform any Reiki Healing session.

There are many different ways to balance and clear Chakras, and most are effective. I find the following steps (which show me performing clearing and balancing Chakras on another person) to be the best and quickest way for me. To clear and balance Chakras on yourself, just use the same steps. All Reiki Levels can use this method.

Clearing and Balancing The Chakras

1. Prepare like you normally would for a Reiki Healing Session.

2. Have the person on his or her back.

3. Channel Reiki with the intent to clear and balance 1st Chakra for 15-30 seconds. (Photo 112)

4. Channel Reiki with the intent to clear and balance 2nd Chakra for 15-30 seconds. (Photo 113)

5. Channel Reiki with the intent to clear and balance 3rd Chakra for 15-30 seconds.(Photo 114)

6. Channel Reiki with the intent to clear and balance 4th Chakra for 15-30 seconds. (Photo 115)

7. Channel Reiki with the intent to clear and balance 5th Chakra for 15-30 seconds. (Photo 116)

8. Channel Reiki with the intent to clear and balance 6th Chakra for 15-30 seconds. (Photo 117)

9. Channel Reiki with the intent to clear and balance 7th Chakra for 15-30 seconds. (Photo 118)

10. Have the person turn over on his or her stomach.

11. Channel Reiki with the intent to clear and balance back 1st Chakra for 15-30 seconds. (Photo 119)

12. Channel Reiki with the intent to clear and balance back 2nd Chakra for 15-30 seconds. (Photo 120)

13. Channel Reiki with the intent to clear and balance back 3rd Chakra for 15-30 seconds. (Photo 121)

14. Channel Reiki with the intent to clear and balance back 4th Chakra for 15-30 seconds. (Photo 122)

15. Channel Reiki with the intent to clear and balance back 5th Chakra for 15-30 seconds. (Photo 123)

16. Channel Reiki with the intent to clear and balance back 6th Chakra for 15-30 seconds. (Photo 124)

17. Finish like you would your normal Healing Session, or continue on with a Reiki Healing Session for a specific purpose.

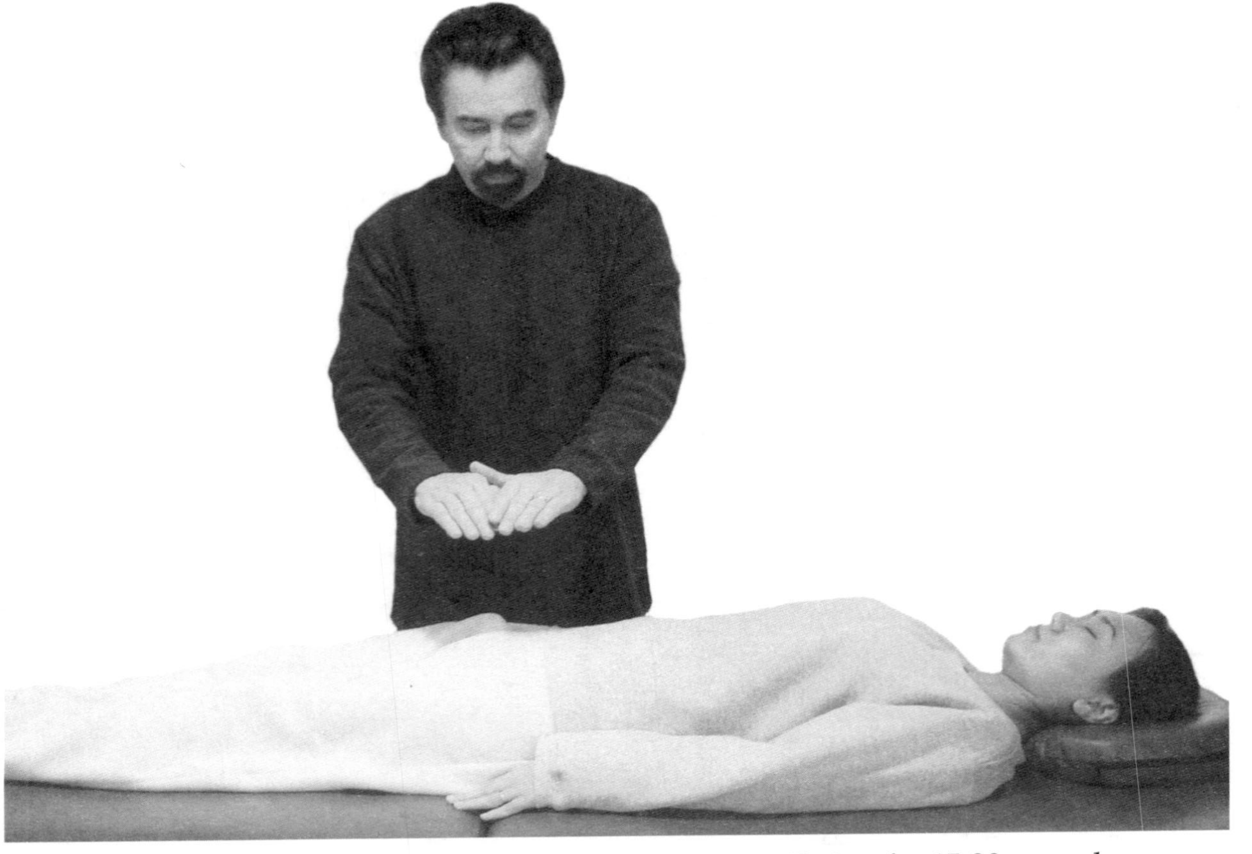

(Photo 112) Channel Reiki with the intent to clear and balance 1st Chakra for 15-30 seconds.

(Photo 113) Channel Reiki with the intent to clear and balance 2nd Chakra for 15-30 seconds.

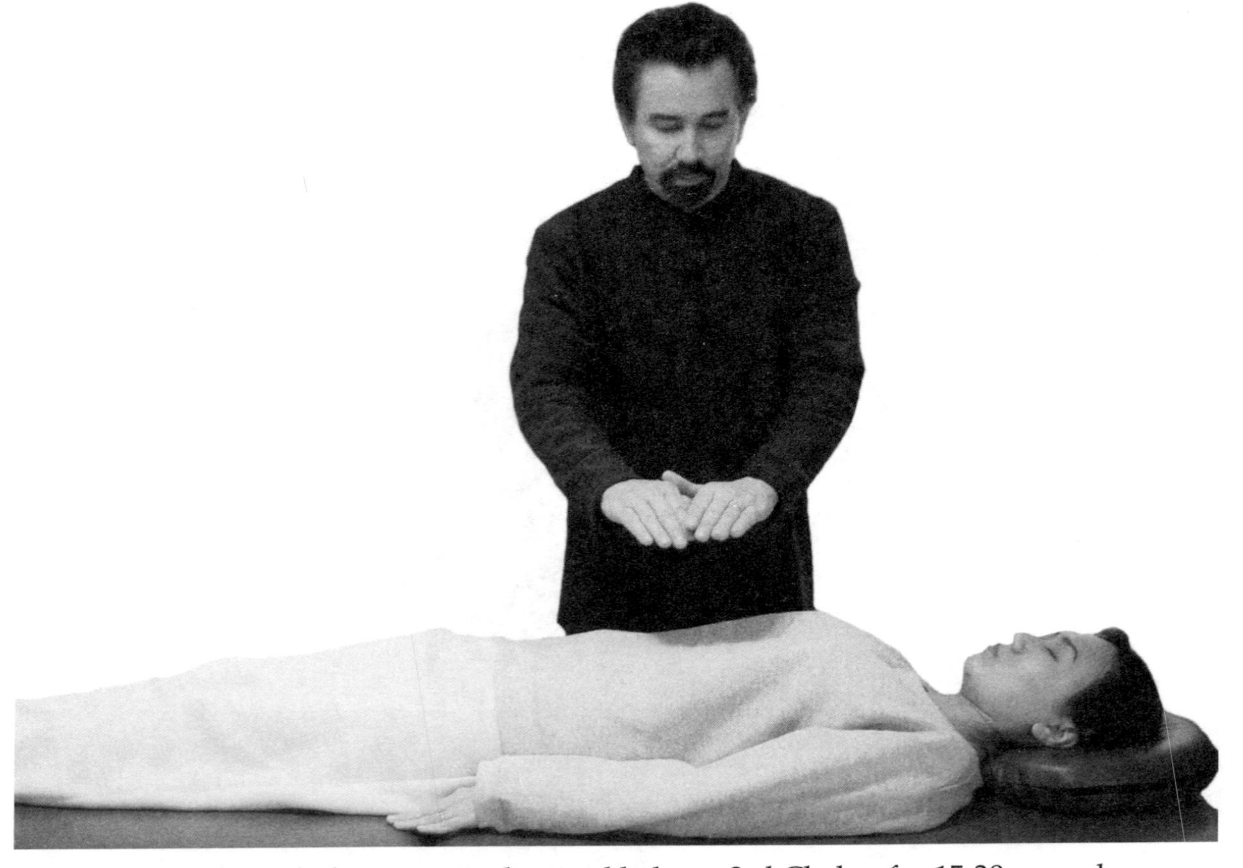

(Photo 114) Channel Reiki with the intent to clear and balance 3rd Chakra for 15-30 seconds.

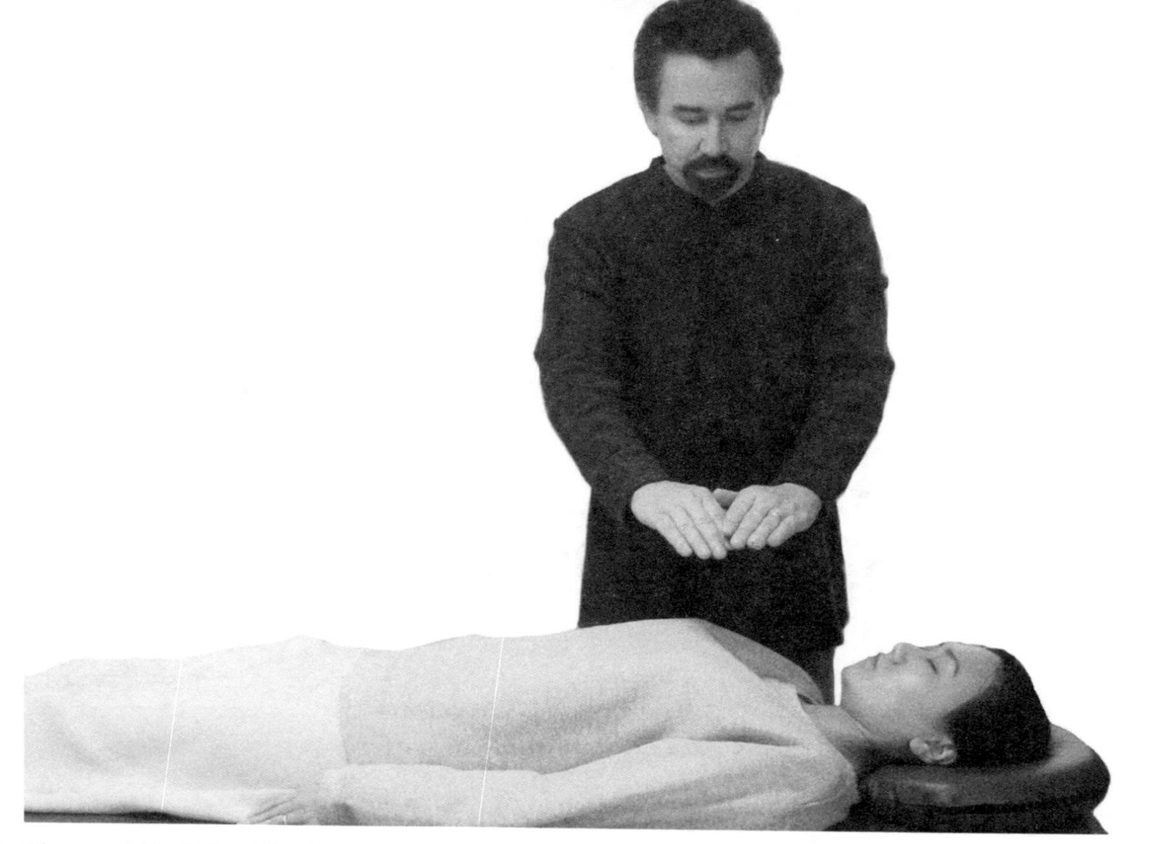

(Photo 115) Channel Reiki with the intent to clear and balance 4th Chakra for 15-30 seconds.

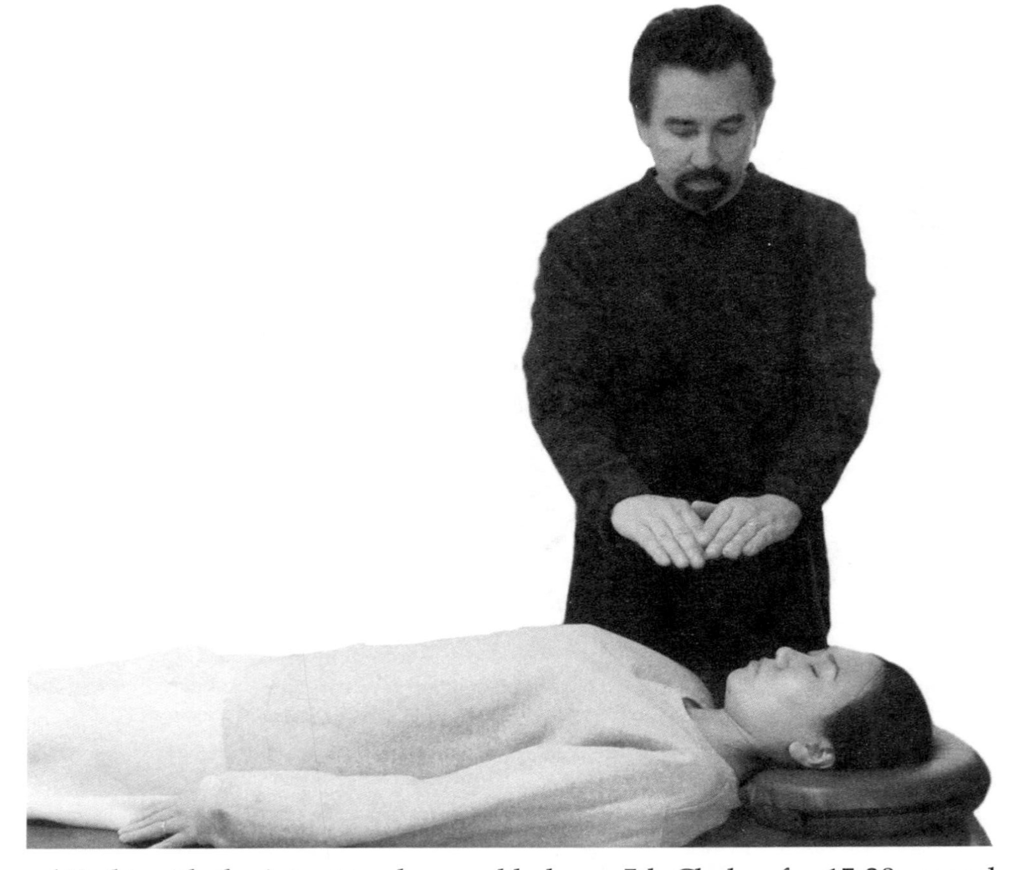

(Photo 116) Channel Reiki with the intent to clear and balance 5th Chakra for 15-30 seconds.

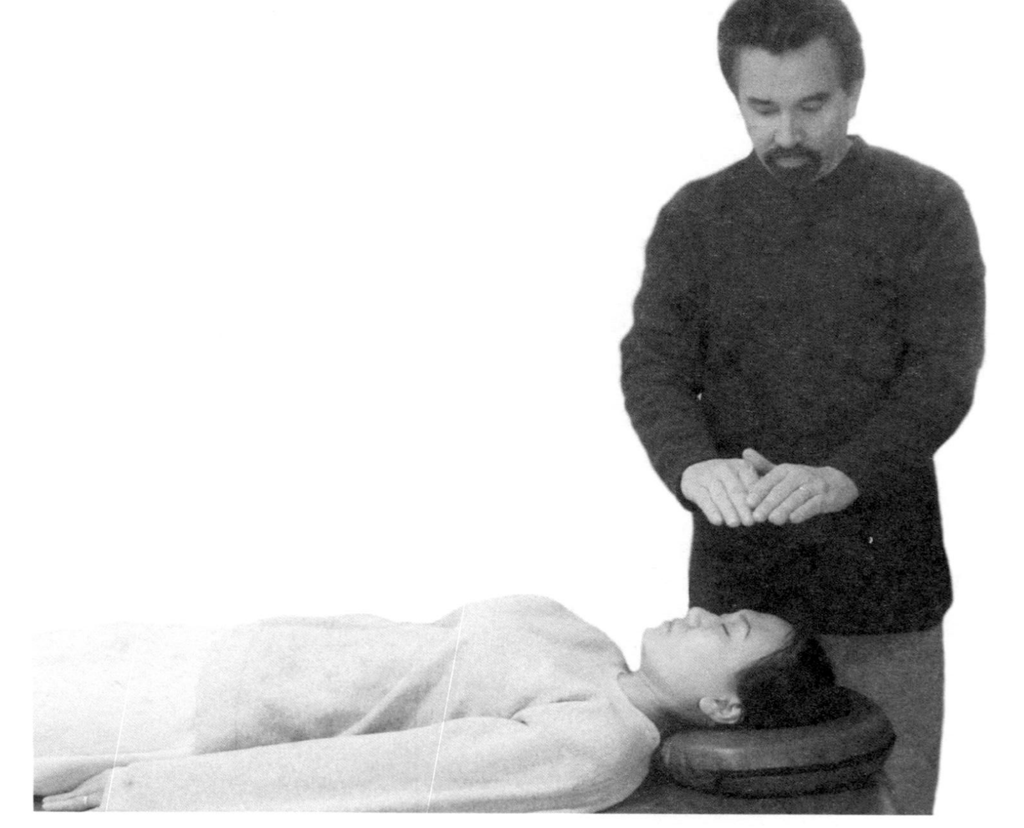

(Photo 117) Channel Reiki with the intent to clear and balance 6th Chakra for 15-30 seconds.

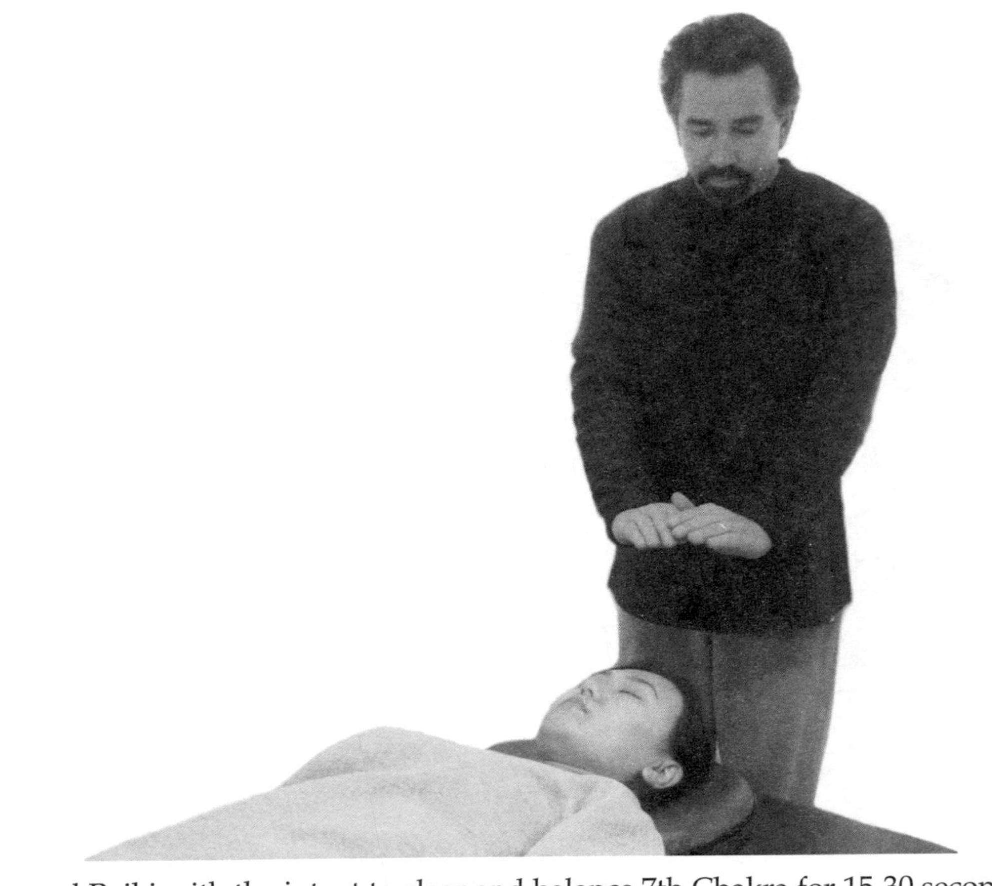

(Photo 118) Channel Reiki with the intent to clear and balance 7th Chakra for 15-30 seconds.

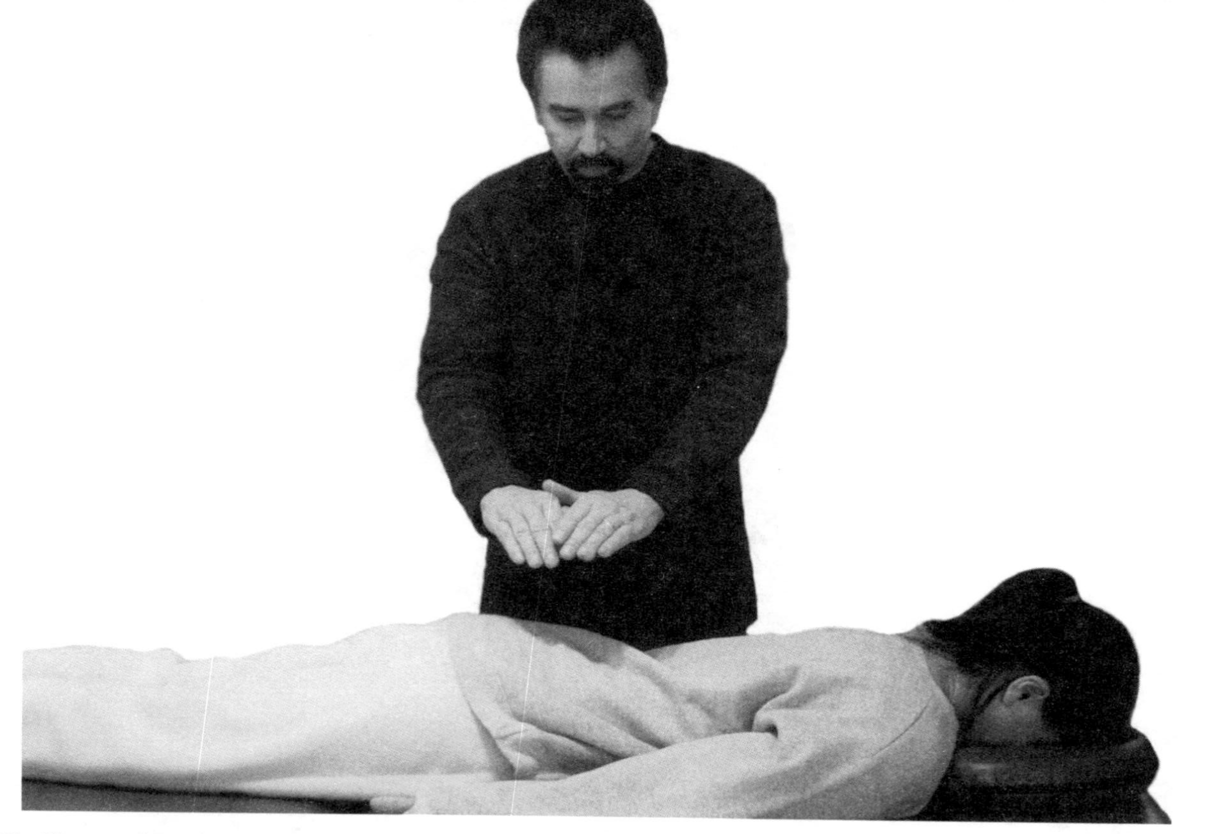

(Photo 119) Channel Reiki with the intent to clear and balance back 1st Chakra for 15-30 seconds.

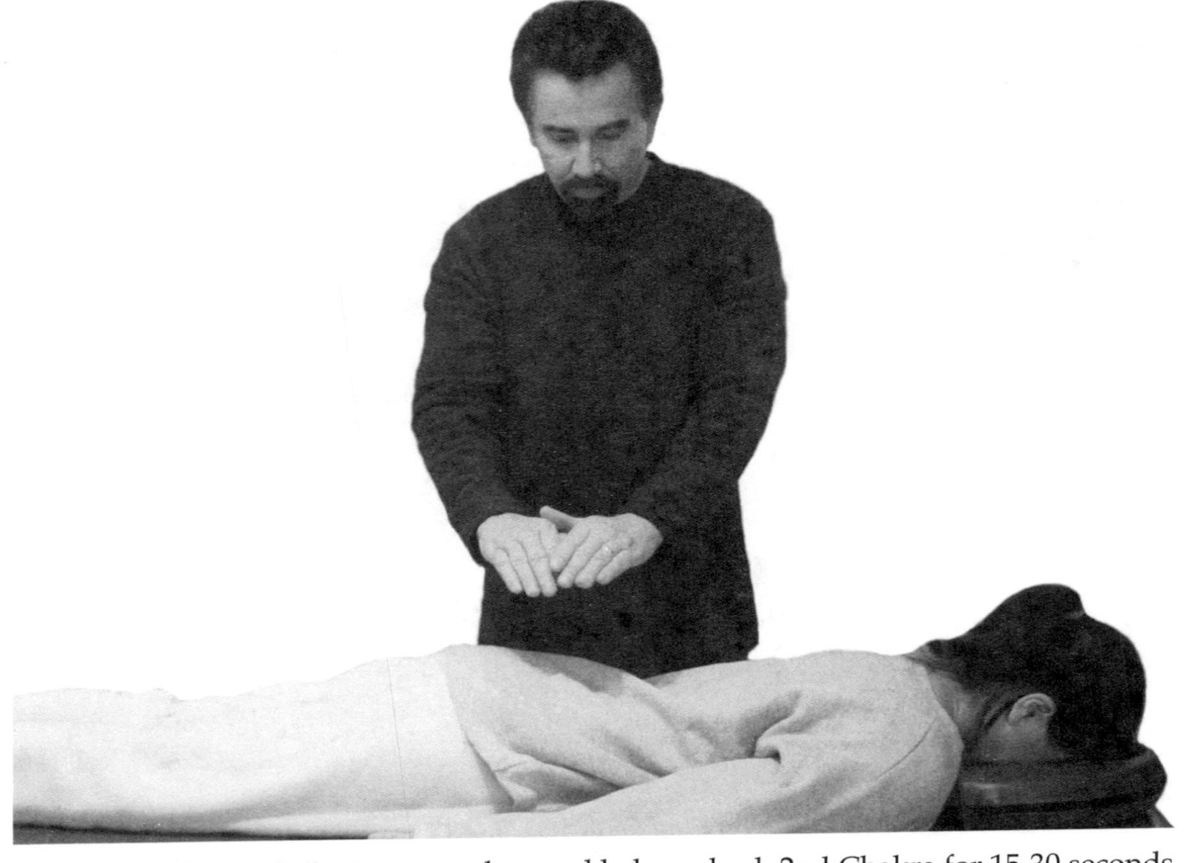

(Photo 120) Channel Reiki with the intent to clear and balance back 2nd Chakra for 15-30 seconds.

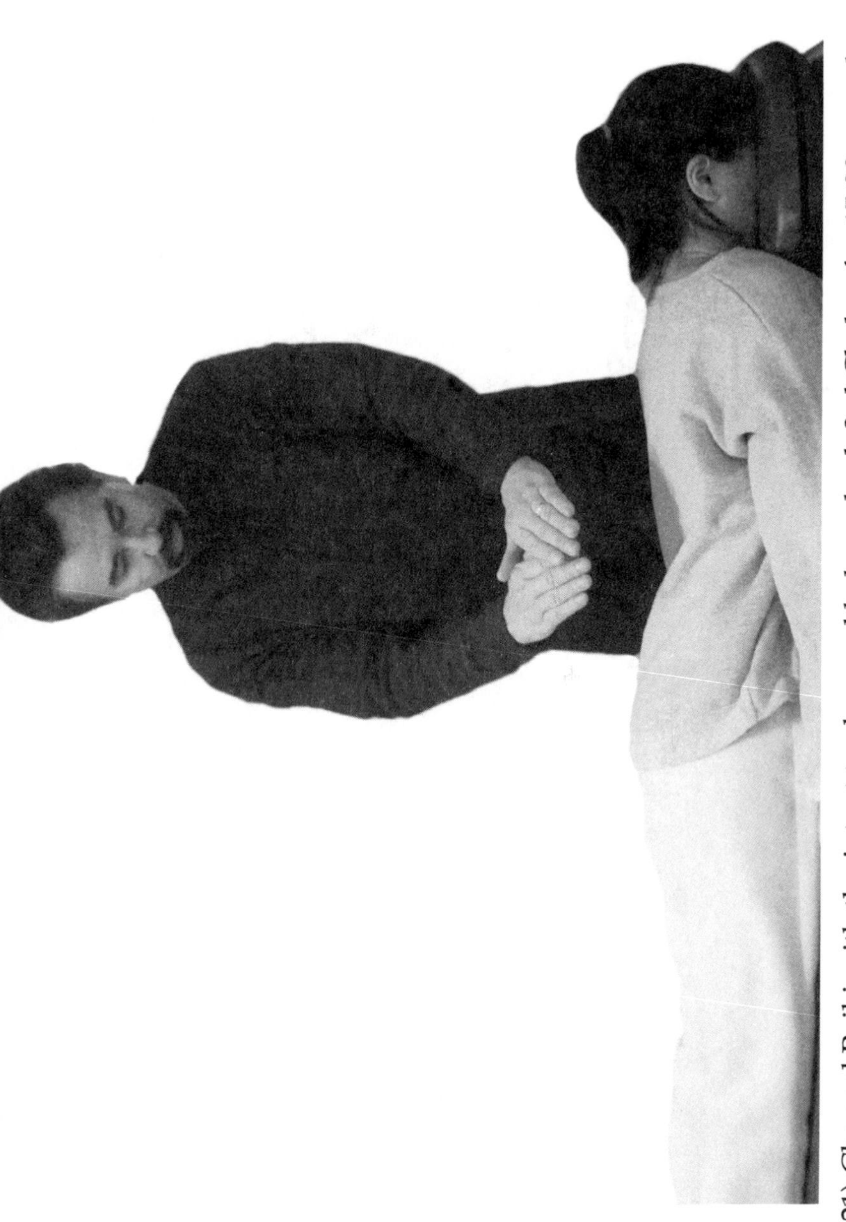

(Photo 121) Channel Reiki with the intent to clear and balance back 3rd Chakra for 15-30 seconds.

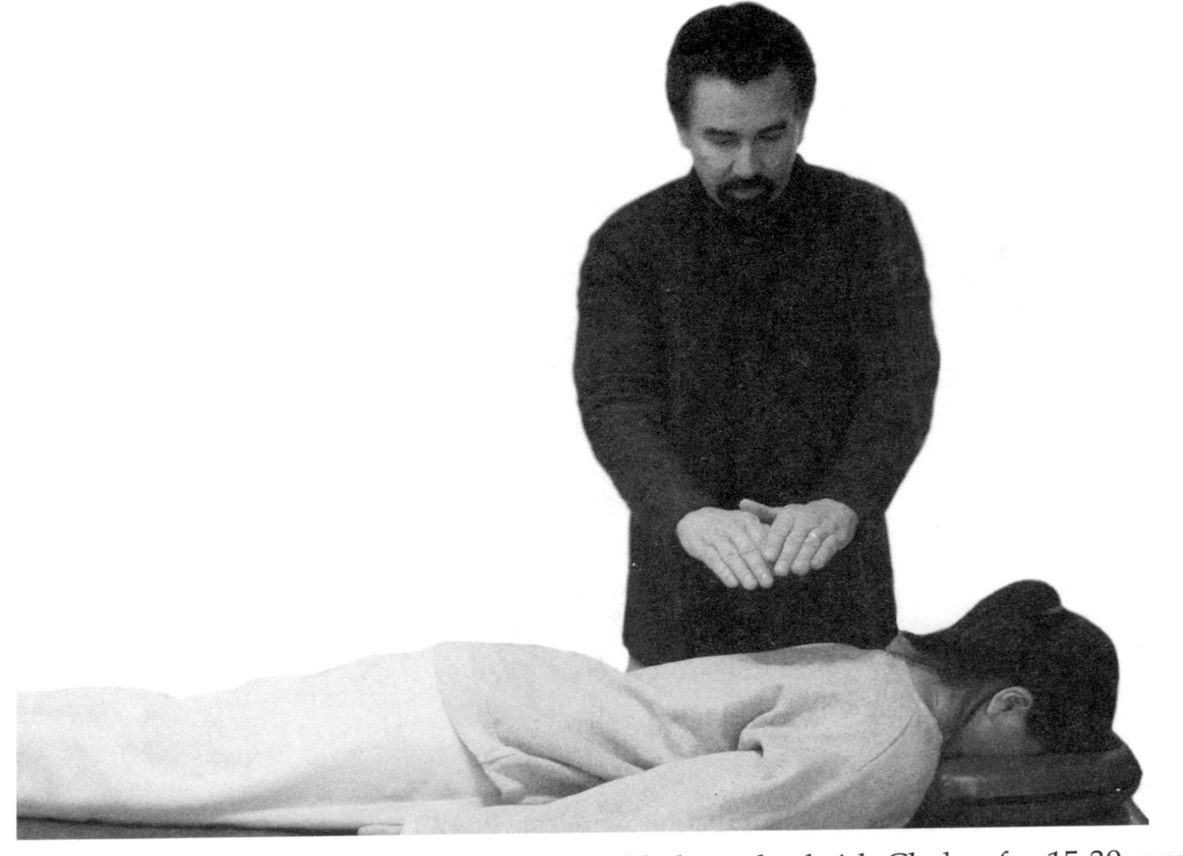

(Photo 122) Channel Reiki with the intent to clear and balance back 4th Chakra for 15-30 seconds.

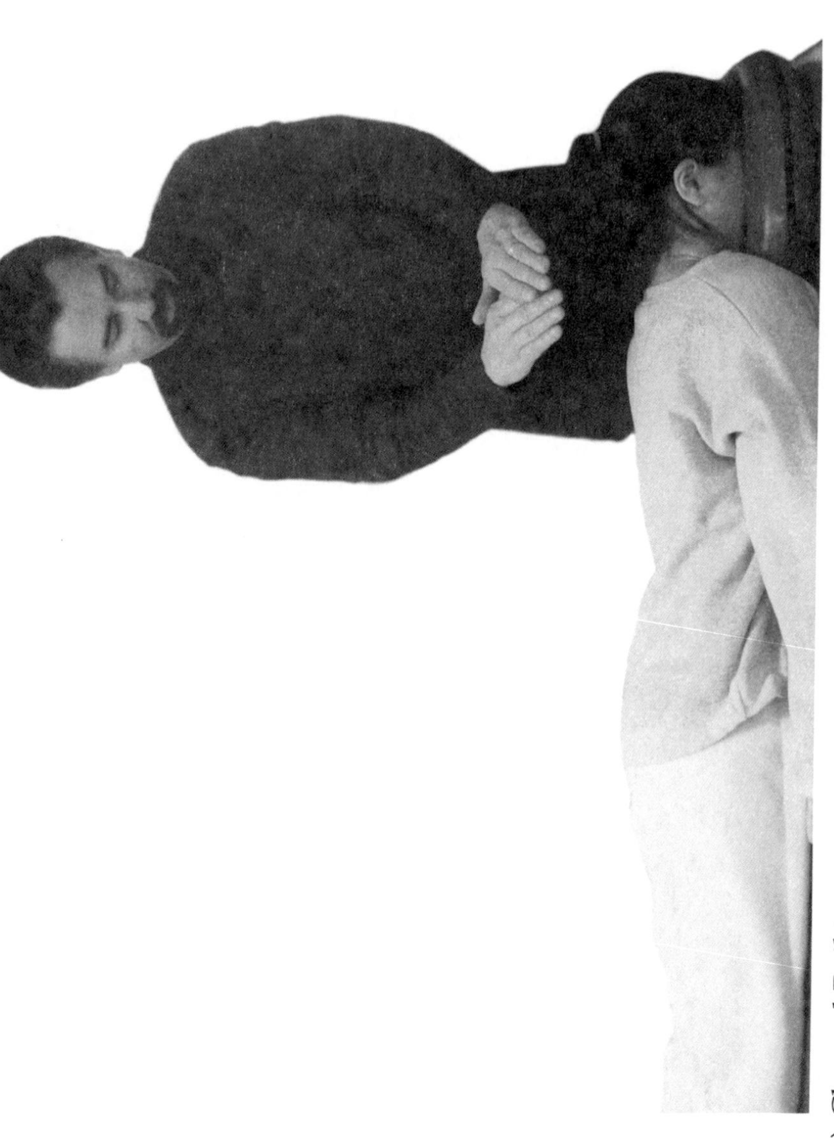

(Photo 123) Channel Reiki with the intent to clear and balance back 5th Chakra for 15-30 seconds.

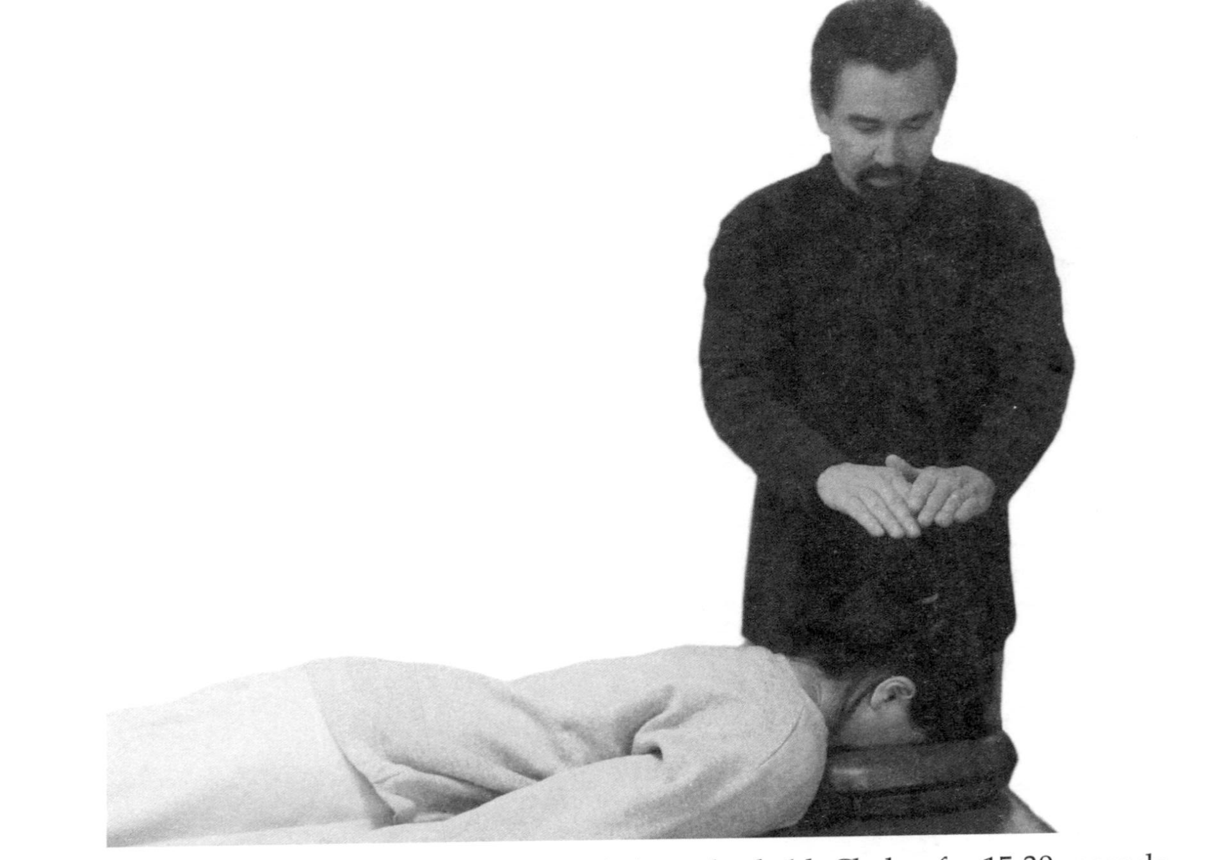

(Photo 124) Channel Reiki with the intent to clear and balance back 6th Chakra for 15-30 seconds.

“Beware! Don’t allow yourself to do what you know is wrong, relying on the thought, ‘Later I will repent and ask God’s forgiveness.’ ”

-Rumi

"Be occupied, then, with what you really value and let the thief take something else."

-Rumi

Reiki Healing Stones

Many people have requested I write a chapter about Reiki Healing and Chakra balancing stones and how to use them. These stones unite the metaphysical properties of gemstones with Reiki Symbols and Chakra Symbols and colors to create unique and powerful healing tools.

The stones are not required for Reiki Healing Attunements or Reiki Sessions to be effective, but they are great options you can blend into your Reiki Healing when appropriate.

An artist who happens to be a Reiki Master crafts my healing stones individually for my students and clients. You should be able to find similar stones in a local metaphysical or spiritual store. If you have problems finding any of the items that I describe, just visit my website or contact me for information on obtaining these stones.

The black and white photos on the following pages do not really show the full beauty of these stones, but they will give you a general idea of their appearance.

You can use the healing stones any way in which you intuitively sense you should. There is not a right or wrong way. I will give suggestions on using them, but it's up to you to discover what works best for you and your clients.

Clearing Stones

Remember to always clear any healing stone(s) before and after you use them. Usually Healers have their own preference for doing this. A quick and easy way is to hold the stone(s) in your hands and use Reiki with the intent to clear and purify for a minute or two.

Reiki Healing Stones

The Reiki Healing Stones (Photo 125) are made with different gemstones with the Reiki Symbols engraved on them. They are flat and can be placed on the body. The gemstones option are Jade, Fluorite, Ammonite Fossil and large natural Quartz points.

Suggestion for Healing Reiki Stones

Here are just a few examples of ways to use the stones:

- Place on the body for healing when performing a Reiki session.
- Place on photos when sending Reiki Healing to the past, present, or future.
- Place on paper with writings of goals you need to manifest.
- Place on documents before they are signed.
- Carry one or all with you on special occasions.
- Leave with a person for healing.
- Leave in a room for healing.
- Place in room, car, etc. for protection.

The stones can also be used as a teaching tool, and in passing Reiki Level Attunements to students by placing the appropriate symbol in the palms of the receiver.

Reiki Stones and Healing Attunements

In a Reiki Healing Attunement, you can place a stone with the appropriate symbol you are activating on the Chakra. Just replace each stone on the Chakra as you activate the next symbol. When working with the 7th Chakra, just hold the stone on with one hand or lay it next to the Chakra or work with the Chakra sitting up.

Reiki Crystals with Symbols

I do not place Reiki large natural Quartz points (Photo 126) on the body because of the size and shape. You can use the other methods I suggest for the Reiki stones. Healers also use the Reiki engraved crystals in Crystal Grid Healing. I have been told this intensifies the results dramatically.

Reiki Pendants with Symbols

The great benefit with Reiki pendants (Photos 127 & 128) is they can be utilized constantly by simply wearing them. They come in two gemstones, Amethyst and Rose Quartz, plus two shapes, oval and heart. Also, they have Reiki Symbols engraved on them. Pendants can be used in many, many ways, which include healing and for protection. They can be worn hidden from view, if desired.

Here are just a few examples of ways to use the pendants:

- Wear during meditation.
- Wear in a Healing Session for yourself or others.
- Wear in an important meeting or event, while traveling, or for special occasions.

The reasons for wearing the pendants are endless. If you have the set, you can wear the symbol that is needed at the time. People do wear more than one pendant at a time.

Chakra Balancing Stones

The Chakra gemstones (Photo 129) have engraved symbols for each Chakra, and each is a gemstone of the color that correlates with each Chakra. This combination gives them maximum clearing and total balancing abilities, especially when used together. The stones are also made flat for placing on the body.

You use the stones with all Chakra balancing and healing modalities. They can be heated briefly and used in a hot stone massage fashion as well.

In a Reiki Healing Attunement, place the Chakra stone on the Chakra to which it corresponds during the Attunement.

(Photo 125)

(Photo 126)

(Photo 127)

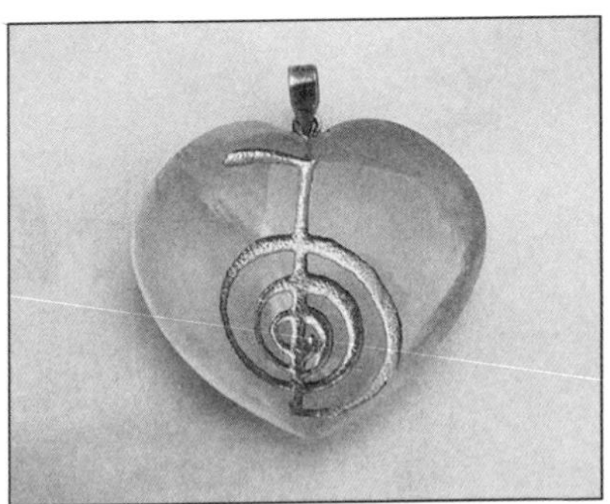

(Photo 128)

(Photo 129)

Shanti

Steve Murray

Index

Selected Bibliography

Davies, B. *The 7 Healing Chakras*. Group West. 1998 ISBN 1-56975-168-4

Diemer, D. *The ABC's of Chakra Therapy*. Samuel Weiser. 1998 ISBN 1-57863-021-5

Dale, C. *New Chakra Healing*. Llewellyn. 1996 ISBN 15678-200-3

Gardner, J. *Color and Crystal*. Crossing Press. 1988 ISBN 0-8954-258-5

Ritberger, C. *Your Personality, Your Health*. Hayhouse. 1998 ISBN 1-56170-538-1

Arewa, C. *Way of the Chakra*. Thorsons. 2001 ISBN 0-7225-4039-6

Borang, K. *Principles of Reiki*. Thorsons. 1997 ISBN 0-7225-3406-X

Baginski, B. & Sharamon, S. *Reiki Universal Life Energy*. Life Rhythm. 1985 ISBN 0-940795-02-7

Waites, B. & Naharo, M. *Reiki a Practical Guide Astrology* Publishing. 1998 ISBN 965-494-046-9

Lubeck, W. *Reiki Way of the Heart*. Lotus Light. 1996 ISBN 0-941524-91-4

Morris, J. *Reiki Hands That Heal*. 1996 ISBN 1888196-05-X

Nevius, S. & Arnold L. *The Reiki Handbook* PSI Press. 1982 ISBN 0-9625500-1-9

More of what people are saying...

This is a great book! The author keeps it straightforward and simple. It can be used to review what you learned when you were attuned to Reiki. It can be used to hand out to students as they are being attuned. The illustrations are very easy to understand and the author explains the different levels of attunements in a simple manner. This book takes all the mystery out of a wonderful healing modality and makes it easy for anyone to understand. This guide, when used in conjunction with Steve's Attunement videos, enables anyone, anywhere to become a Reiki Healer, and the world needs as many as it can get. ***CD***

I would like to say that this book is really amazing. I am happy I found it. I just became a Reiki Master in December and I have been practicing Reiki a lot. I did the initiations already but I found this book has so much information I don't know yet. I would really recommend it to anyone who is interested in Natural Healing, Or even to people who have never had experience with Reiki. It's a great new Journey of your life. Reiki has changed my life a lot, and it will change yours too. I want to thank Steve for his wonderful work. ***LG.***

I am a recently attuned Reiki student. This is a good reference book and it's good to see someone make this information available in a very clear and well-written format. I would highly recommend this book and his video series to anyone who is interested in Reiki and looking for answers. My heartfelt thanks to the author, Steve Murray. ***PM***

Steve's book is openly revealing many things that many others don't. Also, his style of writing has a very personal touch. I surely recommend people get to know this Reiki Master. You'll start feeling warm and good after reading this. ***DR***

This is a marvelous book and a "must have" for the serious Reiki practitioner regardless of whether your training was formal or informal, or a mixture of both. I frequently use the principles of Reiki in my work as a legal professional and as Reiki is healing energy, we must promote and encourage healing on all levels. After exploring and reviewing numerous Reiki reference books, I believe this is one of the best. ***PL***

Anyone who wishes to read a book about Reiki that is straightforward, easy to read and has great "how to" pictures, this is the book for you. The symbols are clearly defined and explained in a way that makes the process easy to duplicate. The tone of the book is educational, yet open-minded. The author never forces his own views or uses for Reiki on anyone else, but instead gently guides his readers along for the journey. This reader appreciates it. Thank you, Steve, for all your efforts. ***CK***

Having practiced Reiki at 1st and 2nd degree levels for the past three years and constantly searching for the answers to many Reiki questions, Steve Murray has produced a book that should be on the bookshelf of everyone who is interested in or practicing Reiki. Having purchased and read many Reiki books, I still found myself searching for answers, but this book has answered many questions and explains in an understable and simple fashion the secrets of Reiki that many Reiki books and masters, for whatever reason, were reluctant to share with everybody. ***FS***

I have been involved in the Healing Arts and metaphysics for over 30 years, starting back in the 1970s. I have taught courses, lectured in many cities and had the pleasure of listening to and studying with teachers from a wide range of spiritual disciplines. To be blunt, I was born a skeptic and a cynic--I know a “con game” when I see one--and again, I say that Steve Murray's earnestness as a Reiki teacher is straight from the heart. ***LO***

Steve Murray--and those who walk the same Maverick road--are to be applauded for putting resources of healing into the hands of those who need it most. Shanti! ***LW***

HOW TO ORDER DVDS, CDS, & BOOKS

To buy any of the following Books, DVDs or CDs check with your local bookstore, or www.healingreiki.com or email bodymindheal@aol.com, or call 949-263-4676.

BOOKS BY STEVE MURRAY

Cancer Guided Imagery Program
For Radiation, Chemotherapy, Surgery And Recovery

Reiki The Ultimate Guide
Learn Sacred Symbols and Attunements
Plus Reiki Secrets You Should Know

Successfully Preparing for Cancer Chemotherapy
Guided Imagery and Subliminal Program

Reiki The Ultimate Guide Vol. 4
Past Lives and Soul Retrieval
Remove Psychic Debris and Heal your life

Stop Eating Junk!
5 Minutes A Day-21 Day Program

Reiki The Ultimate Guide Vol. II
Learn Reiki Healing with Chakras
plus New Reiki Attunements for All Levels

Cancer Fear and Stress Relief Program

Reiki The Ultimate Guide Vol. 5
Learn New Psychic Attunements to Expand Psychic Abilities & Healing

DVDS BY STEVE MURRAY

Reiki Master Attunement
Become A Reiki Master

Reiki 2nd Level Attunement
Learn and Use the Reiki Sacred Symbols

A Reiki 1st
Aura and Chakra Attunement Performed

Successfully Preparing for Cancer Radiation
Guided Imagery and Subliminal Program

Reiki 1st Level Attunement
Give Healing Energy To Yourself and Others

Reiki Psychic Attunement
Open and Expand Your Psychic Abilities

Reiki Healing Attunement
Heal Emotional-Mental Physical-Spiritual Issues

Reiki Psychic Attunement Vol. 2
New Attunements to Expand Psychic Abilities

Preparing Mentally & Emotionally For Cancer Surgery
A Guided Imagery Program

Preparing Mentally & Emotionally For Cancer Surgery
A Guided Imagery Program

Preparing Mentally & Emotionally For Cancer Radiation
A Guided Imagery Program

Destroying Cancer Cells
Guided Imagery and Subliminal Program

Fear & Stress Relief Subliminal Program Let Your Unconscious Mind Do The Work!

Cancer Fear and Stress Relief Program

30-Day Subliminal Stop Smoking Program Let Your Unconscious Mind Do The Work!

Preparing Mentally & Emotionally For Cancer Chemotherapy
A Guided Imagery Program

Preparing Mentally & Emotionally For Cancer Recovery
A Guided Imagery Program

Pain Relief Subliminal Program
Let Your Unconscious Mind Do It!

30-Day Subliminal Weight Loss Program Let Your Unconscious Mind Do The Work!

Successfully Preparing for Cancer Chemotherapy
Guided Imagery and Subliminal Program

MUSIC CDs BY STEVE MURRAY

Reiki Healing Music Attunement Volume I

Reiki Psychic Music Attunement Volume I

Reiki Aura Music Attunement

Reiki Healing Music Attunement Volume II

Reiki Psychic Music Attunement Volume II

Reiki Chakra Music Attunement

DVDS BY BODY & MIND PRODUCTION

Learning To Read The Tarot Intuitively

Learning To Read The Symbolism Of The Tarot

How to Contact Spirits, Angels & Departed Loved Ones:
A step-by-step Guide

How to Contact Spirits Vol. 2
Learn to use a Spirit/Ouija Board and Hold a Séance

Mind Fitness Workout:
"Program the Mind for Weight Loss as you Exercise" Dance Workout

Mind Fitness Workout:
"Program the Mind for Weight Loss as you Exercise" Walking Workout

Mind Fitness Workout:
"Program the Mind for Weight Loss as you Exercise" Fitness Workout

About the Author

Steve Murray is the author of the best selling *Reiki The Ultimate Guide* books, and has a series of self-healing programs on DVD. The DVD subjects include Reiki Attunements, Cancer Guided Imagery, weight loss, pain, fear, and stress relief to name just a few. He has produced four Reiki Music CDs for healing, meditation and psychic work.

Steve is an experienced Usui Reiki Master, Tibetan and Karuna Reiki® Master. One of his most powerful attunements came from the High Priest of the Essene Church, which made him an Essene Healer. The Essenes have been healers for more than 2,000 years. Steve is also a Hypnotherapist and a member of the National League of Medical Hypnotherapists and National Guild of Hypnotists.